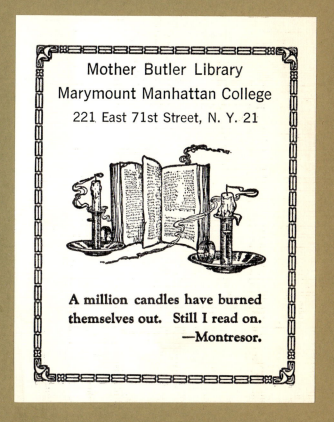

The Panama Affair

Maron J. Simon

The Panama Affair

Charles Scribner's Sons · New York

for Helen

This acknowledges a considerable debt of gratitude to several generous, patient, and highly competent men and women who helped me dig out material for this book:

. . . to Miss Claire Schumacher, Miss Shirley Dakin, Mrs. Katherine Lundell, Mrs. Alice Plowitz, Timothy Field Beard, Frank E. Bradley, jr., Philip Falco, Miles Jefferson, Joseph Mask, and Norman Petteway, of the New York Public Library;

. . . to Miss Sylvia C. Hilton and Miss Helen Ruskell, of the New York Society Library;

. . . to David Finch, librarian of the French Institute, New York;

. . . to Byron Scott, of the Francis Lynde Stetson Library at Williams College;

. . . to Mitch Havemeyer, owner of Mitchell's Book Corner, Nantucket, Mass., for bringing to me the monograph his grandfather, Henry Mitchell, wrote on Ferdinand de Lesseps for the American Academy of Arts and Sciences;

. . . to Herbert C. Rothschild and Erwin B. Steiner, of New York, for hours of translation;

. . . to Maurice Prince, of Barnstaple, Devon., England, for his diligent checking of details in Bournemouth and London.

The Panama Affair

1

*J*ust in time for Christmas in 1880 the foremost living Frenchman offered his countrymen the ownership of an undertaking with the greatest prospect of material reward in the history of private enterprise.

The venture he offered them was the construction and operation of a ship canal across the Isthmus of Panama; when opened to commerce in just eight years its presence would rearrange the earth's geography.

The canal, scarcely 45 miles long, would cut the distance from Calais to California almost in half and shorten the sea route from the Atlantic coast of the United States to its Pacific ports by 10,000 miles.

On a clear day, from a 300-foot height in the middle of the isthmus, a man with normal vision might see both oceans; but to move freight from Colon on Panama's Atlantic side to Panama City on the Pacific meant either a costly and cumbersome transshipment by rail or a four-week sea voyage by the fastest ships afloat.

With the cost of operating a 4,000-ton steamship running from 1,500 to 2,500 francs a day (300 to 500 United States dollars) the burden this geographic barrier placed on world commerce, and the bonanza the breaching of it would bring, were elemental considerations. The magnitude of the undertaking would make its achievement another monument to the grandeur of France; and its authorship attested the likelihood of its success, for the man who proposed it had already proved himself by means of a pertinent achievement that Anatole France came to call "the greatest affair of the civilized world."

1

He was Ferdinand de Lesseps, who had cut the Suez Canal through a hundred miles of Egyptian desert in the face of the bitter opposition of the Turkish empire, nominal owner of the right of way, the antagonism of the British, who dominated the Turks, the doubts of his countrymen, and the tardiness of his emperor's support.

Now everyone honored de Lesseps, even the English. Governments and learned societies throughout the world festooned him with decorations. Empress Eugenie's confessor, preaching the principal sermon at the Suez opening, equated his achievement with that of Columbus. Leon Gambetta, chief accoucheur of France's Third Republic, if not its founding father, bestowed on him the catchy title, *"le Grand Français."*

There would, of course, be some risk and sacrifice in following "The Great Frenchman" to his new triumph. Shares in Monsieur de Lesseps's Universal Panama Interoceanic Canal Company would cost 500 francs each, almost the average yearly wage for half the working population of France, for it was a time when men in heavy industry averaged 5 francs 27 centimes a day, women 2.67 francs, (in Paris); in the provinces the pay was almost a third less. A faceman in the bituminous mines near the Belgian border earned 4.50 francs for a day's work; his landlord received not quite 33 centimes a day for renting him a six-room brick house with hardwood wainscoting, a cellar, and a garden. Even half a decade later, when the workmen building Alexandre Gustave Eiffel's great tower in the Champ de Mars went on strike, their objective was a pay raise of one half franc a day.

The Suez shares had also cost 500 francs, and de Lesseps's *petites gens de bas de laine*, his "little wool-stockinged people," who had taken the plunge with him in Egypt, could revel in their foresight; Suez shares were selling at more than 2,000 francs on the Bourse, and dividends flowed at the rate of 17 per cent. Even the British had scrambled aboard the Suez bandwagon; in 1876, when Ismail, the spendthrift Khedive of Egypt, had been compelled to sell his 44 per cent slice of the Suez equity to get himself out of a financial squeeze, Queen Victoria's government had raced to pay him 100,000,000 francs for his shares.

Some of de Lesseps's countrymen challenged the validity of his Panama enthusiasm, both on economic and political

grounds, but he met their doubts head on and routed them sin-
glehandedly. He went to the New World to remove any com-
plications that might arise from a venture into a vital sphere
of interest of the United States of America and to lead a committee of technical experts in an on-the-spot study of the entire
undertaking—route, requirements, and working conditions. On
his return his reassurance was decisive.

Once the digging started, he said, the task would take only
six years of 250 working days a year; 8,000 laborers would excavate 50,000 cubic meters of earth a day, with the help of machinery and steam power. "As for the salubrity of the climate
of Panama, whither I accompanied the committee with my
family," he reported, "the perfect health whereof we presented
living proof on our return to Europe shows how unjustly that
beautiful climate has been condemned by those who know
nothing of it—*omne ignotum horrendum.*"

With this, the public fell upon his offering of Panama
shares with the voracity a hot stock issue excites among investors of every time and market place. Eighteen months later,
though the start of excavations was still half a year away,
Panama shares were up 40 francs, as much as a Paris concierge
earned for three weeks' work. This was far better than Suez
shares had done at the same stage, de Lesseps pointed out; Suez
shares had averaged only 300 francs during construction and
had once dropped to 180.

"The Panama stock has never been below par, and I believe
the day will come when it will stand higher than Suez stock,"
he said. "I buy Panama for my children, and you know I have
nine, the youngest fifteen months old and the tenth expected
soon, because it is cheaper than Suez and because it is surely
destined to be worth more."

His countrymen thought so, too. In eight years, as the company's financial needs zoomed, several hundred thousand
French men and women came forward with a billion francs
more to buy its bonds. All that lay between the risk and the
reward were a 300-foot mountain of almost solid rock, a capri-
cious river that sometimes rose more than thirty feet a day, and
swarms of *Aëdes aegypti* and *Anopheles* mosquitoes on which
epidemics of yellow fever and malaria rode the construction
zone on unremitting patrol.

Long before de Lesseps took up the task, the prospect of

creating and commanding a short cut from the Atlantic to the Pacific at the New World's slender waist had enticed generations of famous Europeans. The corporation de Lesseps drew together was simply the first with sufficient financial muscle to launch an organized attempt.

The earliest Spanish explorers of the Western Hemisphere had contemplated the advantages of an interoceanic canal through the Central American isthmus as soon as they became aware of the wasp-waisted profile of the newly discovered land mass. Balboa, having spotted the Pacific from a peak in Darien, looked for a natural passage. Angel de Saavedra proposed to Charles V, the Holy Roman Emperor, the construction of a canal through the Isthmus of Darien at what is now the Colombia-Panama border. Cortez urged the Emperor to dig a canal through the isthmus of Tehuantepec. Antonio Galvao, a celebrated Portuguese navigator, published an essay in 1550 in which he suggested two more routes: one through the Lake of Nicaragua and one through the Isthmus of Panama.

Thus the principal routes were known to Europe's most powerful monarch, but he did not act on any of them. After Charles's death, Lopes Gomera, the Spanish historian, proposed that Philip II, his son, build a canal, saying: "It is quite true that the mountains obstruct these passes, but if there are mountains there are also hands. Let but the resolve be made and there will be no want of means; the Indies, to which the passage will be made, will supply them. To a king of Spain, with the wealth of the Indies at his command, when the object to be attained is the spice trade, what is possible is easy." But Philip shelved the idea imperiously; "that phenomenal bigot and tyrant declared it was a sacrilege to undo what God had created, and therefore wicked to cut through the mountains for a canal."

After Philip, the idea of the canal languished for two centuries; but in 1780 another Spanish monarch, King Charles III, sent out Manuel Calistro, whose expedition made the first substantial exploration. From then almost until the moment de Lesseps arrived, so many explorers combed the thin strip of land between the two American continents that in a region of less luxuriant vegetation their footsteps might have tramped out a clear path from shore to shore.

4

They searched at the behest of Louis Philippe, King of the French, of William I, King of the Netherlands, and of three French companies, a Belgian group, and of a firm of London contractors. Alexander von Humboldt, the German naturalist, surveyed the area extensively. Napoleon III, having read a series of Berlin Geographical Society lectures on the subject, became fascinated with the idea of a Nicaragua canal and wrote an English-language pamphlet on it; repeatedly during the building of the Suez Canal he told de Lesseps, "When you have severed Asia from Africa you must sever North from South America the same way."

Goethe, who had read von Humboldt's findings, told his secretary, J.P.Eckermann, with clairvoyant precision on February 21,1821: "I should wonder if the United States were to let an opportunity escape of getting such a work into their own hands. It may be seen that this young state, with its decided predilection to the West, will in thirty or forty years have occupied and peopled the large tract of land beyond the Rocky Mountains. It may furthermore be foreseen that along the whole coast of the Pacific Ocean, where nature has already formed the most capacious and secure harbors, important commercial towns will gradually arise for the furtherance of a great intercourse between China and the East Indies and the United States. In such a case it would not only be desirable but almost necessary that a more rapid communication should be maintained between the eastern and western shores of North America, both by merchant ships and men-of-war, than has hitherto been possible with the tedious, disagreeable voyage around Cape Horn. I therefore repeat that it is absolutely indispensable to the United States to effect a passage from the Mexican Gulf to the Pacific Ocean, and I am certain they will do it. Would that I might live to see it, but I shall not. I should like to see another thing—a junction of the Danube and the Rhine. But this undertaking is so gigantic that I have doubt of its completion, particularly when I consider our German resources. And thirdly, and lastly, I should wish to see England in possession of a canal through the Isthmus of Suez."

The United States was not forty years old when it began to investigate ways and means of eliminating the continent-encircling detour in the Atlantic-Pacific route. The new republics to the south were active, too. Simon Bolivar sponsored an exploration. Mexico commissioned an English explorer to reconnoitre the Tehuantepec route. The President of the Central American Federation ordered a study of the San Juan River route.

One of the most persevering dreamers of a transisthmian canal was Frederick M. Kelley, a young Wall Street financier who had become entranced with the idea in his boyhood, when he read von Humboldt's account of a passage called the Raspadura. Nicaraguan Indians had dug this course in 1783 at the behest of a Spanish monk, Brother Antonio de Cereso. Intended initially as a drainage ditch to mark a disputed boundary between the holdings of two families in the parish of Novita, it ran for three miles through a ravine, known as the Quebrada de la Raspadura, and linked the headwaters of the Atrato River, which empties into the Gulf of Darien on Nicaragua's Atlantic coast, and the San Juan River, whose mouth is on the Pacific. In rainy seasons the ditch held water deep enough to clear small canoes, and cargoes were soon moving from Pacific ports to the San Juan's mouth, transferred to bogues, or large canoes, for the journey upriver, carried through the Raspadura canal in small canoes, reloaded into bogues, and hauled down the Atrato to ocean-going ships. Eventually the tropical rains eroded the banks of Brother Antonio's little ditch, and by the time von Humboldt arrived, it was almost forgotten; but its promise of a practical route was sufficient to beguile Kelley. He started in 1852, when he was twenty-eight years old, and spent $125,000 of his own money in the next twelve years on surveys and explorations of the isthmus. Ultimately he tried to induce the governments of the United States, France, and Britain to join in building a canal.

Commodore Cornelius Vanderbilt supported another private canal venture that came to nothing. He and several associates formed the Atlantic & Pacific Ship Canal Company, got a concession from Nicaragua, and commissioned Colonel O.W. Childs to conduct a study conforming to true engineering standards. But the A & P Canal Company never raised the necessary funds, and Nicaragua canceled the concession after the filibustering expedition of William Walker, the restless Tennessean who surrendered to a British fleet in his final attempt to conquer Central America and died before a Honduran firing squad in 1860.

The United States government took up intensively the quest of an interoceanic short cut in 1869, soon after General Ulysses S. Grant became President. His administration got Colombia's permission to conduct canal surveys on its territory, Congress appropriated funds, and between 1870 and 1875 United States-financed expeditions surveyed nine routes.

A Presidential commission, named to evaluate their findings, reported that the route known as the Nicaragua route "possesses both for construction and maintenance of a canal greater advantages and offers fewer difficulties from engineering, commercial, or economical points of view than any one of the other routes shown to be practicable by surveys sufficiently in detail to enable a judgment to be formed of their relative merits."

Commander Chester Hatfield had studied the Nicaragua route first, and then Commander E.P.Lull, both making an examination, study, and definite instrumental location of a line in the vicinity of San Juan del Norte (Greytown) on the Atlantic side, then through Lake Nicaragua and the Medio and Grand rivers to Brito on the Pacific. The recommendation for this route was never acted on.

A lengthy procession of chance and coincidence attended the selection of the route de Lesseps came to follow. Long before Goethe, cosmic thinkers projecting a new geography had contemplated the construction of canals through the Suez and Central America isthmuses as related undertakings.

One of these visionaries had firsthand knowledge of the New World. He was the Count de Saint-Simon, the French social philosopher, who in his youth had his servant wake him each morning with the exhortation: "Get up, Count, you have big things to do!"

Saint-Simon served with distinction through five campaigns of the American Revolution, was decorated with the Order of the Cincinnati, and was present at the siege of Yorktown and Cornwallis's surrender. In the French Revolution he renounced his title, saying "Count" was inferior to "Citizen." When he died in 1825, he left a set of socio-economic principles that his followers built into a system known as Saint-Simonianism, embraced by some of the foremost economists and industrialists of the time, men such as Michel Chevalier, the free trade champion who negoitated the first Anglo-French trade treaty in 1860 with Richard Cobden.

Another believer was Barthelemy Prosper Enfantin, an effective businessman whose career had been interrupted by a brief jail term for his leadership of an eccentric moral-religious cult of free love advocates that evolved among some of the Saint-Simonians. Discharged late in 1833, Enfantin hurried to the Middle East to join a pilgrimage of his associates, and there made the first detailed proposal for the present Suez Canal to a ruler of Egypt who owed his exalted rank to Ferdinand de Lesseps's father, Count Mathieu de Lesseps.

The pilgrims Enfantin followed into Egypt journeyed there aboard the brig *La Clorinda*, under the leadership of the playwright Emile Barrault, one of the most persuasive orators of their sect. *La Clorinda's* mate, exposed to Saint-Simonianism by the chance of his presence on the two-week voyage, and steered by Barrault's eloquence into directions in which his life touched importantly on those who became prime movers in the Panama enterprise, was Giuseppe Garibaldi.

The Saint-Simonian apostle convinced him that "the man who defends his own country or who attacks another is but a soldier—pious in the one just cause, unjust in the other; but that a man who makes himself a cosmopolitan, and who offers his blood up to every nation struggling against tyranny, is more than a soldier—he is a hero."

Sixteen years later, after a flamboyant career as a revolutionary in Brazil, Argentina, and Uruguay, Garibaldi's path and that of Ferdinand de Lesseps crossed at Rome. Garibaldi was the commander of a small force defending the newborn Roman Republic against besieging French forces sent to restore papal rule, and de Lessseps was the French Ambassador striving to negotiate a peaceful accommodation.

When the French army descended on Rome and the Republic collapsed, de Lesseps, after a rebuke from his government for having shown too much favor to the republican cause, resigned from the diplomatic service and went into a protracted rustic retirement, from which he emerged to build the Suez Canal.

De Lesseps's canal, which cut the distance of the sea voyage from Liverpool to Singapore almost in half by eliminating the loop around the Cape of Good Hope, was not the first waterway from the Mediterranean to the Red Sea, but merely the first channel dug through the Isthmus of Suez, which separated them. Two millenniums before the birth of Christ, according to the fragmentary evidence of antiquity, a branch of the Nile was linked with the Bitter Lakes, from which another passage was dug to the Red Sea. Archibald Ross Colquhoun, a nineteenth-century British colonial administrator who was a student of interoceanic communication, credited Rameses II with joining the Red Sea and a Nile branch in the thirteenth century B.C. by means of a canal "wide enough to admit the passage of two vessels abreast, the passage occupying four days."

Darius I was said to have enlarged and improved the canal of the Pharaoahs, and Cleopatra to have tried to move her fleet through it to gain refuge in the mountains of Africa after the defeat by Octavian at Actium. For a time the canal was called Trajan's Stream. A succession of Ptolemaic, Roman, and Arab dynasties maintained the passage with varying diligence until the eighth century A.D., when an Abbasside caliph—a member of the dynasty claiming descent from Abbas, the uncle of the prophet Mohammed—filled it in for strategic reasons.

"It was a work of peace suppressed by war," Anatole France said in his address to the French Academy in 1897, when he assumed the seat left vacant by the death of Ferdinand de Lesseps.

Among the accidents of history from which the present-day Suez Canal evolved were those that produced the staunch friendship of the families of Mathieu de Lesseps, the accomplished Napoleonic diplomat, and Mohammed Ali, an illiterate Macedonian who became the most effective ruler of modern Egypt.

After Napoleon ended his occupation of Egypt, which he had undertaken ostensibly to restore Turkish rule and to end the power of the Mamelukes, he and Talleyrand, his Foreign Minister, directed Mathieu de Lesseps to find among the Turkish militia a troop commander whom the Sultan could be induced to appoint as the Pasha at Cairo, a hitherto nominal dignity. The Mamelukes, the warrior caste of slaves' descendants who had been dominant in Egypt for seven centuries, were hostile to French policy, and the man Napoleon wanted for the job was one with sufficient force and brains to throw them out.

Mohammed Ali, whom de Lesseps chose, not only routed them by the practical expedient of massacring their leaders, but made Egypt virtually independent of Turkish dominion, won the right of hereditary succession for his family in the pashalate, and founded an Egyptian royal line of which Farouk was the end product. His gratitude to de Lesseps was enduring, and years after he had become a feared and powerful ruler, he was pleased to acknowledge instances of the Ambassador's kindnesses to him when he was an insecure young soldier.

"The father of this young man was a great personage when I was a very small one," he once told a companion of Ferdinand de Lesseps. "He had one day invited me to dinner. The next day I learned that some silver had been stolen from his table, and as I was the only person who could be suspected of the theft, I dared not return to the house of the French agent, who was obliged to send for me and reassure me." The Khedive's high regard for Mathieu de Lesseps opened the way for Ferdinand de Lesseps, in turn, to win a friendship that would bring him the privilege of building the Suez Canal.

Ferdinand de Lesseps became enchanted with the idea of the canal when he arrived at Alexandria in 1831 to take up his own post as a young vice-consul. His inspiration lay in a book on Napoleon's Egyptian expedition that he read while languishing in quarantine after a thirty-seven-day voyage from Tunis; it was the famous illustrated work by the painter and antiquarian, Dominique Vivant Denon, and it contained the report of Charles Lepere, the expedition's chief engineer, who had been ordered to trace the route of the ancient canals.

When de Lesseps emerged from his quarantine to be received by Mohammed Ali, he found his father's old friend subjecting an enormously overweight young son, Said, to a reducing regimen consisting of a starvation diet, rope-skipping, hikes around the city walls, and two hours a day of climbing masts of ships. Young de Lesseps was the only person the Khedive permitted to receive the flabby heir.

"When he came to see me he would throw himself on my divan quite worn out," de Lesseps said. "He had come to an understanding with my servants, as he confessed to me later, to obtain from them secretly meals of macaroni to make up for the fasting imposed on him."

When Mohammed Ali died in 1849 after a year of insanity, his evil nephew, Abbas, succeeded the regency that ruled the pashalate, and drove Said into exile. The corpulent refugee fled to Paris, living for a while in a lodging house in the rue de Richelieu, where he found that Ferdinand de Lesseps, eminent diplomat and second cousin of Empress Eugenie, had not abandoned him. "His situation, the welcome I gave him, and the recollection of his childhood established between us from that moment a truly brotherly friendship," de Lesseps said.

Although Mohammed Ali's interest in trans-Egypt commerce had prompted him to build the Mahmoudieh Canal from Alexandria to the western arm of the Nile delta early in his rule, giving ships of light draft a sheltered water course from Cairo to the coast, he would not consent to an interoceanic canal through the Suez isthmus; he feared, and correctly, Britain's opposition, Said told de Lesseps. Even painstaking projections based on investigations by a *Société des Etudes* that Enfantin had raised 150,000 francs to form failed to convince the Khedive.

After the old Khedive's death Enfantin armed de Lesseps with the data he had developed, and induced him to sound out the new one; but Abbas, who was a Francophobe, was dead set against the project, too. His nominal chief, the British-dominated Sultan of Turkey, was equally antagonistic to proposals made on behalf of de Lesseps by his friend, Benoit Fould, a banker whose brother, Achille, Minister of Finance for Napoleon III, had borne the Emperor's official proposal of marriage to Eugenie de Montijo.

But in 1854, two servants murdered Abbas, and Said became his successor. When the news reached de Lesseps, he was perched on a scaffold helping to restore his family's country home, the old castle of La Chesnaye, which Agnes Sorel, mistress of Charles II, had once owned. He had retired to the country to act as agent for the extensive agricultural holdings of his mother-in-law, Mme. Delamalle, in the Berry district.

De Lesseps wrote at once to congratulate Said on his elevation, and received a delighted reply urging him to hurry to

Egypt. He accepted, and accompanied the new Pasha on maneuvers in the desert before the investiture. The experienced diplomat foresaw that the adventure would offer him an exceptional opportunity to plead the cause of a Suez canal, but recognized that a gingerly approach was indispensable, for Said was an unpredictable man, generous but violent, who had to be convinced that a good idea was his own. De Lesseps waited patiently for an opportune moment. It came on November 15, 1854, and when Said heard his proposal he replied: "I am satisfied and I accept your scheme. We will arrange all the details during our journey. But understand that it is settled and you may count upon me."

Recounting the omen of success he had seen that morning in the sky over the camp at the oasis of Ghell, on the site of ancient Marea, a famous garrison town in the days of the Pharaoahs, de Lesseps wrote in his journal: "The camp begins to be astir. The morning freshness of the air heralds sunrise. On my right the East is in all its glory. On my left the West is gloomy and cloudy. All at once I perceive a brilliant rainbow, its extremities extending from East to West. I confess that I felt my heart beat and I had need of checking my imagination, which in this sign of the Covenant spoken of in the Scripture was already greeting the advent of the veritable link between the East and the West and the day assigned for the success of my scheme."

He came to command of the Panama enterprise by a much more mundane route.

When the Congress of Geographical Sciences convened at Antwerp in 1871, not quite two years after the opening of the Suez Canal, the question of a waterway through the other great isthmian barrier in Central America was a natural choice for a high priority on the agenda, and de Lesseps the natural choice of France as delegate to the meeting.

The congress, however, did no more than recommend for consideration of the maritime powers and of all scientific bodies a survey that Anthoine de Gogorza and Louis de Lacharme had made during a French-financed expedition to Panama in 1865.

A second congress took place in Paris in 1875, at which de Lesseps expressed the opinion that all those who had advanced plans up to that time had made a serious error by examining routes suitable only for canals with locks. To meet all the requirements of commercial navigation, he said, the canal would have to be a sea-level passage, as was the Suez Canal.

The congress confined itself to the following equivocation: "The congress expresses the wish that the governments interested in the construction of an interoceanic canal should have surveys for it made as fast as possible and that they will adhere to the routes that offer navigation the greatest facilities for access and traffic."

Rather than wait for governments to get around to it, the Commercial Geography Committee of Paris took steps to get a canal started promptly. Convinced that all the existing topographical information on the Central American isthmus was inadequate for intelligent selection of a route, it established a special French committee, on March, 24, 1876, to study the canal problem. De Lesseps was named president, with Admiral La Ronciere-le Noury, president of the Geographical Society of Paris, and Admiral Meurand, president of the Commercial Geography Committee, as vice-presidents. But the Geographical Society had no means of financing the expensive explorations that were needed. At this point the undertaking passed from the savants to the speculators. Istvan Türr, a venturesome Hungarian, and his brother-in-law, Lucien Napoleon Bonaparte Wyse, a twenty-nine-year-old lieutenant in the French navy, stepped in to nurture and promote a scheme to build an Atlantic-Pacific canal.

Sixteen years earlier, Türr had been Garibaldi's aide-de-camp in the conquest of the Kingdom of the Two Sicilies, the climax of the struggle to unify Italy as a kingdom under the rule of Victor Emmanuel II, King of Sardinia. When Garibaldi decided that Italy's best hope for unification lay with Victor Emmanuel rather than with the republican cause, Türr offered pertinent qualifications for his service. He was not only a general of the Hungarian army but an in-law of monarchs. His wife, Adeline Marie, was the daughter of Napoleon Bonaparte's niece, Princess Laetitia, whose father was Lucien Bonaparte, Prince of Canino.

Mme. Türr, her brother, and their older sister, Marie Laetitia Rattazzi, a voluminous writer with the unfulfilled ambition to be the successor to Mme. de Stael, were born during their mother's lifelong separation from her husband, the Right Honorable Sir Thomas Wyse of Waterford, Ireland, a British diplomat. She had walked out on Sir Thomas in 1828, and when she refused to return to him and their two young sons, he not only swore that he would never see her again but insisted that their separation agreement contain a clause forbidding her even to live in the same town he lived in.

Türr's first step in the Panama adventure was to get in touch with de Gogorza, who had organized the 1865 survey under de Lacharme. Türr sent him back to Colombia, where, on May 26, 1876, he obtained a ninety-nine year concession from Colombia authorizing them to make a new survey of the Panama isthmus, and in the event it demonstrated the practicability of a canal without locks or tunnels, to form a company that would build a canal and an auxiliary railroad.

Türr then put together a company to own and exploit the concession. This outfit, known as the *Société Civile Internationale pour le Percement du Canal Interocéanique à travers de l'Isthme de Darien* (International Non-Commercial Company for the Cutting of the Interoceanic Canal Across the Isthmus of Darien), had a capital of 300,000 francs, represented by sixty shares sold for 5,000 francs each and ten distributed free—two each to Türr, de Gogorza, and Wyse, two put at Türr's disposal, and two reserved under the company's bylaws "for a purpose known to the interested parties" but not revealed to history.

It raised its capital from men of an enormously varied background and celebrity. Two of them were among the forty Immortals of the French Academy—Senator Emile Littre, the renowned lexicographer, and Octave Feuillet, the novelist and playwright from whose name the word *feuilleton* derived to characterize his newspaper serials. One was the curator of the Opera, Jules Bourdon, and one was General Claude Davout, Duke of Auerstaedt, grandnephew of the Marshal of France for whom Napoleon I created the dukedom. Others included a former Colombian Consul General at Paris, Eugene Rampon, and a director of the Bank of Bogota, Joachim Sarmiento. The money they risked went to finance the survey stipulated in the concession de Gogorza had obtained.

The Panama Affair

The survey party sailed from St. Nazaire on November 6, 1876, aboard the steamship *Lafayette*. The co-commanders were Bonaparte Wyse and Armand Reclus, also a lieutenant in the French navy, whose brother was Elisee Reclus, the well-known geographer and anarchist. The party's secretary was Oliviero Bixio, a young ordnance officer in the Italian army; he was a nephew of Nino Bixio, one of Türr's comrades at arms in Garibaldi's force.

Three members of the expedition died, among them Bixio, and the rainy season disrupted operations. The survivors returned to France, and set out again in November, 1877.

Dr. W. E. Johnston, a New York physician who was the American Geographical Society's delegate to a subsequent international congress—from which the de Lesseps undertaking emerged full-blown—made the following report on the new expedition two years later: "After some months consultation, in which M. de Lesseps took a large part, it was decided that Lieutenant Wyse should return to the isthmus and look at the Panama route with the view of making that the affair on which they were finally to settle, and as the affair to which the public in France would be most likely to subscribe.

"The survey was made—how imperfectly was afterwards shown in the congress by the abandonment of all the figures and even of the plan; the party returned to Paris, and last winter the plan of campaign putting through the Wyse scheme was organized."

Whatever Wyse's merits were as a surveyor, his horsemanship was superb. He rode out of Panama City on February 25, 1878, and arrived at Bogota fifteen days later. "The inhabitants of the capital, accustomed to long ridings, were astounded," he reported. "It is true that I rode sometimes twenty-two hours in a day, but at any rate I arrived in time to treat with President Parro, who, well aware of our efforts, had shown himself favorably disposed to discuss the modifications which I was commissioned to ask in the concession of May 28, 1876."

Three days after Wyse creaked out of the saddle, he submitted a new concession contract for discussion, and the Colombian government accepted it on March 23, 1878, just a week before President Aquileo Parro's term expired. The Colombian Congress then discussed it until May 17, by which time all the

15

amendments had been disposed of, and the new President signed it the next day.

This contract, which Wyse negotiated with Eustorgio Salgar, Columbian Minister of Foreign Affairs and Minister of Interior, gave the canal company a ninety-nine-year concession in return for a down payment of 750,000 francs as earnest money and an annual compensation based on a percentage of the company's gross income, starting at 5 per cent and going up 1 per cent every twenty-five years thereafter, with a guaranteed yearly minimum of $250,000.

The concession also gave Wyse's group all the lands needed for the canal and its dependencies: a strip of land 200 meters (almost 220 yards) wide on each side of the canal for its entire length, and 500,000 hectares (1,235,500 acres) of public lands, including mineral rights.

An international commission was to examine the route and report to the Colombian government by 1881. Within two years thereafter a corporation was to be formed to build a canal that would accommodate vessels approximately 550 feet long, 58 feet 6 inches abeam, with a draft of 28 feet 3 inches. The canal had to be completed and in operation within twelve years of the formation of the company. Should the canal be routed through territory in which the Panama Railroad had exclusive right of way, the canal company would have to work out an agreement with the railroad, which had been built twenty-five years earlier with United States private capital.

With the signing of the concession, two and a half years remained for the delivery of the international commission's report to the Colombian government, and two years more to form the construction and operating company, but the push to launch the undertaking proceeded with all deliberate speed.

The committee assigned to complete the canal-route studies convoked a *Congrès International des Etudes du Canal Interocéanique* for Thursday, May 15, 1879, at the home of the Paris Geographical Society at 184 boulevard St. Germain.

While preparations for the historic event in the boulevard St. Germain were being organized, another event of incalculable historic importance took place at Versailles, where the Chamber of Deputies was sitting. On March 1, Georges Clemenceau, the thirty-eight-year-old Deputy for Montmartre, attacked police methods and conduct in a speech so devastating that the responsible cabinet member, Emilc dc Marccre, Minister of the Interior, left the Chamber almost in shock and resigned two days later. It was the first Ministerial kill in a combative legislative career that brought Clemenceau his world-renowned nickname, The Tiger, and brought him, too, a tangential role in the Panama story that, in the words of the official biographers of the French parliament, was never quite cleared up.

The demeanor of the canal congress was not so openly abrasive as the Chamber's, but the convocation produced a considerable body of eyewitness testimony that questioned its scientific detachment.

It was evident to J. G. Alger, a long time member of the Paris bureau of the *Times* of London, that "the conference was a sham convened to register a foregone conclusion." He wrote: "The hall of the Geographical Society, where the conference sat, was decorated with a large placard stating the estimated cost of the various routes, with the number of locks required, but that of Panama the only one which promised a level waterway to the sea."

Dr. Johnston reported to the American Geographical Society: "It was hardly dignified for men holding the high rank of government delegates to take their seat in a congress which had been gotten up for a certain limited and well-defined object —and in which no proposition outside the program stood the least chance of adoption."

Admiral La Ronciere-le Noury opened the first session and turned the gavel over to de Lesseps, who announced that five committees would perform the work of the congress. "I ask the congress to conduct its work *à l'américaine,*" he told the delegates, "that is to say, with speed, in a practical manner, without losing sight of the necessary maturity. Perhaps in this way we will finish in eight days."

The meeting lasted a week longer than he had hoped.

There were 135 delegates, 68 from France and the rest from other countries, including 11 from the United States, of whom only two were official delegates. One of these was Admiral Daniel W. Ammen, who had been a member of the Presidential commission to evaluate the United States-financed route sur-

veys. The other was Aniceto G. Menocal, a distinguished civil
engineer. Together with one of the nonofficial delegates, Commander T. O. Selfridge, who conducted four of the nine government-financed surveys, they constituted pre-eminent authority
on the problems of canals across the isthmus of Central America. When their turn came to give figures and estimates of the
various routes, "a complete revolution took place."

Ironically, Wyse claimed all credit for the presence of the
official United States delegates. The young lieutenant boasted
that by standing up to an uncooperative Secretary of State,
William M. Evarts, and warning him that with or without
American representation the congress would take place and
the canal be built, he had "shown the Yankees that I was as good
as they at bluffing it out."

Menocal, in a blow-by-blow report of the infighting at the
congress, said: "Lieutenants Wyse and Reclus were not members of the congress, but took a very important part in its deliberations and organization, and on one occasion when a
subcommittee was to be appointed to consider and report on the
question of locks, Lieutenant Wyse stood side by side with the
president of the technical committee urging the appointment
of such delegates as might be in favor of a canal without locks.
The result was that the majority of the subcommittee was uncompromisingly in favor of the proposed Panama canal.

"Those delegates who attended the congress only for the
purpose of examining the different projects that might be presented for examination and deciding in favor of the one possessing the greatest advantages as to facilities of construction,
permanency, cost, and facilities for navigation, confined themselves to the presentation and discussion of the facts which
were understood by them to be the object of the meeting. They
were, however, in the minority and their opinions had little
weight with the opposition, composed of interested parties and
their friends."

Another subcommittee, composed of eight of the most eminent engineers at the congress, examined the relative merits
and probable cost of the various routes before the technical
committee. They said that the proposed canal, without locks,
presented so many doubtful construction elements that they
could not reach any conclusions as to its ultimate cost or per-

manency. They reported favorably on the Nicaraguan route.

"An excited discussion followed these reports, the friends of the Panama scheme attacking the Nicaraguan route in every possible way and advocating their plans no matter what the cost," Menocal said. "A resolution was passed to the effect that those who had introduced projects for a canal should not be permitted to take part in the debate, thus virtually excluding from the deliberations the delegates from the United States government who advocated the Nicaraguan route on its own merits."

Crisanto Medina, the Guatemalan Minister to France, who was his country's delegate to the congress, offered an insider's view of the pressure build-up that finally produced the vote for the Panama project.

The United States, Dutch, and Belgian delegates favored the Nicaraguan route, he said, and gradually every foreign delegate joined them, even though a letter was read to the congress in which Joaquin Zavala, the new President of Nicaragua, announced his determination not to enter into any contract for a canal through his country.

"At this juncture," Medina said, "during one of the last meetings of the congress, de Lesseps called me aside and said: 'The majority seems to be in favor of Nicaragua. I have personally no interest one way or the other, especially as any outlay for expenses incurred by the Türr-Wyse surveying party can be refunded by the new company. It would, however, be necessary to come first to an understanding with the Nicaraguan government as to the general bases of a contract; otherwise, if the congress votes in favor of Nicaragua and we then send a commissioner to deal with that government, without any previous understanding, the result will be that Nicaragua will demand such conditions and terms as to render the entire project out of the question. Is there anyone here authorized to make an offer in the name of the Nicaraguan government?' "

"Unfortunately, I knew too well there was not," Medina said. But as a friend of Nicaragua and a citizen of a neighboring republic, he assured de Lesseps that Nicaragua was too well aware of her own interests to attempt such a hold-up.

"I used every effort to persuade him to allow the convention to make a free and impartial decision," the Guatemalan diplomat said. "All my arguments were, however, of no avail in the face of the fears entertained by de Lesseps and the pressure brought to bear by the Colombian syndicate whose every energy was at work in an effort to secure a decision in favor of Panama."

At last it was agreed, "amid great confusion and marked anxiety on the part of many of the delegates," as Menocal put it, that "the (technical) committee, standing on a technical point of view, was of the opinion that a canal, such as would satisfy the requirements of commerce, is possible across the Isthmus of Panama, and recommends, specially, a canal at the level of the sea."

On May 29 the congress voted on the following proposition: "The congress thinks that the construction of an interoceanic canal on a constant level, which is so desirable in the interest of commerce and navigation, is possible, and that such ship canal in order to meet the indispensable facilities of access and utilization which should be offered especially by a communication of this kind, should be directed from the Gulf of Limon to the Bay of Panama."

The vote was: Yes--78, No--8, Abstaining--12, Absent--37.

It was a roll-call vote, and when the name of de Lesseps was called, he set off an explosion of applause when he cried: "Yes! And I accept the command of the enterprise!"

"This announcement electrified the house," Dr. Johnston told the American Geographical Society, "not only because M. de Lesseps is much loved and is really the best man for the work, but because it was a plank of safety thrown to a scheme which was being saved with difficulty."

"When it did finally come to what seemed to be a positive selction of a route," said J. Lawrence Smith, of Louisville, Kentucky, one of the nongovernmental delegates, "it appeared that at least one-half the affirmative votes were based on a mere sentiment not to oppose an enterprise so earnestly pressed by that most remarkable man, M. de Lesseps."

Menocal, analyzing the affirmative vote professionally, reported: "Only nineteen were engineers, and, of this last number, eight are at present or have been connected with the Suez Canal. Five are not practical engineers and only one, the delegate from the State of Panama, had ever been connected with any surveys of the isthmus, and it is believed that with that exception, not one of the nineteen had ever visited the locality."

He said that the five delegates from the French Society of Civil Engineers "either voted nay or absented themselves from the last two meetings of the technical committee and the congress."

One of the French delegates who voted No was Eiffel. It was his first association with the Panama Canal, an engineering problem that turned into a legal one and troubled him for years after his tower became the emblematic landmark on the Paris skyline.

Of the Americans, Admiral Ammen, Dr. Johnston, and Menocal abstained. Five kept away from the voting: W.W. Evans, an engineer; Cyrus W. Field, promoter of the Atlantic cable, an old friend of de Lesseps, who attended as representative of the New York Chamber of Commerce; Frederick Kelley, Commander Selfridge, and Smith, a member of the National Academy of Sciences who had been vice-president of the congress's committee on navigation and meteorology. Three voted Yes: Nathan Appleton of Boston, who went to work for de Lesseps soon thereafter, and Christian Christiansen and Eli Lazard, who represented the San Francisco Chamber of Commerce.

When the vote had been tallied and the momentous decision announced, de Lesseps took leave of his guests with characteristic sanguineness: "At the moment of parting I should confess to you some of the questions I have pondered while the congress was in session. I did not think fifteen days ago that I would have to put myself at the head of a new enterprise. My friends tried to talk me out of it, saying that after Suez I ought to relax. Ah well, if you ask a general who has won the first battle if he would like to gain a second, he can scarcely refuse."

2

Ferdinand de Lesseps repeatedly made plain that he was neither businessman nor financier nor engineer. By training he was a diplomat; by nature he was an energetic optimist. He mined an inexhaustible lode of silver linings and vaulted over obstacles with acrobatic grace. He had a flair for the dashing action, and the skill to bring it off. A moment after he had won Said Pasha's consent to build the Suez Canal, he put his horse over a parapet in a reckless jump that won him the admiring support of the Khedive's entourage. The same day, when a whole Egyptian regiment had missed the bull's-eye at a target shoot, he seized a musket and hit the mark with his first shot, and then knocked down a cruising eagle with a second pull.

He had as great a flair for the encouraging word. Late in 1870, on the eve of the battle of Champigny, he was dining with General Auguste Alexandre Ducrot, commander of the committed forces, when an officer arrived from the *Journal Officiel* with proofs of the general's proclamation to his troops. Asked to comment on the message, de Lesseps told Ducrot: "It's very good but it lacks something. You speak to your troops too much of the obstacles they will meet with and of the confidence you have in them. You do not speak to them enough of yourself."

"What shall I say?" the general asked.

De Lesseps thought for a moment, then wrote quickly at the bottom of the printer's galley a phrase that was famous in Paris the next day as the general's peroration: "As for me, I declare that I will only return to Paris dead or victorious." The battle raged three days, then the French had to withdraw. The general died in 1882.

Ernest Renan, the philosopher and moralist, welcoming de Lesseps to a chair in the French Academy, exclaimed: "You convince the Turk, the Arab, the Abyssinian, the Paris speculator and the Liverpool merchant by reasons which differ only in appearance. The true reason of your ascendancy is that people detect in you a heart full of sympathy for all that is human, a genuine passion for ameliorating the lot of your fellow creatures. You have in you that *'misereror super turbas'* ('O have pity upon the masses') which is the sentiment of all great organizers. People love you and like to see you and before you have opened your mouth you are cheered. Your adversaries call this your cleverness; we call it your magic."

His adversaries often showed great affection for him, too. Smith, the Louisville delegate, opposed him at the Paris congress but called him "one of nature's great men, born to the accomplishment of enterprises that repel even those accustomed to contend with great difficulties."

With a jaunty gesture and plain hard work de Lesseps won Englishmen over in his Suez venture despite the implacable opposition of the Prime Minister, Lord Palmerston, and such eminent British engineers as Robert Stephenson, who called the project "one of those chimeras so often formed to induce English capitalists to part with their money." He simply hung a French flag from the window of his hotel room on Piccadilly and went from town to town throughout the United Kingdom, holding thirty-two meetings in forty-five days. He would arrive loaded down with maps, pamphlets, and prospectuses, call on the Mayor and offer him the chairmanship of the meeting, visit the editors of the local papers, spend the night correcting proofs of the previous day's speeches, and take away a thousand copies to hand out the next day.

De Lesseps was sixty-four years old when he opened the Suez Canal to commerce, and in the same year, 1869, he married eighteen-year-old Louise Helene Autard de Bragard, a Creole beauty of Provençal descent who was twelve years younger than Charles de Lesseps, his son by his first marriage. They had twelve children, and he saw to it that they were raised ruggedly; he felt that the children of the well-to-do were "overdressed, overfed, and underexercised." Almost the first play-things the de Lesseps youngsters had were ponies, and "the merry procession of children and small ponies scampering out of the Bois de Boulogne at breakneck speed, accompanied by their father," was a heartwarming Parisian spectacle for many years.

De Lesseps was not a rich man. His father had been ruined financially in the diplomatic service of Napoleon, whom he last represented as imperial commissioner to the Ionian Islands. When a British squadron stood off Corfu and demanded its sur-render in May, 1814, a month after Napoleon abdicated, Math-ieu de Lesseps and the military commander refused, having had neither orders to capitulate nor even word of the abdica-tion. They held out until Louis XVIII sent a commissioner to relieve them, de Lesseps meanwhile paying the garrison with his own drafts on his Paris banker. During the Hundred Days of Napoleon's resumed reign after his escape from Elba, he conferred the title of Count on de Lesseps, and the government repaid the determined diplomat in *rentes*, its long-term securi-ties. But in paying him, it computed the *rentes* at par, and Mathieu de Lesseps was wiped out when he had to sell them to raise cash, because the market price then was only 30 francs, a fraction of their face value.

Ferdinand de Lesseps fared just as badly in the service of Napoleon III; when he abandoned his own career in diplomacy in 1849, he owed his bankers 30,000 francs—his posts in Madrid and Rome having cost him everything he could make.

Although his Emperor was slow in approving the Suez un-dertaking, de Lesseps's second cousin, Empress Eugenie, was one of its early champions; and when the canal was opened, she led the ceremonial procession through it aboard the imperial yacht. De Lesseps had a deep affection for Eugenie, and the day the Second Empire fell, while the Emperor was a prisoner of the Prussians, he rushed to the Tuileries to make certain that she was safe. When a lady in waiting told him there was no cash at the palace to finance her flight, and nobody to send for money, he raced home, grabbed up 500 francs from his desk, and hurried back. When he reached the Tuileries he found that the lady in waiting, Mme. le Breton, and the Austrian and Ital-ian ambassadors, Prince Metternich and Count Nigra, had taken her to the home of Dr. Thomas W. Evans, her American dentist, where she remained until Evans escorted her to England.

When de Lesseps took up the challenge of the Panama canal he was seventy-four years old, but he went into action with a show of confidence and vigor that never abated in the ten years he led the enterprise.

Owners of small hoards of cash, beneficiaries of his earlier venture, waited hungrily for his new one. To have his cab driver grab his hand and tell him gratefully; "M. de Lesseps, I am one of your stockholders," was a frequent experience; there was "scarcely a small tradesman or peasant who has not his share in the Suez Canal," de Lesseps wrote in his memoirs.

"Everybody had imagined that the Panama enterprise was destined to prove the same kind of gold mine as the Suez Canal, and was convinced the de Lessepses were simply rolling in wealth, an impression confirmed by their reckless expenditure and extravagant mode of life," a *New York Tribune* writer said.

First step in the formation of a company to build and operate the Panama canal was the organization of a syndicate to supply the money needed to nurse the venture along until it was ready to go public, at which time these founders would reap a special reward. This syndicate consisted of stockbrokers, financiers, publishers, and other suppliers of venture capital.

Next, de Lesseps bought out the Türr-Wyse group, paying ten million francs for the Colombian concession. Payment, half in cash and half in his corporation's stock, was due as soon as de Lesseps succeeded in organizing the company.

This rich return, a profit of more than 3,000 per cent, spurred two of the Türr-Wyse adventurers on to other isthmus-piercing enterprises.

Türr parlayed his own happy experience into a concession from King George I of Greece to build a canal from the Adriatic to the Aegean across the five-mile Isthmus of Corinth, the connective tissue between central Greece and the Peloponnesus.

Baron Jacques de Reinach, Türr's colleague on the board of directors of his Panama venture, went on to participate in the de Lesseps company's financing from the start and to become its financial agent in 1886, at a moment when the company was seeking passage of legislation considered indispensable to its survival. For his efforts on the canal company's behalf *The Spectator* of London bestowed on him the title of "Patronage Whip" of the Panama canal. He was a fun-loving, freewheeling operator, involved in a multitude of financial ventures, many of them in association with Cornelius Herz, one of the deftest contrivers in the wire-pulling world of Europe.

Herz, who was born in France in 1845 and grew up in New York, returned to serve in the French army as an assistant surgeon major in the Franco-Prussian War, then went back to the United States to win a stake. After a three-months residency at Mount Sinai Hospital, New York, he resigned rather than take examinations the hospital insisted on when he could not produce a medical school diploma. He moved to San Francisco, established a spectacularly lucrative medical practice there, and returned to France three years later, leaving behind a host of outraged friends, patients and brother Masons who said he had drained them of $300,000 by various confidence tricks. In a few years he was a tycoon in the newly-emerging electrical and telephone industries of France, publisher of a leading magazine of the electrical profession, an important investor in Clemenceau's newspaper, and, before he was forty, the first United States citizen to become a Grand Officer of the Legion of Honor, France's highest award. But when Ferdinand de Lesseps was putting together the canal enterprise, Herz was still a shadowy figure, though rapidly increasing in substance.

In the summer of 1879 de Lesseps announced that he would form a corporation called the *Compagnie Universelle du Canal Interocéanique de Panama* with a capital of 400,000,000 francs, to be obtained by the sale of 800,000 shares at 500 francs each. Then the nimble patriarch hit the road to sell the enterprise to the provinces.

"In these provincial tours," Dr. Johnston said in his report to the American Geographical Society, "he everywhere gave the impression that the governments of France and the United States were equally favorable to the enterprise; the flags of the two nations were everywhere united over his head when he spoke; and the following extract from one of his speeches, published in a provincial paper, is but a repetition of what he said at all the towns where he spoke: 'The Monroe Doctrine,' he said, 'has nothing to do with our enterprise because it is a private affair, because it is international in character, and therefore neutral. The opposition of the United States is not serious because their representatives at the congress declared that the United States came to the congress to submit themselves to the verdict of the majority, and this verdict has been rendered in favor of the Panama route.'

"I need not assure you, perhaps," Dr. Johnston added, "that no authorized delegate of the American government made any assurance of the kind to the congress."

At Lyon, where the press gave a breakfast in honor of de Lesseps, Nathan Appleton, one of the three Americans who had voted Yes at the congress, replied to the toast to the United States with the statement that the country of George Washington would give unlimited assistance to the country of Lafayette and would second the canal project heartily.

Appleton went about France with de Lesseps that summer, making speeches on behalf of the Panama venture. Presently he went on the payroll at $4,000 a year, reporting personally to de Lesseps and drawing his monthly pay through J. & W. Seligman, New York investment bankers. His duties consisted of lecturing and writing newspaper articles—when he could get them published.

On August 6 and 7, 1879, the Universal Panama Interoceanic Canal Company offered its shares to the public, in America as well as Europe, and de Lesseps discovered suddenly a magic arrayed against him that was even more powerful than his own. The public bought only 60,000 of the 800,000 shares offered, and he had to give back the down-payments the few purchasers of his stock had made.

On August 14 he issued a circular blaming the failure of the issue on opponents who, he said, exaggerated the cost of the project, minimized the receipts the canal would produce, and attempted to "create uneasiness by representing the United States of North America to be hostile to the scheme." Later he identified the opposition, saying: "The financial organs were hostile because they had not been paid."

Undismayed by the setback, de Lesseps declared he would sail right ahead. He announced in the circular that Couvreux & Hersent—the contractors who had cleared the entrance of the Suez Canal, regulated the course of the Danube, and enlarged the ports of Antwerp—had undertaken at their own expense a study of the work required to build the Panama Canal and had decided to take on the construction job "either by contract or for a royalty, as I may prefer, and thus to leave no doubt as to the real amount of the expenses."

As to the matter of diplomacy, he said, "I shall solve that myself by an early voyage to America." He would go to Panama, too, he said, at the head of an international technical commission that would survey the entire project.

While preparations for the expedition were under way, a noteworthy event in the canal company's history took place: the debut of its external house organ, the *Bulletin du Canal Interocéanique,* which appeared regularly on the first and fifteenth of every month for the next ten years.

"M. de Lesseps has a newspaper organ of his own or rather of his canal company, in Paris," the *New York Tribune* said of it, "and it is quick to make the most of everything occurring in this country which seems favorable to his project. Every expression of opinion in the press which can be construed to mean that the Administration does not represent the sentiments of the people on the canal question is reproduced by this journal, which of course takes good care not to print the other side."

On December 30, 1879, de Lesseps, his gorgeous young wife, three of their children, Victor de Lesseps, a son by an earlier marriage, and the members of his international technical commission who had been in Europe, reached Colon on the steamship *Lafayette*.

"The visit of M. de Lesseps to the isthmus is a genuine ray of sunshine to the simple natives," the *Tribune*'s correspondent reported. "He has kindled their hopes, and whatever may be the opinion elsewhere of his canal scheme, the natives of Panama have given it their implicit confidence. From the moment the news reached the isthmus of his coming, their minds were made up. The scant supplies of the government for the fiscal year were unhesitatingly appropriated for his entertainment, and the poverty-stricken inhabitants of Panama were compelled under heavy penalty to scrub, whitewash, and paint their dwellings, and set their streets and alleys in order. Such an air of neatness has not pervaded this city of pigs and smells within the memory of the oldest inhabitant."

The impact of de Lesseps's personality was enormous. Seeing him in action it was difficult to realize that he was almost seventy-five. He was just under middle height and somewhat stout, but he stood with soldierly erectness; and with his air of self-assurance, his snow-white hair accentuated by his dark, florid complexion, the bright glance of his black eyes, his square chin, prominent nose, and drooping, grandfatherly mustache, he brought a commanding yet kindly presence to speakers' stands across the world. He spoke rapidly, with constant gestures. He had warmth and enthusiasm, and displayed a brand of courtesy that could not be ruffled.

Tracy Robinson, a York State transplant who had lived on the isthmus since 1861 and was editor of *The Panama Star & Herald,* was one of the first to greet him in Panama. De Lesseps's confidence, joyfulness, and vigor impressed him deeply.

"He would ride over the rough country through which the canal had been or was being located, all day, would then dance all night, like a boy, and be ready for the next day's excursion 'fresh as a daisy.' " Robinson wrote. "His good nature and the optimism of his character were phenomenal and unfailing. Nothing ever seemed for an instant to dampen the ardor of his enthusiasm, or to cloud the vista of that glorious future which he had pictured in his imagination."

The old Panama hand was even more profoundly moved by his first sight of young Mme. de Lesseps, and years later when he was nearly eighty he still recalled with fervor that "her form was voluptuous and her raven hair without luster contrasted well with the rich pallor of her eastern features."

On the second night of 1880 there was a banquet for the visitors at the Grand Hotel in Panama City. To the toast of the evening, the health of M. and Mme. de Lesseps, the canal builder made a response of remarkably limited scope: "The press!" Then he paused an instant, and added: "The press of America, Europe, Asia, and Africa!"

In Panama he expounded the philosophy of optimism that had sustained him through the tribulations of the Suez undertaking. There had been very little capital in hand when he started at Suez, he said, but if he had waited to start until the money came in, the canal would not be finished yet. There would be unsolved problems at Panama, just as there had been at Suez, he said, and he would solve them just as he had solved them in Egypt; when difficulties arose, men of genius would spring up to overcome them, just at they had at Suez.

He already knew that more trouble lay ahead than the Türr-Wyse reports had led him to expect. "Lesseps himself told me," Mrs. Emily Crawford, the Paris correspondent for the *London Daily News* and the *New York Tribune,* wrote years later "that Wyse's report was daringly mendacious and that he ought to have known it could not be otherwise because there was an inborn hostility in everyone of the Bonapartean race whom he had ever known to the truth. But he was in for the enterprise, and as he thought it feasible, he meant to go on with it."

There already had been one abrupt departure from the data of Wyse and Reclus at the Paris congress. It had raised their 427,000,000-franc original estimate of the canal's cost to 1,070,-000,000 francs for the work and 130,000,000 francs more for interest on the investors' funds.

The technical commission that de Lesseps led to Panama handed him another revised estimate of cost on February 14, 1880, cutting the congress figure to 843,000,000 francs, including 10 percent for contingencies; it also cut the congress's twelve-year estimate of the time needed for the job to eight years.

The survey party sailed for New York the next day aboard the Panamà Mail steamship *Colon,* and at sea de Lesseps composed a note on the commission's cost estimate, cutting it to 658,600,000 francs.

The *Colon* docked at Canal Street on February 24, and de Lesseps checked in at the Windsor Hotel, Fifth Avenue and Forty-seventh Street, and composed a prospectus, in which he cut the cost figure still further.

"In the program which I presented to the commission," he explained in the prospectus, "I recommended a heavy maximum for the cost per cubic meter of execution and works, whenever the nature of the ground was not thoroughly known in its depth and breadth. Thus it was that we arrived at a total estimate of 843,000,000 francs, but I am convinced, and most of the members of the commission likewise, that the final operations shall show a considerable reduction. This is the reason that induces me to fix the capital for the company at 600,000,000 francs. The European capitalists, having shown their intention to take a share in the undertaking as they did formerly in the Suez Canal, one half of the public subscription, say 300,000,000 francs, shall be reserved to the capitalists of all the States of America.

"From statistical reports published by the international congress of Paris, during the month of May, 1879, there should be upon the opening of the canal traffic of at least six million tons annually. The transit duty having been fixed by the act of concession at 15 francs per ton,* and more if it becomes necessary, the annual revenue (minimum) would be ninety million francs. Therefore, six million tons, which will increase progressively, would give a revenue of 10 per cent a year on a capital of 900,000,000 francs.

"Actually as the merchandise in transit through the Isthmus of Panama, including the expenses of landing, storage, railway transportation and cold storage, lighterage, without counting delay, pays an average of about 80 francs per ton, it is easy to see the benefit when cargoes coming either from the Atlantic or the Pacific will be able to cross from one ocean to the other without any delay. An interest of 5 per cent will be paid to the shareholders on the sums paid by them during the progress of the work, and also during one year after the opening of the canal to large vessels."

The traffic forecasts that de Lesseps referred to had been published in the following statement by Emile Levasseur, the geographer and economist, who was president of the Paris congress's committee on statistics: "In ten years (1889) before which time the canal, in all probability, will not be opened to traffic, 5,250,000 tons at least will probably represent the commercial movement of the two oceans, and about two million tons will represent that fraction of the commercial movement between the east and Europe, which as it seems, may be diverted from the route now followed in order to take that of the American isthmus; 7,250,000 tons in the aggregate."

Levasseur pointed out that this did not mean that the canal

*(Article 14 of the concession stated: "Tolls may be such as the concessionaires fixed, not exceeding 10 francs per cubic meter of the submerged hulls of vessels using the canal.")

would get 7,250,000 tons of business in the first year of operation, or even in the next years; he only wanted to show the capacity of the double reservoir of shipping that was to supply the canal with tolls.

Throughout the New York visit de Lesseps never seemed to tire; he received every visitor graciously and fielded every question with élan. But he also made it clear that he was a single-minded, stubborn man, with a conviction that the authority of command was indivisible—a philosophy he had acquired in his youth from Mohammed Ali, who told him: "Remember in the course of your lifetime, whenever you have anything important to do, if you are two there is one too many."

At a special meeting of the American Society of Civil Engineers at the Union League Theater, Madison Avenue and Twenty-sixth Street, he told a huge and admiring audience: "If the committee had decided to build a locked canal, I would have put on my hat and gone home. Locks are very good for small vessels, but they would not do for large ships. There is a ship on the stocks now that I know of, 120 feet in length. It would take a very long time to get a ship of this size through a canal of this length with a single lock. If there were to be a system of double locks it would be much more expensive than any deep cutting on the route."

Distinguished New Yorkers lavished on de Lesseps their customary distinguished hospitality for distinguished visitors, mixed with some gritty food for thought with which Whitelaw Reid, editor of the *Tribune,* augmented the menu at a dinner at the Lotos Club: "For what he *has* done we give him our most cordial welcome and the homage of our heartiest applause. What he proposes to do is another matter, not to be dealt with here, not to be dealt with lightly anywhere, a matter of national and international concern, a matter affecting the policy which the government has maintained for nearly a hundred years, and to which our people are likely to adhere as tenaciously in the future as we have done in the past."

De Lesseps hastened to Washington to deal with United States government policy. On March 8, appearing before the House of Representatives Select Committee on an Interoceanic Ship Canal, at the committee's invitation, he emphasized that his project was entirely a private enterprise. Replying to a question by Representative Conger of Michigan as to an earlier statement that control of the company's administrative, judicial, and financial affairs would be in Paris, he said: "The assembly of shareholders is sovereign and can dispose of the question. If the majority of the stock is held by Americans, they can have the headquarters either in New York or Washington."

He told the Congressional committee that the 840,000,000-franc estimate of the cost of the canal included some work for finishing touches that would be necessary only after the canal was open to navigation. He said that if he were an engineer he would ask for eight years as a reasonable time to build the canal, but that it could be done in six.

When he emerged from the hearing room, having been invited to continue his discussion the next day, he found that President Rutherford B. Hayes had just sent a message to the Senate in which he declared: "The policy of this country is a canal under American control."

The President said in his message: "The United States cannot consent to the surrender of this control to any European power or to any combination of European powers. If existing treaties between the United States and other nations, or if the rights of sovereignty or property of other nations stand in the way of this policy—a contingency which is not apprehended, suitable steps should be taken by just and liberal negotiations to promote and establish the American policy on this subject consistently with the rights of the nations to be affected by it.

"The capital invested by corporations or citizens of other countries in such an enterprise must in a great degree look for protection to one or more of the great powers of the world. No European power can intervene for such protection without adopting measures on this continent which the United States would deem wholly inadmissible. If the protection of the United States is relied upon, the United States must exercise such control as will enable this country to protect its national interests and maintain the rights of those whose private capital is embarked in the work.

"An interoceanic canal across the American isthmus will essentially change the geographical relations between the Atlantic and Pacific coasts of the United States and between the United States and the rest of the world. It will be the great ocean thoroughfare between our Atlantic and our Pacific shores and virtually a part of the coastline of the United States. Our merely commercial interest in it is greater that that of all other countries, while its relations to our power and prosperity as a nation, to our means of defense, our unity, peace and safety, are matters of paramount concern to the people of the United States. No other great power would under similar circumstances fail to assert a rightful control over a work so closely and and vitally affecting its interest and welfare.

"Without urging further the grounds of my opinion, I repeat in conclusion that it is the right and the duty of the United States to assert and maintain such supervision and authority over any interoceanic canal across the isthmus that connects North and South America as will protect our national interests. This I am quite sure will be found not only compatible with but promotive of the widest and most permanent advantage to commerce and civilization."

In this explicit statement of national policy, the chronically optimistic de Lesseps perceived cause for rejoicing. He told his Congressional hosts that he had not appeared before them to talk politics, but he could not refrain from expressing his delight with the President's message. He said that it would certainly be advantageous for the United States to protect the canal during construction and after it was opened and that he had just advised his son in Paris that the President's message "assured the security of the canal."

Having thus solved the problems of diplomacy that beset his Panama enterprise, he embarked on a three–week promotional trip across the country, which left prospective investors in Philadelphia, St. Louis, Omaha, San Francisco, Chicago, Niagara, and Boston marveling at his imperishable vitality.

While de Lesseps was on tour, France's Minister to Washington, Maxime Outrey, presented a note to Secretary Evarts saying that his government was "in no way concerned" in the Panama Canal enterprise and "in no way proposed to interfere therein or to give it any support, either direct or indirect."

3

*O*n *its second attempt to go public the*
Universal Panama Interoceanic Canal Company succeeded
beyond the flashiest hopes of its venturesome founders.

The offering of its stock, 590,000 shares at 500 francs a
share, was substantially smaller than the stillborn issue of the
year before—not even a half of the 600,000,000-franc capital de
Lesseps had set as his objective when he distributed his prospectus to the bankers in New York. This time he could have
reached the larger goals easily; applications for 1,209,609
shares poured in, and the company had to ration the stock.

Opening of the subscription of December 7, 1880, set off a
three-day stampede from which 86,230 men and 16,000 women,
almost all of them French, emerged as shareholders in the new
de Lesseps enterprise. Their clamorous response made the
Panama Canal Company one of the most populously owned
businesses in corporate history. Odd-lot transactions, or orders
for fewer that 100 shares, made up a vast majority of the pur-
chases; 80,000 of the stockholders received five shares or fewer.

After the promoters' experience with the unsuccessful issue of 1879, the company had developed several pragmatic solutions to the problems to which de Lesseps had attributed the
fiasco. A month before the new stock offering de Lesseps met
the doubters of his cost and revenue projections with a trium-
phant proclamation in his *Bulletin:* "My forecasts are completely realized. An international technical commission,
meeting on the spot at Panama, confirms the practicability of
the maritime canal. The contractors Couvreux & Hersent have

presented their schedule and declared that the construction of the canal will not cost 500,000,000 francs. The evaluation of the annual traffic, certainly 90,000,000 francs of revenue on 6,000,-000 tons, is considered conservative. The revenue will be much larger than supposed."

At that moment the actual cost of the canal was a matter of conjecture. A 512,000,000-franc figure had been mentioned widely. Abel Couvreux, one of the contractors, had used it in a speech at Brussels on May 6, 1880, arriving at the total by adding an estimate of 466,098,000 for excavation and dam construction and 45,902,000 for contingent work. He said it was "certain that these prices are still in excess of the truth, and if the future shows that the estimates now adopted have not been reached, the wisdom of those who have prepared them must not be impugned, but their wise foresight must be recognized in the performance of so gigantic a task, which is to be accomplished in such new and unknown regions."

But no contract price had been specified, for the contract was not executed until March 12, 1881, and even then it provided only the means of arriving at a price.

On the diplomatic side, the Panama Canal Company had recruited the United States Secretary of the Navy, R. W. Thompson, right out of President Hayes's Cabinet to serve as president of the company's American committee, composed of representatives of the banking houses of J. & W. Seligman, Drexel, Morgan & Co., and Winslow, Lanier & Co. General U.S. Grant had refused the job, describing his reasons in a letter to Admiral Ammen from Galena, Illinois, dated June 22, 1880: "Today I received a letter from Seligman enclosing a cablegram from de Lesseps offering me the presidency of the Panama Canal (New York presidency) with the same salary he is to receive, namely 125,000 francs per annum. The letter also says that the Seligmans with some other bank or banks they can associate with them will have the business of receiving the American subscriptions for performing the work. I telegraphed back my nonacceptance and wrote giving my reasons. I gave work that had been done in the way of surveys, what had been proved wrong by these surveys, and that while I would like to have my name associated with the successful completion of a ship canal between the two oceans, I was not willing to connect it with a failure and one I believe subscribers would lose all they put in."

The press, which de Lesseps had accused of opposing the earlier issue because he had not paid off, was no longer so antagonistic. Charges under the head of *publicité* were 1,595,-371.20 francs this time. Emile de Girardin, the press lord who had owned the *Petit Journal*, with its enormous circulation, and a string of provincial newspapers, and had invaded the field of finance by founding the *Banque Nationale,* had waged a particularly violent campaign against the Panama project the year before. Now he was a member of the canal company's first board of administrators.

The promoters did not limit their merchandising efforts to advertising space and editorial cultivation. They plastered Paris walls with colorful handbills, induced merchants to stuff advertising flyers in the orders they delivered, and conferred silver medals worth five francs each on five-share stockholders. They also offered the stock on easy and alluring terms: one quarter down, the next due a year later, the last two, five years later. Stockholders were to receive interest of 5 per cent a year on their paid-up installments until the opening of the canal.

The issue was not only a triumph for the company but a bonanza for the underwriting group that had brought it out and for the syndicate that had nursed the venture along from takeover of the Türr-Wyse concession, through the 1879 setback, up to the moment the public rushed in.

This syndicate consisted of 172 men and women who had chipped in a total of 2,000,000 francs in 5,000-franc units. They were rewarded with founders' shares of the Universal Panama Interoceanic Canal Company, of which there were 900 in all. The syndicate members received 400 of them, one for each 5,000-franc unit they had ventured. The founders' shares did not represent any ownership of the company, but they carried a claim in perpetuity on a large piece of the action. Article 60 of the Panama company's bylaws reserved 15 per cent of net profits for the owners of the founders' shares.

The founders' shares of the Suez Canal Company, each of which also rewarded an original investment of 5,000 francs, were selling at 380,000 francs at the time. The Panama company's founders' shares, not yet admitted to the Bourse, rose rapidly to 70,000 to 75,000 francs in the over-the-counter market, where they could be bought or sold in tenths of a share to facilitate trading.

The largest holder of the founders' shares was Jules Lebaudy, with fifty. He was a member of the rich family of sugar refiners whose name was identified with spectacular financial ventures for decades. Next, with twenty founders' shares, was Paul Dalloz, proprietor and director of the *Moniteur Universel,* the government's official organ until 1868, and member of the famous French publishing family of Panckoucke.

Ninety founders' shares were put at Ferdinand de Lesseps's disposal, and eighteen went to Marc Levy-Cremieux, vice-president of the Franco-Egyptian Bank, who put together the consortium that brought out the successful issue. Three large commercial banks—the *Société Générale, Crédit Lyonnais,* and *Crédit Industriel*—the investment banking house of Seligmann Frères, and the Suez Canal Company comprised a managing committee of this underwriting group. The underwriters split fifty-nine of the opulent founders' shares, one for each 10,000 of the canal company's shares they committed themselves to issue. The remaining 333 founders' shares were earmarked for cooperating newspapers and bankers.

Not all the press or all the banks cooperated. A Paris correspondent of the *New York Tribune*, for one, commented harshly that "although numerous banks here allured by the prospect of gain have lent themselves to the scheme, some men of high standing, like M. Christophle,* the director of the *Crédit Foncier*, and the Rothschilds, refused to allow their counters to be used for such a flytrap."

Banks and other financial institutions that climbed on the Panama bandwagon and booked subscriptions for the stock at their windows cut up a total commission of 4,224,918 francs for the service, an average of slightly more than seven francs a share.

The underwriters had advanced four francs a share to meet the expenses of the issue on the proposition that if they failed to sell it in toto they would lose their advance, but if they suc-

*Albert Christophle, Governor of *Crédit Foncier de France.*

ceeded they would get back the advance, plus a bonus of twenty francs a share. With the issue a sellout, their combined 2,360,000-franc risk brought them an 11,800,000-franc profit.

The actual capitalization of the company was 300,000,000 francs, represented by the 590,000 shares sold to the public at 500 francs each and 10,000 paid-up shares handed to the Türr-Wyse combination as half the purchase price for its Colombian concession.

The sale of its stock cost the Panama Canal Company slightly more that 20,000,000 francs. When it had paid the underwriters' fees, commissions to the subscription agents, charges for purchased cooperation of various financial institutions, expenditures listed as *publicité*, the 5,000,000-franc cash half of the Türr-Wyse price for its concession, and the 750,000 francs of earnest money due Colombia, not quite 271,500,000 remained of the 295,000,000 the enthusiastic public had subscribed.

At the company's first general meeting, on the afternoon of January 31, 1881, de Lesseps assured the subscribers that he had no intention of diluting their equity when the time came to seek more money to complete the canal; he said he would get an additional 300,000,000 francs by borrowing it.

The exultant crowd that jammed the Cirque d'Hiver in the rue Amelot for the historic occasion represented every order of the French economy: big financiers, small shopkeepers, women turned out by haute couture and, white-bonneted maids who fetched and carried for them, provincials in their blouses, men of the *Garde Républicaine* who had managed to stretch their small pay far enough to handle the down payment on a few shares. They gave de Lesseps an ovation, approved his entire report unanimously, and shouted that he was "*le plus grand génie de l'univers.*"

De Lesseps rewarded them by announcing that the company's first executive party had arrived on the isthmus and recalling how he had forecast in 1860 the great profitability of the Suez Canal. He said the Panama canal's prospects were even brighter because so many fresh reservoirs of traffic were waiting to be tapped.

He had still better news for the second meeting, on March 3. The engineers had established five survey camps in the first days of February, and de Lesseps reported that recent borings had reduced the estimate of necessary excavation from 75,-000,000 cubic meters to 72,900,000. In the mountain ridge to be cut through, no part was untested, he said, and French contractors had learned at Suez how to dig economically in soft soil and at Cherbourg how to attack submarine rocks. The rough estimate of work on the canal proper—excavation and the construction of lateral dikes—amounted to 430,000,000 francs. Building the weirs and deepening of trenches to carry fresh water to sea would come to 46,000,000, and another 36,000,000 for a waiting dock and tide gates on the Pacific side, which de Lesseps did not think necessary, brought the total up to Couvreux & Hersent's estimated 512,000,000 francs for the canal complete and open to navigation.

In the autumn, he said, the cutting of the Culebra Mountain would start, and before the year's end excavations at the lower level would be under way, while a marine dredge would scoop out an access channel in the bay at Limon on the Atlantic side. At peak periods the job would not require more than 8,000 to 10,000 laborers, and they would be found easily among the colored population of the region, he told the investors.

On May 4 the *Times* of London brought the English-speaking world an even more confident report, quoting a dispatch from the *Journal des Débats*: "A broad road already connects the two oceans. The engineers concluded from the survey that has been made that the construction of the canal will be a comparatively easy matter."

The company created a superior consultative committee to act as a technical board and give its opinion on all plans. Some of the most eminent engineers in Europe accepted the invitation to serve on it.

The job was going so well that in June de Lesseps was able to lend the services of an outstanding engineer to his old friend, General Türr, to help out on the Corinth Canal project.

Panama shares entered the new year a favorite on the Bourse at a time when the Bourse was a favorite preoccupation of the jealously demarcated microcosm known paradoxically as *tout Paris*, and of considerably more inclusive worlds.

A writer for the clerical journal, *Le Monde*, was astonished to find that none of the guests at a fashionable reception "thought of or deemed it opportune to utter a gallant phrase, but all, without exception, talked of 'Timbale,' 'Union,' 'Suez,' 'Panama.' "

"I fancied I was dreaming, thrown by a nightmare among brokers, surrounded by young couples ready to dance, and witnessing some enchantment which altered the words on their lips," he wrote. "One wished to ask for a waltz, and against his will spoke of nothing but stocks. The lady, instead of promising him the third, replied, 'I sell at so much.' I pinched myself in the hope of waking up to see people and things in their normal condition. Vain effort. Some left; others took their places; and the subject of conversation did not vary. Let me be hung on the highest tree in the Champs Elysées if ever during my entire youth I thought of holding such a conversation with a pretty woman."

For the canal company's shareholders the year 1881 had been almost a honeymoon. There had been casualty reports and a few engineering disappointments, but Panama, where they had occurred, was a remote place, little comprehended.

4

The first men engaged in the actual work of building the canal across Panama arrived on the isthmus on January 29, 1881—forty pioneers led by Armand Reclus, the canal company's general agent, and by Gaston Blanchet, chief engineer for Coureux & Hersent who was to be the director of works.

Reclus had been in Panama with Bonaparte Wyse, and Blanchet had been there twice, once for the contractors' initial survey and later with de Lesseps. For the other members of the party, who had never been out of France, the isthmus was the New World not only in nomenclature but in every environmental aspect.

They stepped down the gangplank of the *Lafayette*, three weeks out of St. Nazaire, into the sweltering, smelly town of Colon, a community consisting of two streets lined with bars, stores, and tenements. There was no drainage system whatever, and refuse of every sort lay piled everywhere. The Panama Railroad had built the town and had initially named it Aspinwall, a dubious honor to William Henry Aspinwall, one of the road's founders.

Obligingly, H.A. Woods, superintendent of the railroad, got the newly arrived canal builders out of town at once on a special train bound for Panama City, forty-eight miles away, on the Pacific side of the isthmus.

The railroad, opened in 1855, had been built at a heavy cost both in lives and money; there was a local legend that at least one body lay beneath each sleeper tie along the entire route.

Halfway across the isthmus, the canal builders had their

first glimpse of the Chagres River, control of which was indispensable to any canal built along their chosen route. Shallow and sluggish then, in the midst of the dry season, its flow was known to multiply 140 times, to almost 70,000 cubic feet a second, during the long months of heavy rainfall.

As they crossed the river on a 625-foot iron bridge, the Chagres waters, oozing across the marshland and simmering in the blazing sun, brought a disturbing reality to the frequent and fearful tales of "Shagress fever" with which ships' stewards filled every Panama-bound passenger. (Less picturesquely but more functionally, Americans referred to malaria simply as "the shakes.")

Occasionally a huge alligator slithered out of the Chagres mud, small monkeys popped down from the trees, and white pelicans waddled along the spongy right of way. The vegetation was wild and lush, and beyond the swamp, south of the line of the railroad, brightly flowering shrubs, cocoa, banana and breadfruit trees, covered the gradually rising hills.

The newcomers from France learned later that the long, strange-looking ribbons they saw hanging in the doorways of the huts along the riverbank were strips of jerked beef. In the yards of the huts they saw flocks of turkeys and chickens, monitored possessively by vultures. Now and then they passed a well-built, green-shuttered white house, its yard surrounded by mango trees and planted with red and white hibiscus and everlasting rose. It was the home of a railroad executive.

After a three-hour run they reached Panama City, an ancient, sun-broiled Spanish town. An important Pacific port and capital of the Colombian state of Panama, it was already a cosmopolitan though languid place to which the canal's construction had not yet bought boom prices and bustle.

The French party put up at the Grand Hotel, which charged them 15 francs a day for a room, breakfast and dinner included. Soda water, in constant demand, was as much as 1.25 francs a bottle. The Grand, which the canal company bought a year later for 1,030,000 francs as a headquarters building, was a large, airy structure in the form of a hollow square, the bedrooms opening onto interior galleries from which the guests could look down on an enormous bar and billiard room where men from every part of the world were at the tables day and night.

"Two billiard tables, the biggest I have ever seen, stood in the middle," said Henri Cermoise, a young engineer who came out from France a few weeks later. "They were so huge that there were four balls to a game; with three it was impossible on most of the shots to reach the ball you were playing, lost in the middle of this steppe of green cloth. Beyond the billiard tables, at one end of the room, one of those vast bars that have such a place in American life was erected. In front of these rows of bottles with their multicolored labels most of the business in Panama was transacted while standing and gulping down cocktails, always the eternal cocktail. Then, if the customer had the time and, above all, money to lose, all he had to do was to cross the hall to find himself in a packed little room where a roulette wheel was in operation. There is every diversion at hand in this hotel lobby. Besides, it would be useless to go out to look for other pleasures; they were nowhere to be found. In this city there is neither theater nor concert nor café, nothing but the lobby of the Grand Hotel, to which one must always return."

Opposite the hotel stood the cathedral with its façade of rich brown stone, its passing bell tolling all day long during yellow fever epidemics as funeral processions plodded continuously through the city's narrow streets.

Blanchet, the engineer in charge, lost no time getting the job under way and establishing work camps across the isthmus. He was a prodigious worker, completely dedicated to the creation of the canal. "He did not give a thought to taking care of himself," Cermoise said. "He ran constantly from one work camp to another, not taking any rest, trying to pursue an European schedule of activity in a country where this is a sure guarantee of sickness if not of death."

At first the pioneers made do with crowded, inconvenient barracks; but these were replaced as soon as was possible with more spacious demountable houses that the company had bought in the United States. In these prefabricated chalets, erected on high pilings coated with tar to repel snakes, everyone had a room of his own, furnished with chairs, a washstand, and a frame on which to sling a hammock—"all the refinements of modern luxury," Cermoise said cheerfully.

Fortunately for the first party, they arrived in the dry tropical winter, but as the malarial months of the rainy season approached, they learned to live with the constant quiver of nerves that the daily dose of quinine produced—and even to endure the sensation of being near to bursting that came with the double or triple dose the slightest feverishness warned them to take.

Moving out to plot the route of the canal, they learned many dishes of a strange cuisine. Indians, who made their way to some coastal town to barter for their annual supply of salt, bringing along as payment their pots of honey and wax and the colorfully beaded bags they had crocheted with great skill, introduced the builders to a broth made of water or milk mixed with *pinole*, a powder of toasted corn and cocoa. Occasionally, along the trail, the canal builders met an American or English mining engineer and his native guide, the guide's mount loaded down with saddlebags, blanket, shotgun, and a pair of fighting cocks. From such encounters they learned to make a ragout of freshly killed armadillo stewed with *ñames* and *ototes*, roots that are vaguely like potatoes.

They did not, however, forsake the European cuisine. The Gamboa encampment, for example, had a Belgian cook, and for a long time its mess hall was famous among the company's camps as "the *summum* of luxury and elegance."

It was at the Gamboa camp, sixteen miles northwest of Panama City, that Ferdinand de Lesseps's right-hand man, Henri de Bionne, was guest of honor on the night of July 9, 1881, at a gala dinner that was the high-water mark of canal company society for a brief time, but soon came to be regarded as a tragic augury. "There was never a banquet so gay and warmhearted," Cermoise recalled.

De Bionne, who had accompanied his chief to Panama eighteen months earlier, was back there on a confidential mission for him. He was a poised and courteous man of thirty-eight, a former naval officer, with degrees both in law and medicine. He was the last to arrive at the dinner, having stopped to look through his baggage for a quinine tonic, which he always took before each meal. He walked into the dining hall just in time to hear one of the guests, a Norwegian woman, exclaim: "We will be thirteen at table!"

45

"In this case it is the last to come who pays for all," he reassured her cheerfully.

De Bionne sailed for home two weeks later, on July 24. Forty-eight hours out of Colon he fell ill of yellow fever and died. He was buried at sea in the Gulf of Mexico.

Scarcely four months later Blanchet mounted his horse and rode into the interior on an exploration that exhausted him; he was stricken with yellow fever on his return and died in three days.

Blanchet's short term in Panama had not been a particularly happy one. He was disappointed and mortified when the home office rejected two of his most important proposals. These became, in paradox, a lasting monument to his engineering competence, for their wisdom ultimately came to be recognized.

The first concerned the most fundamental aspect of the construction job: the plotting of the canal's exact course. Preliminary selection of the route, according to *Le Génie Civil*, a highly regarded French technical magazine, had been made on the basis of maps so small in scale that they furnished only vague, approximate indications of the country's features. Blanchet proposed to clear a strip 400 feet wide along this provisional route, for he was confident that the earlier maps were at least sufficiently accurate to assure discovery of the practicable line within a clearing of that extent; such a clearing not only would afford ample room to determine precisely the canal's line by means of an instrument survey, but would also open up cross-country communication and remove acres of malarial forest.

Instead, Blanchet was ordered to clear a strip only 40 feet wide, which provided nothing but a crooked, narrow trail that had to zigzag constantly around minor obstacles. It yielded no comprehensive picture of the terrain, made the use of precision instruments extremely difficult, and was finally abandoned. The location of the canal ultimately was fixed by reference to the line of the Panama Railroad, and a strip many times 40 feet in width had to be cleared.

The second proposal by Blanchet that his board of directors rejected, a *Génie Civil* correspondent reported, was his initial selection of a site for a company town on the isthmus.

Colon, near the mouth of the Chagres, offered no suitable location for wharves, warehouses, residences, machine shops and other necessary facilities. Seeking an accessible and relatively healthy location, with firm soil on which to build, Blanchet had chosen a spot eight miles upriver and set to work to construct an industrial town.

High ground overlooking the river had just been staked out and graded, and construction started, when sickness swept the work force, killing several men and stampeding the rest. The directors ordered immediate abandonment of the location, and Blanchet obeyed, although subsequent experience proved his initial choice to have been correct, said *Le Génie Civil*. Since Colon, with its many defects, was the only other place on deep water that the railroad touched, he had to return there and create a site for a headquarters town, named Christophe Colomb, with a fill of dry earth hauled down from the nearby Mindi Hills.

The actual digging of the canal began on January 20, 1882, just seventy-four days after Blanchet's death. The scene of the operation was the Emperador work station, on the incline leading up to the rocky heights of Culebra Mountain. A throng of Colombian government officials, local celebrities and admiring townspeople turned out. The City of Panama staged a grand fete to celebrate the beginning of the dig, for it was an event of special significance; all the work until then had been preparatory, and the Emperador excavation was the premiere of a series of test digs that the contract with Couvreux & Hersent stipulated as the basis for determining the ultimate cost of building the canal.

The contract was such a monument to mutual trust and esteem that it named de Lesseps, one of the parties to it, the final arbiter of disputes that might arise between the contractors and the canal company. It divided the job into two stages: an organizational period expected to last about two years, then a period of the work proper. During the first stage most of the material would be mobilized and installations built, and the digging attacked at numerous points to provide an exact understanding of costs on which unit prices would be established.

The canal company would pay for all expenditures, which had to adhere to itemized budgets submitted by the contractors;

any budget alterations would require approval by the company's directors or, in an emergency, its chief agent in Panama.

As a first-stage remuneration, the contractors would receive 6 per cent of the total expenditures after deduction of specified administrative charges.

For their second-stage pay, the contract established a formula under which to compute it. Couvreux & Hersent and the canal company would split the difference between the cost of excavating the verified cubic yardage at the unit price agreed on and the total of actual expenditures computed without interest and after deduction of the specified administrative costs. The canal company then would distribute 20 per cent of its share among its own and its contractors' employees on the basis of their salaries and length of service.

Work moved along steadily. Captain Meade, commander of the U.S.S. *Vandalia*, reported to the American Secretary of the Navy that a 300-yard-wide strip along the entire length of the canal had been cleared of trees and underbrush. Blanchet's proposed strip would have served as the foundation of this clearing.

Meade also reported a high incidence of sunstroke among the white employees, and said the Frenchmen on the job took little care of themselves and ate and drank just as though they were at home. But he thought the death rate among canal personnel remarkably low, and said newspapers in the United States had exaggerated the figures greatly.

The shareholders heard more of the company's accomplishments at the annual meeting on June 29. The directors reported that they had decided on the canal's exact course—it would run right through territory in which the Panama Railroad had exclusive right of way under agreements in force until 1966. On April 13, 1881, Reclus had written to de Lesseps: "It is necessary at any price to settle the question of the railroad, because on its possession or not depends the accomplishment of the canal."

More than a year earlier, rumors of negotiations between the canal company and the railroad company had become so noisy that the Colombian Minister at Paris, M.C. Holguin, had asked de Lesseps what was going on. De Lesseps wrote to him on June 14, 1881: "We have not pursued any negotiations for the purchase of the Panama Railroad nor have we had occasion to offer an indemnity to the directors of the said railroad company. We have simply negotiated the acquisition of a certain number of shares of the Panama Railroad Company, discussing with the holders the purchase price of their shares. If our proposition shall be accepted and our negotiations succeed, we shall become stockholders of the railroad company, which will continue to exist." On July 1, 1881, the first day of the canal company's new fiscal year, he made this letter public in its biweekly *Bulletin* and disclosed that the negotiations with the railroad had ended happily. A purchase contract, drawn on June 10, 1881, was authenticated on July 8.

The highlight of the stockholders meeting of June, 1882, was de Lesseps's disclosure of the details of the purchase, and the plans for financing it. Early in 1879 Bonaparte Wyse had negotiated an agreement with the railroad's management under which, among alternative methods of cooperation, the canal company acquired the right to buy at least a majority of the road's shares at $200 a share. Through its so-called American committee the canal company had acquired almost the total equity, 68,534 of the road's outstanding 70,000 shares, at approximately $250 a share, plus $41 a share for some unidentified assets. De Lesseps asked authority to float a loan to pay the bill.

He also asked approval to borrow 300,000,000 francs more, which, together with the company's capital, would make up the 600,000,000 francs needed to open the road in 1888—a completion date that was now a certainty, he said. The stockholders approved both borrowings.

Describing the health of the working force, de Lesseps said that the year before, when yellow fever had struck hard in the West Indies and along the Gulf of Mexico, Panama had escaped unscathed. From February to June, 1881, when the work force grew from 425 to 588, there were eleven deaths; in the next five months, when the payroll increased to 1,928, fifty-one died; in the first four months of 1882, when the force rose to 2,652, only twenty-four died.

These casualties included the loss of de Bionne, Blanchet, Etienne, the canal's subdirector, and his secretary, Bertrand, but they did not diminish the public's zeal to lend money to the company. On September 7, 1882, men and women enticed by a municifent rate of interest from an elegant company gobbled up the first bond issue—the borrowing to pay for the Panama Railroad. The issue consisted of 250,000 bonds, redeemable at 500 francs each on maturity in 1957 and bearing yearly interest of 25 francs, or 5 per cent, until then. Since the bonds were offered to subscribers at only 437.50 francs, the 25 francs a year they yielded represented an actual interest rate of 5.71 per cent on the investment.

Marc Levy-Cremieux, so successful for the canal company in its stock issue, also managed the underwriting syndicate for its first bond issue and for the next two it floated. In these three borrowings the syndicate acted under a two-phase agreement with the company. One phase consisted of their commitment to buy a portion of each issue for resale at a specified markup, a perfectly straightforward assumption of risk, although official scrutinizers of their operations came to call the underwriters excessively timid in the portion they took. The other phase granted them options to buy a substantial part of each issue at a somewhat smaller discount than they received on their committed portion, but did not require them to exercise the options until after they had sold the bonds to the public, thereby guaranteeing them a profit with no risk.

The public's voracious response to the first bond issue was noted at great distances, the *New York Tribune* commenting on the de Lesseps appeal: "With $30,000,000 already invested in the enterprise and with applications for shares showering him from all quarters of France whenever he faces the market with a direct proposal, he can now reckon with confidence upon the resources required for so vast a scheme. He can get the money, and unquestionably he has the genius requisite for surmounting the engineering difficulties. Englishmen and Americans may as well reconcile themselves to the situation. M. de Lesseps, if he lives, will undoubtedly cut his way through the rocky buttresses of the Panama isthmus as he did through the shifting sands of the Suez desert. It is a matter of money, labor, and explosives."

Three months later Couvreux & Hersent asked to be released from their contract. They said that while they were ready to go ahead with the second stage, the so-called period of work proper, on the basis of the unit prices established during the first stage, they felt it their duty to point out that such an arrangement would be a burden to the company. Their experience had shown them, they said, that it would be more efficient to parcel out the jobs among a large number of contractors, both European and American, who would be able to work independently of one another and therefore prepare the ground more quickly.

De Lesseps obliged. The canal company cancelled the contract, paid Couvreux & Hersent 1,200,000 francs, and in this amicable atmosphere retained Hersent as a consulting contractor.

The withdrawal of Couvreux & Hersent meant that the canal company now had to supervise directly all operations on the isthmus, line as well as staff, recruit its own technical staff there, divide up the work, and let new contracts. To boss this complicated task it hired the highly competent Chief Engineer Jules Dingler of the French government's Department of Bridges and Highways. He sailed for Panama on February 6. A few months later he was back in Paris with his plan for the work that lay ahead.

Starting from the bay of Limon, at Colon, on the Atlantic side, the canal was to run through the Chagres River valley for a distance of 45 kilometers to Obispo, cut through the Cordillera Mountains in the next 11 kilometers, then follow the Rio Grande valley to Pacific deep water near the island of Naos in the Bay of Panama. To control the Chagres floods, the engineers planned a huge dam across the valley of the river at Gamboa, creating a reservoir that could store part of the floodwaters. With their flow reduced, deflections on each side of the canal would channel the waters of the unpredictable river and its affluents to the sea.

To carry out this plan, Dingler estimated that he would have to excavate 120,000,000 cubic yards of earth and rock, an increase of almost 65 per cent over the reduced requirement reported to the stockholders early in 1881.

The canal across Panama was not the only canal de Lesseps had on his hands. The year before, Britain had become the sole protector of Egypt and *de facto* master of the Suez Canal when the French refused to join them in military action to put down an antiforeigner uprising in Alexandria. Now, in the middle of the major changeover at Panama, de Lesseps had to rush to London to negotiate with the Gladstone cabinet; he obtained a highly favorable agreement covering the Suez operations; then hurried home to the bedside of his ninth child, who was ill of typhoid fever, and to be present at the birth of his tenth.

Despite all these concerns, the old man never lost sight of the target date at Panama. At the Panama Canal Company's annual meeting, on July 17, 1883, he reiterated that the canal would be finished by 1888, and the next month, in a speech before the Geographical Congress at Douai he announced: "Our works director, M. Dingler, Engineer of Bridges and Highways, who has just gotten our personnel and materiel organized, is coming to Paris to report on his plans and preparations for the inauguration of the sea canal in 1888."

In October the company made the first borrowing of the funds which he had said it would need to complete the canal promptly. The company's administrative council decided to issue 600,000 bonds bearing 3 per cent interest and redeemable at 500 francs on maturity in 1957. The council set the price at which they would be offered to the public at 291 francs but the directors cut it to 285 francs, thus making the actual rate of interest slightly more than 5¼ per cent per annum—15 francs on a 285-franc investment. The council ratified the directors' action two days after the bonds were issued.

The bonds seemed such a bargain that the *Times* of London correspondent wrote: "M. de Lesseps is being twitted, and, I think, rightly, with offering the subscribers too favorable conditions, with a view to favoring the existing stockholders, to whom half the issue is reserved."

"An enterprise like the Panama Canal," he said, "ought not seemingly to pay such high interest but should be able to raise money at 4 percent at most. It cannot be supposed that the bonds of such a company will not be regularly met."

In the same dispatch he reported that de Lesseps "very dextrously confided the execution of the two entrances of the canal to leading American contractors" and that "as all American travelers of mark, and they are very numerous, are received in the most cordial manner, public opinion at New York has become very favorable to the enterprise."

The Panama Affair

The *publicité* for the October, 1883, bond issue rose to almost 2,500,000 francs and included a special commission of 375,000 francs to eight banks, at the rate of 5 francs on each of 75,000 bonds, and a 100,000-franc payment to the *Société Générale*, whose receipt stated simply: "Stipulated for our cooperation in the issue."

Men and matériel poured into Panama. The Royal Mail Steam Packet Company ferried so many hired hands across the Caribbean from Jamaica that soon the Jamaican planters found their operations crippled by a labor shortage, their daily shilling or one-and-six holding no attraction for workmen hurrying to get on a canal contractor's payroll for $1 or $1.50 a day.

Suddenly, trouble began to come in bunches. Chief Engineer Dingler built a house for his family on a magnificent hillside at Ancon, but they never occupied it. In scarcely a month early in 1884 yellow fever killed his wife, his son and daughter, and his daughter's fiancé. Commandant Richier, the company's superior agent on the isthmus, quit in a rage because the home office was slow in acting on his report that he had discovered fraud in an excavation payment: a contractor had been paid for work never done.

The *Times* of London, in a dispatch from Panama published March 12, 1884, announcing the death of an English missionary, one of several victims of yellow fever, reported that "the Europeans who have lately arrived in connection with the canal scheme are apprehensive of the danger from the disease, and several of them are leaving the place." But it added, "The work of construction is progressing satisfactorily."

Two months later, however, the *American Architect & Building News* commented pessimistically that the work was "proceeding more slowly than surely toward completion," and that "the statements which are published from time to time in the American, English, and especially in the French papers are vague and contradictory, based upon information derived from official sources and possibly not less confused for that reason."

"We do not venture to suggest for a moment that M. de Lesseps will make a wreck of his fortunes or of those of his supporters by the failure of the project," the publication insisted, "but we believe that future success is only possible by a vast expenditure in money and, unfortunately, in life, on account of the very fatal climate through which the canal passes."

In September, for the first time since the canal company had become a going concern, it failed to sell out a bond issue. The sticky issue consisted of 387,387 bonds maturing in seventy-five years. They were offered to the public at 333 francs, priced to yield 6 per cent per annum. The company spent almost 1,700,000 francs to promote the issue, but when the subscription books closed on September 25, 1884, almost a fifth of the bonds remained unsold.

A special syndicate, formed to take over the unsold securities, needed another eighteen months to get rid of them, and then was able to sell them only at a substantial markdown from the original issue price. These unsold bonds hung over the market like a nimbus cloud beneath whose gloomy presence the progress reports of the Panama canal turned into an increasingly shrill, discordant dialogue between witnesses uttering testimony so contradictory that at times it seemed improbable they were talking about the same things.

Two comments of the effects of a new misfortune exemplified the conflict.

Early in 1885 an insurrection swept several areas of Colombia. The rebels burned Colon. Fire destroyed the Panama Railroad's headquarters and the canal company's docking facilities and repair yards.

On May 8 a *New York Tribune* special correspondent at Panama wrote to the paper: "The Panama canal is in such a state that its ultimate completion is beyond question, but it appears equally certain that the present company can never complete it. . . . In going over the canal route, one gets the impression that the work is practically stopped, and from the best information to be got at here, I believe such to be the case. The last revolution here, of course, has had something to do with this state of affairs, for when bullets fly spades drop. But revolutions have their benefits too, for they afford the canal company a reasonable excuse for giving up the work, and give it up they must, before long, or get a large amount of new capital."

M. de Lesseps, reporting on the insurrection at the annual meeting of his company on July 29, 1885, told his stockholders: "The fire at Colon destroyed some buildings, which we had on the site of the old town, and a dredging machine, which was on the stocks, was injured. The destruction of our buildings caused us only a very limited material injury, a decision being taken to transfer for some months all our operations to the new town called into existence by us at the entrance of the canal—Christophe Colomb. We shall be able to save some parts of the burned dredging machine. At Culebra the injury done falls on the contractors. Their workmen, panic-stuck, had left the yard. Those in charge, having remained steady at their post, the laborers, reassured, have now returned to their work. . . . The fire at Colon, which has only caused us comparatively unimportant material injury, by the almost complete destruction of the means of landing and repairing materials, caused the difficulties of which we shall note the effects during the second half of 1885. With the utmost energy and ready decision our agents at once made up for the insufficiency of the wharves by the employment of floating material. It has been possible to carry out our landing operations in a sufficient manner."

He also reported confidently on the progress of excavations: "Considering the first excavations are the most difficult to extract and that our general manager makes a point of attacking the difficult ones first, there is reason to be satisfied with the progression of the amount of the monthly excavations since the beginning of the year. In January this amount was 550,000 cubic meters, in February 590,000 meters, in March 627,-000 meters, in April 775,000 meters, and in May 798,000 meters. We had thought that the monthly figures would speedily reach a million meters. We had included in our calculation the product of the large American dredges which on the Colon and Panama sides were at work in land generally soft. We shall explain later on how the American contractors have been delayed. The part to be executed by them being the easiest, this delay will in no way hinder the completion of the canal."

The *Tribune* man, who had seen the same January-April figures in the company's *Bulletin* published on June 1, wrote to his paper on July 15: "The figures are simply astounding."

"Now January, February, and March were favorable for work on the canal, and the isthmus was comparatively quiet," he recalled. "On March 28 occurred the burning of Colon, and chaos ensued. All through April and far into May there was little work done on the canal, the officials giving as an excuse the disturbed state of the country. Thousands of laborers left off work and fled in alarm to Jamaica, so that whole sections were almost denuded of them. Added to this, heavy rains fell in April and the weather was unfavorable for work. The most 'guileless young Marine' that went to the isthmus with the American forces would hesitate before believing that under all the unfavorable circumstances, with scarely enough men on the canal to keep up a semblance of labor, 775,000 cubic meters were excavated, while in January, under the most favorable conditions, only 550,000 cubic meters could be taken out."

In addition, he said, "already this season several landslides have occurred, and at the divergence of the Rio Grande a landslide of very serious proportions has almost undone the work of the preceding months at that place."

M. de Lesseps retorted bitterly. The canal company, under the terms of its concession from Colombia, had been given the right to a strip of land 200 meters wide along each side of the canal and 500,000 hectares of public lands wherever it chose, title to them to be surrendered to the company as work on the canal progressed.

"The Colombian government," M. de Lesseps told the stockholders meeting, "was called on to estimate the degree of advancement of the works. The declaration of the government, dated the twenty-sixth of December, 1883, was in these terms: 'The Panama Canal Company is entitled to be adjudged, according to the provisions of the act of concession, 150,000 hectares of land as the equivalent of more than one third of the execution of the work.'"

Adding the work done in the nineteen months since that declaration, de Lesseps said, "the efforts actually put forth may be considered as more than half the total efforts necessary."

"This considerable amount of effort, which ensures the execution of the work, being undeniable," he declared, "the opponents of the Panama Canal Company, as formerly those of the Suez Canal, resort to puerile discussions, utter absurd criticism, and impotent to injure, they do not shrink from calumny or defamation.

"A fresh band of opponents has appeared. You have hitherto had against you certain capitalists, concerned to delay as long as possible the inauguration of the new highway, either in the interest of existing modes of transportaion or in order to attract capital for the problematical execution of a rival canal. There were also speculators who tried from time to time to influence the Bourse against you. These speculators know well what your resistance has cost them. Unable to do anything against the shareholders, these persons then turned against the company, and by newspapers started for the streets, or by letters and pamphlets, an actual campaign of extortion has been organized. We need not say that these speculators of a peculiar kind will find the Panama Canal Company as disdainful and immovable as the shareholders have been."

Next day, placing the attacks de Lesseps complained of in the perspective of current financial practice, a London *Times* leader observed: "A modern financier, in many instances, looks upon the shares of other people with the sort of feeling which would be entertained for Lowland beeves by a Highlander two or three centuries ago—that is, as desirable things which afford opportunities for the display of dexterity in the art of plunder; and the Panama Canal Company can hardly be surprised, even while they may justly complain, that the greatness of their undertaking has pointed it out as one which is exceptionally calculated to reward the faithful employment of the machinery by which various kinds of value are made to undergo fictitious deterioration or exaltation."

Despite the predatory instincts of the financiers, the company was ready to embark on a new adventure among them.De Lesseps brought his report to a climax with a revelation of the company's intention to borrow 600,000,000 francs more. He announced that amendments in plans and forecasts to effect "a better adaptation of forces," not a departure from the grand design, had now produced a cost figure of 1,070,000 francs. This, he pointed out, was the original construction estimate of the Paris congress of 1879, which had been the canal company's launching platform.

"To lighten our future charges for borrowing under the best conditions the sums necessary to complete the maritime canal promptly," he disclosed, "your president, as he did in analogous circumstances to assure completion of the Suez Canal, has asked the French government for permission to obtain the

600,000,000 francs previously mentioned by means of an issue of lottery bonds."

De Lesseps, almost eighty years old, spoke for an hour, vigorously and confidently, and was still going strong at the finish. The stockholders applauded uproariously his denunciations of the attacks by the press. When one shareholder protested that the canal would cost 3 billion francs and would lose 150,000,000 a year, his co-owners shut him up with demands to know why he held onto his stock if he thought the outlook so gloomy; he couldn't even find anyone to second his motion to appoint an investigating committee. The meeting adopted the president's report enthusiastically, giving full approval to his proposal for the lottery loan.

This was a tried and proved device of Suez financing. In 1867, when a bond issue had failed, the company had obtained permission from the French senate to issue 5 per cent lottery bonds, with four quarterly drawings a year, each yielding a 250,000-franc first prize, two 25,000-franc second prizes, two 5,000-franc third prizes, and twenty-four prizes of 2,000 francs each. The issue was an instant success.

Charles Demole, Minister of Public Works under a republic, was less obliging than the imperial senate had been. He took no action on de Lesseps's new lottery loan request until Christmas Eve, and then he sent Armand Rousseau, Chief Engineer of Bridges and Highways, to Panama to have a look around.

Investors endured the new delay in the taut suspense of a soap opera audience awaiting the next episode. Not only was a tremendous amount of money at stake, but the electoral involvement was vast. Hundreds of thousands of households had dug deep into skinny pocketbooks to buy the Panama Canal Company's shares and bonds.

De Lesseps maintained his air of hardy confidence. A month before Rousseau's appointment he had observed his eightieth birthday by preparing for a Panama trip of his own to "inaugurate the final period of the execution of the maritime canal." He invited delegates from Chambers of Commerce throughout France, as well as observers from the United States, Britain, Italy, and Germany. The canal company was to pay all expenses.

"It is important to a very high degree," he said in his invitation to the New York Chamber of Commerce, "that no doubt should exist any longer upon the completion of the Panama maritime canal, so that at the time of its inauguration ship owners and merchants may be ready to utilize it and that nothing should happen as it did on the eve of the inauguration of the Suez Canal to surprise the universal navy invited to pass through the interoceanic Bosporus when completed."

The European party sailed from Southampton January 28, 1886, and arrived at Colon on February 17, just after Rousseau had completed an eighteen-day inspection and started for home. With de Lesseps, several executives of his company, and the delegates from the Chambers of Commerce at Marseilles, Rouen, St. Nazaire, and Bordeaux were the Duke of Sutherland, the Marquis of Teano, a delegate from Italy, and Leon Peschek, an engineer attached to the German Embassy at Paris. John Bigelow, the New York Chamber's observer, met them at Colon. The welcome they received inspired de Lesseps to say, "With such devotion the canal could not fail to be finished."

He led his guests on a strenuous two-week trip and brought them home in good health. Among the things they had learned was that to his associates on the isthmus his name was something to conjure by, and they had seen the magic *Ferdinand de Lesseps* painted in large letters on the engines, the excavators, the dredges—everywhere.

The drawing power of "the Great Frenchman's" name had also impressed another observer, Lieutenant W. W. Kimball of the United States Navy, who had been on the isthmus just ahead of Rousseau. In a special intelligence report on the progress of work on the canal during 1885, transmitted to the chief of the Bureau of Navigation at Washington on January 20, 1886, from the U. S. flagship *Tennessee* at Colon, he stated: "It is an impressive fact that there is a money value in the prestige of M. de Lesseps, the courage of the French and the determination to finish the canal, for otherwise the company would already have become bankrupt under the showing of 500,000,000 francs practically spent and not more than one tenth of the work accomplished."

In conducting his inspection the lieutenant had received noteworthy cooperation from Philippe Bunau-Varilla, at the time the acting director general of the canal company, to whom he acknowledged his indebtedness for the "more important drawings, for the table of statistics appended to this report, for explanations upon some of the more difficult projects of construction, and in general for unremitting and repeated courtesies." He said that "all the works were freely open to inspection, and there was no evidence of any desire to withhold any information that could be reasonably expected."

"From inspection, investigation, and observation," Lieutenant Kimball reported, "I have become strongly impressed with the idea that if M. de Lesseps succeeds in placing the new lottery loan of 600,000,000 francs, if the money so obtained is expended with the economy that has lately shown itself in the company's affairs, and if the work is energetically pushed by the best methods, the canal will be so far advanced by the time the money of the new loan is expended that the necessity for finishing it will be apparent."

On their return to France, Emile Ferry and Jules Roux, delegates of the Rouen and Marseilles Chambers of Commerce, respectively, also said there was no question that the company, with its anticipated financing, would finish the canal; but they thought it would take another five or six years.

Bigelow, too, thought the company's timetable was overly optimistic. Like de Lesseps, he was not an engineer, but had eminent credentials in other callings; he was a lawyer, was formerly co-owner of the *New York Evening Post* with William Cullen Bryant, had been United States Consul General at Paris and Minister to France, and in 1867 had headed Governor Samuel J. Tilden's commission to investigate New York State canals.

He turned in a frank but friendly report in which he pointed out that "M. de Lesseps has the confidence of the French people to a greater extent than any other citizen of that Republic, for he is justly credited by them with the authorship of the one achievement of this half century in which they feel the greatest amount of unqualified pride."

He remarked that the stock of the Panama Canal Company was held largely by "people of small means, who prefer to confide their little economies to M. de Lesseps than to the bankers, partly because they were rewarded so handsomely for trusting to his representations about the Suez Canal, and partly

because the construction of the Panama canal under his aus-
pices would rank among the half dozen largest contributions
ever made to the permanent glory of France."

The canal, he believed, "will now be prosecuted to its completion without any very serious interruption, for too large a
proportion of its cost has already been incurred to make retreat
as good a policy as advance," and even if the company abandoned the project the contractors would probably find it advantageous to get together and finish it.

But this work, he said, "which for its inevitable cost and, if
accomplished, for the magnitude of its material result, has no
parallel among private enterprise in all history, is attended by
so many uncertain and unworkable conditions that the estimates of the most gifted and experienced engineers are but
conjectures."

He described in detail the magitude of the task of digging
out the Culebra cut through the Continental Divide, "one of the
most formidable obstacles which a sea-level canal here presents to an engineer."

"To cut this hill down to nine meters below the level of the
ocean at low water," Bigelow said, "involves the removal of a
body of earth and rock amounting in the aggregate to some
22,000,000 of cubic yards. This enormous body lies within a span
of only two kilometers, or less than a mile and a half. The
necessity of discharging the excavated material exclusively at
the ends of the cut when the men get below the surface of the
canal must reduce the product of a day's labor.

"The contract for this work was undertaken some years ago
by an Anglo-Dutch company who bound themselves to remove
700,000 meters a month. This contract was subsequently
modified, so as to require the removal of only 610,000 monthly
for the eighteen following January 1, 1886, making 11,000,000
cubic meters and 330,000 a month for the succeeding twenty-
four months to July 1, 1889, making 8,000,000, which amounts
added to the amounts removed before January 1, 1886, say
1,000,000, would give the required result—20 million cubic
meters.

"For this the contractors were to receive eight francs the
cubic meter, or 32,000,000 of dollars, the Canal Company engag-
ing to furnish them, as to the other contractors, their machines

and the men, the contractors only paying the men's wages and a certain rent for the use of the machines. Of course, any failure to supply men enough or machines enough leaves the contractors at liberty to abandon the contract, whenever it ceases to be profitable.

"The results are such as might be expected. Though bound to remove monthly 610,000 meters, they have not yet, I am assured, been successful in getting away in any one month with 100,000 cubic meters. Should they not increase that average it will take from ten to fifteen years to finish their contract, even should they suffer no unforeseen delays or interruptions.

"Doubtless means will be found to expedite this work, which, in its present stage, could be readily effected by an increase of men and machines. The last thirty meters of the cut, however, must necessarily prove tedious and costly. Apprehensions have been expressed that during the later stages of the work at this point the banks might wash or slide and fill up the cutting, as well as endanger the lives of the workmen. That, however, could only result from bad engineering. Perhaps those who give most importance to this criticism do not properly estimate the rapidity with which vegetation would cover the slopes and bind them so compactly that in a few months a yoke of oxen would hardly be able to haul a plow through them.

"I did not hear of any insuperable difficulty in the accomplishment of this work but I cannot but think that M. de Lesseps will be disappointed in his calculations, both in regard to the time and the cost of it. It certainly is not progressing at present at a rate which warrants the hope of its completion in 1889."

De Lesseps, asked to comment, called Bigelow's statements absurd. "He said he would positively guarantee the canal would be opened in 1889 and would have a depth of 6½ meters," the *New York Times* reported from Paris. "He said that further deepening of the canal would be carried on according to the receipts from the traffic, as was done at Suez."

"The Suez Canal was opened sixteen years ago and we are still at work upon it, " de Lesseps wrote in his recollections.

On the Panama isthmus he had seen his forces making use of the fruits of two decades of technological progress since Suez, and from the experience he was able to draw strong reassurance. "At Panama we have the means at our disposal which we did not have at Suez." he wrote, "and according to the estimate which has been made we have 57,000 horsepower, which at the rate of ten men each represents 570,000 men. Add to them the 20,000 workmen on the ground, and it will be seen that we shall be able, by 1889, to open a passage sufficient for the purpose of navigation, while after that we shall enlarge the canal, as we have done for Suez, which yields such a magnificent return to the shareholders, and upon which, nevertheless, we are still at work."

Just before the exchange with Bigelow, the company's administrative council had begun to plan the financing it would undertake when the lottery loan was approved. In quest of the 600,000,000 francs that the last annual meeting had authorized the company to borrow as needed, the council decided to float an initial issue of 362,613 bonds, priced at 333 francs. These would produce a 6 per cent a year interest to the investors and bring the company approximately 120,000,000 francs.

Although there was still no official word of Rousseau's findings, a news leak brought a major shock to the French financial community and the multitude of canal investors, and even disturbed the government. The influential Paris newspaper, *Le Temps*, whose owner, Senator Adrien Hebrard, also published the *Public Works Journal*, printed a story saying that Rousseau had filed an unfavorable report and that the company would have to answer his comments before the government would grant it permission to issue a lottery loan.

De Lesseps, responding to the story, said it would be natural for the government investigator to take a pessimistic view, but the worst thing Rousseau would be able to say would be that "great difficulties have yet to be overcome, and the cutting was contracted for below what the work will cost."

"The contractors will have to suffer if what M. Rousseau says be true, and not the company," he said.

Rousseau's report, delivered on April 30, remained a well-kept secret for three weeks. It stated that the canal could be built and that the enterprise had reached a point at which it should not be abandoned, for abandonment would be a disaster to the investors, all of them French, and also to French influence throughout the Americas. But before sending the lottery loan bill to the Chamber of Deputies, he said, the government should ask the Panama Canal Company to get an opinion on two points from its superior consultative committee, which was composed of men "distinguished by scientific knowledge and moral authority."

These points were:

"1. Does the realization of the company's declared program raise any insurmountable technical difficulties; can it be seriously hoped that this program will be realized under the conditions announced when the public was invited to subscribe to the loans?

"2. From a technical point of view, could not the company introduce changes and simplifications that would facilitate completion of the work?"

"This appears to me all the more indispensable to the present case," he said, "because its completion with the resources contemplated and the delays announced seems to me more than problematical unless the company decided to introduce important reductions and simplifications."

The company asked the consultants for their opinion, and in part they replied: "It follows for us from the data that you have submitted to us that after the loan the company seeks to issue, you cannot fail to guide the enterprise to such an advanced stage that if the passage between the two seas is not open, even the most biased eyes will see, at least, that the final completion of the enterprise is assured, with the help of a final push that then can be calculated precisely, and this last effort, even though relatively considerable, should be unquestionably easy for you to accomplish, because in this situation the capitals of the world will hold in honor those who bring about the crowning of this work of civilization, which should complete the transformation of commerce and shipping already happily begun and partially accomplished by the opening of the Suez Canal."

Three weeks later, on June 17, 1886, Charles Baïhaut, successor to Demole, the Minister of Public Works who had sent Rousseau to Panama, deposited a bill with the Chamber that was designed to authorize the Panama Canal Company to issue lottery bonds. The new Minister's renown was more matrimonial than ministerial. He was known as "the man with the beautiful wife," having won "*la belle Mme. Armangaud*" away from her first husband, who was his friend, engineering-school classmate, and frequent host. For Baïhaut, support of the proposed legislation was a ticket to Etampes, the solitary-confinement prison where prisoners were not even allowed to see each other's faces.

The Chamber referred the measure to committee and the committee began to hold hearings. Chief Engineer Jacquier of the Department of Bridges and Highways at St. Etienne, the company's new works director, told the Deputies that locks would have to be built to finish the canal on schedule and at the prescribed costs. De Lesseps told them it would be possible to complete a sea-level canal in three years, but that he would act according to the requirements of science. He added, however, that a lock canal would be only a temporary device and a sea-level canal would eventually have to be built.

The committee, rejecting a cloture motion by a 6-4 vote, decided on July 8 to continue its investigation, and it asked to see documents such as balance sheets and contracts. This decision meant postponing any final action of the loan application until the Chamber's autumn session. The next day de Lesseps asked the Premier to withdraw the bill, and he told the stockholders and the canal company's correspondents that he intended to get the money by another device.

"I am postponed, I do not accept the postponement," he declared. "Faithful to my past, when it is sought to stop me I work on, not alone, to be sure, but with 350,000 Frenchmen sharing my patriotic confidence."

In other quarters the enterprise in which they had placed their confidence had become the subject of an an almost unrelieved lament. "One cannot but think sometimes how strange a spectacle the wreck on the isthmus by the attempt to build the canal will present to the twentieth century," a *New York Tribune* correspondent wrote. "Most of the machinery will be left and much of it now lies imbedded in mud and encrusted with rust. Belgian locomotives, confessedly useless, now already abandoned, lie canted on broken tracks. With a shamefaced formality the engineer in charge has brushed over the brightwork with some whitewash, but nothing could make those locomotives look as if they were ever to be used again, and as the moonlight falls on these whitened outlines and flecks the vegetation growing up about them with grotesque shadows, the locomotives look like wretched skeletons."

John Heard, Jr., a mining engineer, had sent *Lippincott's Magazine* a mournful tale of an encounter with several old friends of his Paris school days whom he met again as he made his way along the canal line from the Veraguas gold and copper fields to Panama City, which he called a "lazaretto."

"I breakfasted with the fellows at Gordona a few days ago," he wrote, "and while we were at table one of their comrades returned after an absence of six weeks on the island of Coiba. The few words which followed the first greetings are worth recording: they need no comment.

" 'Halphen has not returned from his survey?'

" 'No, he and Kohlbach have decided to remain up there.'

" '*C'est dommage!* They were good fellows. Well, and Duparc?'

" 'Taken off last week.'

"A pause.

" 'Any more?'

" 'Lefevre is gone, and Bontone is down; doctor says he'll last two days at the outside. The rest are well. *Allons! Allons!* the month has been a bad one, but that is no reason to *embêter* Monsieur with our tears and crape. *Quand on est mort c'est pour longtemps.*' "

The building of the canal had brought to the isthmus all the sights, sounds, and activities of a wide-open frontier town, but Tracy Robinson, the *Panama Star & Herald* editor, found that "in the midst of this carnival of depravity, life and property were comparatively safe."

"The state of things," he wrote, "was like the life at 'Red Hoss Mountain' described by Eugene Field, 'When the money flowed like likker with the joints all throwed wide open 'nd no sheriff to demur.' Vice flourished. Gambling of every kind and every other form of wickedness were common day and night."

To an anonymous *Tribune* correspondent the picture was far more depressing than Robinson's and Eugene Field's. "The class of adventurers who are always more numerous—the men who rely upon their supposititious intellect rather than upon their muscle—are today to be found in Panama and Colon literally starving," he reported. "Most of them are swindlers or clerks. The former class, unless they are expert gamblers, find little scope for the exercise of their talents; and the latter oscillate between feeble efforts to emulate the unremunerative practices of the former and a fruitless beggary, until they die in the street or stow away on some homeward-bound vessel.

"It is no unusual matter, either, this sad spectacle of educated men starving in the streets of Panama. Nowhere else does there seem to be less of the milk of human kindness than on the isthmus. Hospitality there is for those who do not need it and who are in a position to requite it. But in the formula, 'I am not down here for my health,' a foreign resident at once expresses a grim recognition of the dangers which surround him and a cool determination to restrict his energies to making money and spending it on himself."

To weigh against chronicle of this shabby society, there was a record of valor, generosity, and sacrifice as impressive to the most detached critics of the enterprise as to its most violent partisans. The heroic kindness of Soeur Marie, for example, the Mother Superior of the Nursing Sisters at the company's 700-bed hospital along the foot of Mount Ancon, and the care she and her assistants lavished on the stricken patients, moved the crusty *Tribune* reporter to write: "There are no long faces, no doctrinal austerities among the Sisters of the canal hospital. They seem to realize that what the sick man needs is a mother's indulgent care, and this they give, and good measure of it. Soeur Marie does not come to talk of death and judgment, does not even express in her face a latent sense of the irrelevancy of these awful considerations. She pats the patient on the shoulder and says, 'Stronger again today, my brave man? Good! And was the chicken broth right? A day or two more and you'll be calling for an *entrecôte*.'

"Such women as these make a home out of a hospital, and when all healing is unavailing they make even the scorched death of yellow fever easy if such a thing can be."

Neither man nor microbe scared Soeur Marie. When the insurrection swept Panama in 1885 and looters milled around the gates of the hospital compound, intent on seizing its stores of liquor, she marched on them and put them to rout with a muscular admonition: "Listen to me, you rioters! Some day you will be sick yourselves, and if you trouble us now, do you think we will have you in the hospital? No! Now go!"

The institution itself was, in the *Tribune* correspondent's words, "a splendid monument to the enlightened liberality of a governing body, most of whose work shows a shocking incapability." It also won high praise from Dr. William Crawford Gorgas, who eventually purged the canal area of yellow fever by eradicating its transmitter, the *Aëdes aegypti* mosquito. The canal company's hospital, he said, is "a very much better institute than any hospital in America that I know of at the same period carried on by a firm or corporation." Still, 1,200 patients died there of yellow fever in nine years.*

When the canal company's shareholders held their annual meeting in the summer of 1886, there was nothing in the bearing or comments of its aging president that even remotely suggested a thought of retreat. He rallied the faithful with an hour-long reading of his report, pausing for a brief rest only when the shareholders begged him to take a break. At the end they cheered him and adopted by acclamation a resolution asserting their complete confidence in him.

He pledged himself to open the canal in 1889, although the company had encountered unforeseen expenses. He said that speculators' attacks on the company's credit had compelled the payment of higher interest rates than had been anticipated, but he reasoned that even this was not all to the bad.

"The greater number of the subscribers to our various loans being already shareholders or those having claims on the company," he explained, "it follows in reality that the advantages offered by an issue of obligations only burden our budget for the benefit of those who are subscribers themselves. At the same time it is true that from this date to the inauguration of the maritime canal, the charges for loans will add to the weight of our accounts and augment the cost of the canal."

Having abandoned its quest for government permission to float lottery loans, the company unveiled its substitute fundraising device. It would issue long-term, low-interest bonds, sell them at approximately half their maturity value, and then hold bimonthly drawings at which several bonds would be pulled out of the hat for immediate redemption at maturity value.

*see Notes

The Panama Affair

The first borrowing by means of this sinuous ploy, which the government never diagnosed as a lottery, took place on August 3. The company, seeking 225,000,000 francs, offered 500,-000 bonds for sale at 450 francs each. The bonds, maturing in 1928, would be redeemable then, or whenever drawn from the bi-monthly pool, at 1,000 francs. Meanwhile, paying interest of 60 francs a year, they would produce a succulent 13⅓ per cent per annum return for those who were not lucky in the drawing.

A new cast of syndicators took on the distribution of these issues. Baron Jacques de Reinach had succeeded Levy-Cremieux, who had died. The earlier syndicates had been recruited almost entirely from the world of finance; the new ones came from far afield. Participants appeared to have been recruited "out of a spirit of camaraderie, sometimes even out of beneficence, out of charity." Some of them, for example, had backgrounds in art or journalism, rather than banking and finance, but they were "members of the Parliament."

Their participation was almost a non-risk effort. They ventured 2.50 francs per bond against the chance of remuneration on a sliding scale: 20 francs a bond on the first 200,000 sold, then 15 per bond on the next 100,000 bonds, 10 on the next and 5 on the last, a topsy-turvy arrangement in which the easiest sales brought the biggest rewards.

Although more than 100,000 subscribers responded, they signed up for only 458,802 bonds, so that after paying the various costs of the issue, including a new reimbursement of 5,-336,412 to the syndicate for its 1,250,000-franc venture, the company retained less than 195,000,000 francs, for which it had contracted to pay back 500,000,000, plus interest, over the next forty-two years.

The failure to achieve a sellout did not disappoint de Lesseps; he said in a circular that the reception of the issue "responded to our hopes." Nor had his great age and responsibilities slowed his drive. On October 16 he sailed for New York on the *Bretagne* to represent France at the unveiling of Frederic Auguste Bartholdi's Statue of Liberty. Standing beside President Grover Cleveland and other dignitaries at Bedloes Island, he declared, in response to loud applause: "Soon, gentlemen, we shall meet again to celebrate a peaceful conquest. Goodby until we meet at Panama, where the flag of the United States, with its thirty-eight stars, will float beside the banners of the independent states of South America and will consummate in the new world for the good of humanity the peaceful and fruitful alliance of the Franco-Latin and Anglo-Saxon races."

Warding off the attacks of speculators, political enemies, and other detractors, the canal builder might have found much to comfort him in a report on the year's progress that Lieutenant Charles C. Rogers, United States Navy intelligence officer on U.S.S. *Galena*, presently compiled. The *Galena* put in to Colon early in March, 1887, a few days after Charles de Lesseps and other company officials had arrived for a personal inspection. On orders of his commanding officer, Commander Colby M. Chester, Lieutenant Rogers asked their permission to gather information for his report. They invited him to join them.

As of the beginning of March, 1887, he reported, 28.8 per cent of the total excavations for the canal had been done. A force of 926 officals and clerks were working for the company, and the contractors on all divisions of the canal had a total of 10,640 workmen. On October 9, 1886, the Colombian government had given the canal company title to another 100,000 hectares of land, bringing to 250,000 the area transferred, or half the total to be handed over as the canal progressed.

"It will be seen that the government of Colombia and the canal company regard the work as half finished," he said. "This does not mean that they claim one half of the necessary excavation has been made, but that the present excavation, plus the installation as now completed, which means the present quarters for officials and workmen, the hospitals, and the present plant of machinery, represents one half of the total work to be done in order to finish the canal."

In collecting his information and arriving at his conclusions, Lieutenant Rogers commented, he had not been guided solely by the figures or estimates of the company. Such statistics as the company gave him, he said, were correct so far as he was able to verify them.

Describing attitudes on the isthmus, he said: "During the stay of the *Galena* at Aspinwall [Colon] I met many residents and foreigners who were not interested in the canal. The most bitter opponents of the enterprise were our own countrymen and a few Englishmen or former employees of the canal who had been discharged or had some other grievance against the company. Many of these opponents were intelligent men who did not hesitate to make the most exaggerated statements, showing either utter ignorance of facts or else malice against the company. Frequently trivial accidents or mishaps that are perfectly natural and must happen to any and every enterprise of such vast extent and difficulty are magnified into insuperable and ruinous obstacles; and such reports are spread abroad without fear of anyone impeaching their trust or the intelligence of the originator. My own personal visit to the works enabled me to test the accuracy of many of these statements and in all cases with the results stated.

"The work of 1886 is very creditable to the company. People of the temperate zone may say that with so many workmen and so large a plant more should have been done, but not one of these critics out of a hundred would go to the isthmus and work in such a climate until the next steamer started on its return home.

"The contractors are young, zealous, and energetic men; the engineers are graduates of the Polytechnic, St. Cyr, or other famous schools of France, and are both clever and capable, and no one can appreciate more than these men the difficulties that lie in their path. Instead of censure and detraction, they deserve the highest praise and respect."

Still, the Culebra remained to be cut through.

"M. Charles de Lesseps said to me," Rogers reported, 'In two years the canal will be finished from Colon to K44 [the Gamboa hills at Matachin], and from La Boca to Paraiso. As to the Culebra, I leave you to form your own conclusions. It is a great and difficult work.' Evidently he regards the Culebra as the great obstacle and prefers not to commit himself about it."

5

In its first six years Ferdinand de Lesseps's Panama Canal Company had borrowed money from the public four times. On the first two occasions its clientele stampeded to oblige; on the next two they showed strong signs of cooling off. Responding to these first four issues, the public had paid the canal company approximately 615,000,000 francs for its bonds. These were bonds that the company was obligated to redeem at various dates from 1928 to 1959 at a maturity value totaling more than 1,000,000,000 francs, all the while paying interest at an annual rate averaging 4.66 per cent on the maturity value but more than 8 per cent on the amount for which it had sold them. The fifth time it passed the hat, the response proved unmistakably that the canal company had lost its old allure: when it tried to borrow 220,000,000 francs on July 27, 1887, again by means of its bimonthly bond raffle, it was able to raise barely half that sum.

On October 31 de Lesseps announced at a meeting of the Academy of Sciences that the canal would be opened about February 3, 1890. He said the works would not be completed then, but would be far enough along to let twenty ships a day be cleared, producing receipts of 90,000,000 to 100,000,000 francs a year. Fifteen days later he signed a contract with Alexandre Gustave Eiffel, the tower builder, for the construction of temporary locks, with the summit level placed above the Chagres flood line and supplied with water pumped from the river. The same day he again asked the government for permission to float lottery loans.

Ever since the return of the government investigator and

the Chamber of Commerce delegates from Panama, there had been a growing discussion of possible changes in the canal's dimensions, structure, and completion date. Testimony at the legislative hearings on the earlier lottery bill renewed an old argument: were the tidal range of the Atlantic and the Pacific the same at Panama; might it be more efficient and economical to lift the canal bed past the Culebra mountain and lower it back to sea level by means of locks, rather than to hack a sea-level passage all the way through the towering mass of rock.

In his petition for a new lottery law, addressed to the Premier and Finance Minister, Maurice P. Rouvier, de Lesseps said he had decided on the temporary locks "to ensure a sufficient passage to the foreseen annual traffic of 7,500,000 tons, and reserve for the future the completion of the definitive maritime canal by means of small levies, as at Suez, on the annual profits of the working."

He added that at the beginning of the next year the company would have 110,000,000 francs at its disposal after meeting all liabilities then due, and he wanted permission to employ the lottery feature "for the 265,000,000 francs which have still to be issued out of the 600,000,000 authorized by the shareholders and for the 300,000,000 francs which might be necessary between this time and 1890, and eventually for the whole or part of the borrowing already made, the conversion of which would be offered to the bondholders."

After two months of consideration, the Cabinet, headed by Premier Pierre-Emmanuel Tirard, who had just succeeded Rouvier, refused to submit the Panama Canal Company's lottery loan bill to the Chamber of Deputies.

De Lesseps responded with a direct appeal to the public. "I cannot and do not accept a silent refusal," he said. "I should have the air of assenting to all the infamous statements with which the Panama Canal shareholders are being flooded, and I am bound in any case not to sanction an indifference which might result in handing over the Panama enterprise on the eve of its completion to the foreigners who covet it."

He distributed to the company's offices throughout France copies of a petition to be signed by the multitude of canal shareholders and bondholders that urged their representatives in the national legislature to submit the bill to a public hearing.

"I reckon upon you for the petitionings which are asked," he exhorted his investors. "The Panama canal will be completed, as the Suez Canal has been, for the honor and profit of our great and beloved France."

A special meeting, called to inform the stockholders of the new technical and financial plans adopted to ensure the canal's opening in 1890, was the most ardent tryst in a corporate love affair that has few counterparts in business history. The enduring devotion of the Panama investors to their aged chief executive brought them the popular designation of "de Lesseps's army," and their loyalty to him continued fierce and unabated —even at a moment when the demand for his photograph in the shops that sold celebrities' pictures had slipped to third place behind Pasteur's and that of the new number one best seller, the theatrical General Georges Boulanger.

A few days before the stockholders' meeting, bear raiders had spread a rumor on the Bourse that de Lesseps had suffered a broken leg. It helped to produce the biggest turnout of any meeting the company had held—more than a thousand stockholders filling the main hall and bondholders crowding the gallery of the Cirque d'Eté in the Champs Elysées Gardens.

Hale and hearty as ever, de Lesseps stood for forty minutes, reading his report rapidly and clearly in a dim light, while his supporters interrupted him repeatedly with applause.

He told them again that attacks on the company had forced it to pay high rates for money, that the original gross estimate of 1,200,000,000 francs put forth by the Paris congress of 1879 had thus proved inadequate, and that the work had been stalled severely in 1887 by heavy rains and the same sort of labor shortage the Suez enterprise had experienced in 1865. But machines had been brought in to supplant manual labor wherever possible, he said, a lock system had been adopted, and the canal would open to shipping in 1890, even though construction would still be in progress.

The stockholders unanimously approved a resolution to issue bonds for the balance of the previously authorized borrowing of 600,000,000 francs, their redemption to be guaranteed by establishment of a special fund invested in *rentes*, the French government's long-term obligations. Investors, pouring out of the meeting, found a handful of intrepid peddlers hawking a pamphlet entitled *"Le Cataclysme Fatal du Panama"* and in a fury chased them away.

On March 4, 1888, ten days before the date of the new bond issue, nine Deputies of various political complexions introduced the bill the government had refused to sponsor—a measure authorizing the Panama Canal Company to run a lottery. In consequence, the new issue provided not only high interest and a chance at fast redemption at more than twice the purchase price, but also convertibility to lottery bonds should the lottery law be passed.

Even with all these enticements and the expenditure of 2,475,000 francs under the heading of *publicité*, the issue was a disaster. The company put 350,000 bonds on sale; the public took fewer than a third of them. Three bond issues, garnished with the chance of a highly profitable, quick redemption, had produced only 372,123,360 francs, not the 600,000,000 intended. Authority to issue a lottery loan, the device that had saved the Suez canal, was now a life-and-death matter for the Panama Canal Company.

Despite this urgency, it took seven weeks of parliamentary maneuvering to bring the bill before the Chamber of Deputies. The committee in charge of the measure had opposed it by a 6-5 vote, but at the last minute the Deputy for Ariège, Charles Francois Sans-Leroy, a hero of the Franco-Prussian War, reversed his position and voted for the bill.

The legislative cliffhanger drew an immense, partisan audience to the Chamber's public galleries. One of the spectators was James L. Boulange, a French civil engineer and former infantry officer then living in New York. He had been a chief of construction on one of the Panama canal sections for two years.

"Every deputy who advocated the lottery scheme was applauded," he reported. "There was an organized claque for this. The opponents of the bill were interrupted and derided at every point."

One who stood up to the abuse, and even won the eventual applause of his opponents, was Leopold Goirand, the radical Left deputy for Deux-Sèvres, who chose the occasion for his maiden speech. "The ruin is getting on fine," he proclaimed from the speaker's stand. "Scarcely more than 50 per cent remains to be lost."

After three days of debate the Chamber approved, by a vote of 284-128, a bill authorizing the lottery loan; but it required the company to state in its loan prospectus that the granting of this permission implied no government guarantee or responsibility. On June 5 the Senate approved the bill, 160-152. For de Lesseps, Boulange said, "it was what theatrical men call a *succès d'estime.*"

The Panama directors moved briskly to make use of their new-won elbow room. Their immediate goal was a loan of 720,-000,000 francs, of which 120,000,000 would constitute the fund to guarantee payment of the numerous and opulent lottery prizes.

Starting in August, 1888, there were to be six lotteries a year until 1913, then four a year until the bonds matured in 1987. First prize would be, alternately, 500,000 francs at one lottery, 250,000 francs at the next. Second prize at each drawing would be 100,000 francs; and there would be one 10,000 franc prize, one of 5,000 francs, five of 2,000 each, and fifty prizes of 1,000 each.

The issue, set for June 26, consisted of 2,000,000 bonds priced to the public at 360 francs, yielding interest at almost 4.5 per cent a year and redeemable at 400 francs on maturity, or on being drawn in the lotteries. They were available on the installment plan, payable over fifteen months.

After the Deputies' overwhelming vote in favor of the bill, Charles de Lesseps obtained a three-months, 30,000,000-franc loan for the company from two leading commercial banks, the *Société Générale* and the *Crédit Lyonnais,* to stave off insolvency. The company agreed to repay them out of the first cash the bond sale brought in, and it put up as collateral its 68,000 shares of Panama Railroad stock, for which it had paid approximately 90,000,000 francs. The lenders charged interest at the rate of 4 per cent per annum, plus the usual ¼ per cent bank commission—but these were the least of their rewards. These two banks, and all the other institutions that accepted subscriptions for the bonds at their windows, received a commission of 5 francs on each bond; but *Société Générale* and *Crédit Lyon-*

nais were granted an additional commission of 10 francs a
bond on a minimum of 200,000 bonds and a maximum of 400,-
000, "in consideration of making available the credit and to
insure for the issue the most active and continuing cooperation." The special commission brought each of them 2,000,000
francs, in addition to ordinary commissions of 1,243,000 francs
each.

The mounting of the lottery issue created several unusual
expenditures. A payment of approximately 2,000,000 francs to
Hugo Oberndoerffer, a banker, was described as his compensation for suggesting the lottery. Costs listed under *publicité*
soared to 7,300,000 francs, including 2,290,000 francs to Baron
de Reinach, the syndicate organizer. A special payment of
3,390,475 francs also was made to de Reinach, whom the *Spectator* of London referred to as the canal's "Patronage Whip."
When an investigator of the company's affairs asked him subsequently, "That was not for you, all that?", he replied: "You're a
naive one."

Despite the extraordinary spending and the lure of the lavish prizes, only 802,119 bonds were sold. Bad timing and a rumor
of de Lesseps's death, which bear raiders spread by wire
throughout the world, were the causes to which the sticky response was attributed.

"Baron de Reinach, who was a shrewd adviser, proposed
bringing out the lottery issue in successive blocks, but the
Crédit Lyonnais made them proceed with the whole amount at
once," said Andre Siegfried, the political historian whose father Jules Siegfried served as the French Minister of Commerce in 1892-93. "This was a very serious mistake, for the
effort asked from the market was obviously too great."

The company did not give up, by any means. The unsink-
able de Lesseps sent a message to his followers announcing his
satisfaction with the bond sale and describing heroic steps the
company was taking to meet its financial needs.

A new syndicate put up almost 26,000,000 francs against
additional sales of lottery bonds to bring the down payments in
hand up to the 120,000,000 francs needed for the prize fund. The
fund was deposited with the *Crédit Foncier*, one of the few big
institutions that had not participated in any of the company's

financing. Another 47,130 bonds were sold. Still the total product of the bond sale, even before deduction of the big costs of the issue, was only 254,596,821 francs, scarcely a third of the amount sought.

On August 1 de Lesseps went before the annual meeting to rally his troops. Their applause filled every pause in his reading of his report, and a delegate of the Corporation of French Commercial Travelers asked permission to express his organization's admiration and respect for *le Grand Français*. He said that the Suez Canal had brought France 2,000,000,000 francs; the Panama canal would bring in some 3,000,000,000 and thus, thanks to their leader, the nation would have recovered the huge indemnity the Germans had extracted for the war of 1870.

De Lesseps summoned all Panama canal investors to join him in a mighty effort to move the unsold bonds. "All France, it may be said, is joined in the completion of the Panama canal," he said. "Actually more than 600,000 of our compatriots are directly interested in the rapid success of the enterprise. If each of them will take two lottery bonds or get them sold, the canal is made!"

The eighty-two-year-old leader and his son, who was the company's vice-president, formed the permanent spearhead of the fight. They toured the provinces tirelessly, organizing hundreds of investor committees, delivering speeches, eating banquet fare, riding the trains night after night, to Lyon, to Le Mans, to Nimes, crossing the Channel to address the British Association at Bath, and always assuring their audiences that the canal would be opened in 1890, which was just ahead of the deadline the Colombian concession stipulated. At Lyon the elder de Lesseps took pains to correct a report that the opening would be delayed until 1891.

"If ever the canal is finished, if ever it yields the result promised, as to which I can make no assertion, it would not be too much to raise statues to these men who have spared themselves no toil but have made almost superhuman efforts to bring the work to a successful close," the *Times* of London correspondent in Paris wrote after a visit to de Lesseps on October 15.

The price of the 1,100,000 unsold bonds was reduced 10 francs, to 350 francs. This was still higher than those already issued could be bought for on the Bourse. At the end of November the price was cut another 25 francs, and the company announced it would cancel the subscription unless at least 400,000 bonds were bought. It set the close of the subscription for Wednesday, December 12; but just before then it cut the price to 320.33 francs, 90 francs down and the balance payable in eight monthly installments.

On December 11 Mrs. Emily Crawford, the *London Daily News* and *New York Tribune* correspondent, went to the Panama company's headquarters building at 46 rue Caumartin to check on the progress of the sale. She found the public hall packed with investors, "flushed and excited, but willing to stake their last penny on the hope of retrieving their fortunes."

"They were like desperate gamblers whose hopes rise highest when their losses have been greatest." she said.

The crowd grew so dense that presently some people had to stand on tables around the room.

"Strangers met and mutually strengthened their faith with words of comfort," Mrs. Crawford related. "A man who ventured to express doubts as to the possibility of the canal found the place too hot for him."

On the climatic day the crush was enormous, but the noisy chatter that filled the hall stopped abruptly as de Lesseps appeared at 4 p.m. He climbed onto a counter at one end of the room and cried out: "My friends, the subscription is safe! Our adversaries are confounded! We have no need for the help of financiers! You have saved yourselves by your own exertion! The canal is made!"

He was so overcome that he wept, but he stayed to shake hands with everyone of his faithful investors who, themselves weeping, cheering, exchanging mutual congratulations, forced their way to his side to assure him of their confidence and affection.

He gave no details of the bond sale, but word spread quickly from the euphoric tumult that subscribers in Paris had taken 410,000 bonds and that Marseilles alone accounted for another 86,000. An official of the company announced that order clerks were being swamped by applications, and the subscription would be kept open throughout the week.

The next day there was the same clamor at the building in

the rue Caumartin. Word got around that the subscription had reached the 800,000-bond mark. The subscribers were cocky with relief and outraged by any suggestion of criticism of the company. They threw out a man who said that if the loan succeeded, the company would only "make a greater crash in a couple of months." Purchase orders continued to pour in.

Late in the afternoon the investors began to call for their leader. Soon the mob surged toward the counter from which de Lesseps had proclaimed the joyous message the day before. Mrs. Crawford, an energetic reporter, was in the front rank.

"After waiting some twenty minutes," she related, "a man got upon the counter whom I recognized to be M. Charles de Lesseps.

" ' Do you wish to see M. de Lesseps?' he asked.

" ' Yes,' said an elderly lady next to me. 'We want to see that good M. de Lesseps.'

" 'My father,' he continued, ' will always be happy to see you, but I suppose you all wish for some information.'

" ' Yes, yes,' resounded from all sides.

" 'We are sitting at an important meeting of directors which I left for a moment to come hither. I do not know what decision may be taken by this meeting, but I am willing to tell you whatever I know. I will be perfectly open with you, only do not hold me responsible if you learn anything else tomorrow. If you would like to wait for another hour, I will let you know the full result of our deliberations, but would you rather know at once what I can tell you?'

"Everybody assenting to this, M. Charles de Lesseps asked what sort of information they wanted, and being told in reply that they wished to know the result of the subscription, he went on in a deliberate tone:

" 'The subscriptions reach a total of 180,000 bonds. This being below the minimum fixed by M. de Lesseps, we will commence returning the deposits tomorrow. You see, I am telling you exactly how things are.'

"Here there were a few cries of 'Yes, that is the best thing. We must subscribe again.' But the mass of the people were much too dazed to express their feelings."

When presently someone asked how the picture had changed so sharply overnight, Charles de Lesseps replied: "My father is younger in spirit than I. His remarks were made on the strength of a hopeful report that I made him. The result is bankruptcy or the winding up of the company."

The company suspended payments on December 14 and deposited a bill with the government designed to give it a three-months moratorium on meeting its obligations. Then de Lesseps and his colleagues in top management resigned, after asking the Civil Tribunal of the Seine Department to appoint provisional administrators.

Finance Minister Paul-Louis Peytral introduced the company's bill, on the strength of which canal shares bounced up 19.5 francs from the 137.5 they had dropped to in a four-week decline of more than 50 per cent. De Lesseps said he was satisfied that the government's action would enable him to complete the canal. The next day the legislative committee considering the moratorium measure turned it down.

A *Figaro* editor brought the news of the defeat to de Lesseps at his home at 11 avenue Montaigne, next door to where the Théâtre des Champs Elysées stands today. The editor found him reading a letter from his old friend, Isabella II, the deposed Queen of Spain who had lived in France since her abdication in 1870.

"Now that difficulties encompass you, I make a point of writing," she said.

When he learned of the Chamber's rebuff he turned pale and cried out, "It can't be so!" But he presently recovered his composure and remarked wryly that the Suez Canal had suspended payment of its coupons for two years and that the Corinth Canal had done the same, without governmental or legislative interference. He said he did not think the investors would petition for a declaration of the company's bankruptcy, since that would only bring about their own ruin.

The investors, in fact, remained steadfast. When the company's offices opened on Monday morning, the 17th, they gathered in long lines in a footpath off the rue Caumartin to wait for hours for their turn to reclaim their deposits. Their quiet, uncomplaining conduct convinced the *Times* of London correspondent, who had gone there to observe them, that if a new company were formed to complete the canal, "M. de Lesseps will have lost very few of his supporters, and those who remain with him will make fresh efforts in his behalf."

The next day their loyalty took a fiercer turn. As Mrs. Crawford approached the canal company offices she heard screams and the crash of breaking glass and arrived in time to see an angry mob chase a man into the street, kicking him and beating him with fists and walking sticks until he managed to escape in the swelling crowd. She was told that he had been caught in the hall spreading false and malicious reports about the Panama canal. A company official whom Mrs. Crawford did not recognize told her: "I too gave the brute a clout as he passed."

"I am sorry there is no chance of ever discovering this victim, who probably spoke more truthfully than any of M. de Lesseps's prospectuses," Mrs. Crawford said.

Two days after Christmas 4,000 shareholders and bondholders, shouting, *"Vive M. de Lesseps!"* and *"Vive la France!"*, poured into the Palais d'Hiver and adopted by acclamation a resolution that stated: "This meeting, declaring its confidence in M. de Lesseps, resolves to cease to claim payment of coupons and annuities until the opening of the canal for navigation; and decides that in order to preserve to the earliest shareholders the profits of the enterprise, it is desirable to come to an arrangement to raise, at once, with the aid of all those interested in the undertaking, the necessary capital to complete the work. The meeting returns its thanks to the principal committees and the press, which so generously defended the enterprise."

As group after group throughout France passed similar resolutions and signed agreements to forego interest on their securities, de Lesseps responded with typical zeal to the renewed call to command.

He began to put together a Panama canal completion company, with 80 per cent of its profits reserved to the investors in the old company, who also would have preference in the purchase of the new shares. Through the small *Banque Parisienne* he arranged a subscription of 60,000 shares at 500 francs each. This time the public took only 9,000 shares,

With this, the old subscribers broke ranks. On February 4, 1889, the Civil Tribunal of the Seine Department approved the application of two of them to dissolve the Universal Panama Interoceanic Canal Company and appointed a liquidator.

When news of the company's collapse reached Panama,

troops were posted along the line of the canal, and British, French, and United States warships converged on the isthmus to be present in the event of disturbances, but there was none. Few believed that the distress would be more than temporary, "but all too soon it became evident that the end had come," said Tracy Robinson, the Panama editor.

The canal payroll had brought hearty prosperity and a zooming inflation to the isthmus; rents and food prices were up 500 per cent from pre-canal days. Withdrawal of the payroll wrecked the economy. The recently teeming streets were deserted. The Panama Railroad ran two trains a day across the isthmus instead of six. Currency was so badly depreciated that commercial transactions were almost impossible. Thousands of imported Jamaican laborers were plunged into such destitution that their colonial government sent a medical officer to assist them and arrange their repatriation at government expense. The Jamaican government brought back almost 4,000 of them. The Civil Tribunal of the Seine Department ordered the liquidator to pay the employees severance compensation, but gave them no preference over any other creditors.

A government-sponsored bill gave the liquidator authority to try to sell the unsubscribed lottery bonds at any price he could get in an attempt to raise funds for maintenance and preservation of the canal works at Panama, pending formation of a successor company.

The lotteries continued to be run, the prizes covered by the fund that had been deposited with the *Crédit Foncier.* True to the odds, the bonds drawn as winners were frequently the unsold ones. At the first lottery the number of an unsold bond had been drawn for the 500,000-franc grand prize. To give the hardy subscribers a break, the company drew the big prize over again at the next lottery, instead of moving on to the scheduled 250,000-franc one. A tailor in the avenue d'Antin won it.

A Deputy's appeal to the government to summon an international conference of engineers and to take some action to protect the interests of the canal company's investors brought a reply from the finance minister, now Rouvier again, that the government had no way and no responsibility to intervene, however much it approved the efforts of the private sector to prevent the collapse of the undertaking.

Maron J. Simon

The Panama canal, launched in dreams of profit and grandeur as a superhighway of ocean commerce, was transmuted into a drainage ditch for the effluent of the power struggle in France—a sort of remote political link of the sewers of Paris, in which some of the most leprous issues in the Third Republic's history began to surface.

A cartoon from a New York magazine shows de Lesseps after hearing President Hayes's declaration that "the policy of this country is a canal under American control." De Lesseps said this delighted him because it "assured the security of the canal."

COMPAGNIE UNIVERSELLE DU CANAL INTEROCÉANIQUE DE

PANAMA

PRÉSIDENT-DIRECTEUR : M. FERDINAND DE LESSEPS

Emprunt de 720 millions (2ᵐᵉ Émission)

Emprunt autorisé, conformément aux prescriptions de la loi du 21 mai 1836, par la loi du 8 juin 1888, mais sans aucune garantie ou responsabilité de l'Etat.

Souscription publique à 1,100,000 Obligations à Lots
ÉMISES A 325 FRANCS
Rapportant 15 francs par an
Payables semestriellement les 1ᵉʳ mars et 1ᵉʳ septembre de chaque année
REMBOURSABLES PAR DES LOTS OU A 400 FRANCS DANS UN DÉLAI MAXIMUM DE 99 ANS

Ces Obligations participeront au tirage du 15 Décembre 1888

TABLEAU DES LOTS TIRÉS CHAQUE ANNÉE
6 tirages par an, du 16 Août 1888 au 15 Juin 1913
3 lots de 500.000 fr. — 3 lots de 250.000 fr. — 6 lots de 100.000 fr., etc.

15 Décembre	Francs	15 Février	Francs	15 Avril	Francs	15 Juin	Francs	16 Août	Francs	15 Octobre	Francs
1 lot de	500.000	1 lot de	250.000	1 lot de	500.000	1 lot de	250.000	1 lot de	500.000	1 lot de	250.000
1 —	100.000	1 —	100.000	1 —	100.000	1 —	100.000	1 —	100.000	1 —	100.000
2 lots de 10.000,	20.000	2 lots de 10.000,	20.000	2 lots de 10.000,	20.000	2 lots de 10.000,	20.000	2 lots de 10.000,	20.000	2 lots de 10.000,	20.000
2 —	5.000, 10.000	2 —	5.000, 10.000	2 —	5.000, 10.000	2 —	5.000, 10.000	2 —	5.000, 10.000	2 —	5.000, 10.000
5 —	2.000, 10.000	5 —	2.000, 10.000	5 —	2.000, 10.000	5 —	2.000, 10.000	5 —	2.000, 10.000	5 —	2.000, 10.000
50 —	1.000, 50.000	50 —	1.000, 50.000	50 —	1.000, 50.000	50 —	1.000, 50.000	50 —	1.000, 50.000	50 —	1.000, 50.000

Par an : 366 lots s'élevant à Fr. 3.390.000

4 tirages par an, du 16 Août 1913 jusqu'à complet amortissement
2 lots de 500.000 fr. — 2 lots de 250.000 fr. — 4 lots de 100.000 fr., etc.

15 Février	Francs	15 Mai	Francs	16 Août	Francs	15 Novembre	Francs
1 lot de	500.000	1 lot de	250.000	1 lot de	500.000	1 lot de	250.000
1 —	100.000	1 —	100.000	1 —	100.000	1 —	100.000
1 —	10.000	1 —	10.000	1 —	10.000	1 —	10.000
1 —	5.000	1 —	5.000	1 —	5.000	1 —	5.000
5 lots de 2.000,	10.000	5 lots de 2.000,	10.000	5 lots de 2.000,	10.000	5 lots de 2.000,	10.000
50 —	1.000, 50.000	50 —	1.000, 50.000	50 —	1.000, 50.000	50 —	1.000, 50.000

Par an : 236 lots s'élevant à Fr. 2.200.000

LES OBLIGATIONS PLACÉES PARTICIPERONT SEULES AUX TIRAGES
La souscription sera annulée, si elle n'atteint pas le chiffre minimum de 400,000 obligations.
Le paiement des lots aura lieu un mois après chaque tirage.

Le remboursement à 400 francs et le paiement des lots sont garantis par un dépôt, dans les caisses du Crédit Foncier de France, de Rentes françaises ou de Titres garantis par le Gouvernement Français, conformément aux termes de la loi du 8 juin 1888.

Indépendamment de l'amortissement qui se fera chaque année par le paiement des lots, l'amortissement à 400 francs commencera à partir de 1913.
Le dépôt en Rentes françaises ou Titres garantis par le Gouvernement Français est administré par une Société civile spéciale, indépendante de la Compagnie de Panama.

Prix d'émission payable comme suit :

		PRIX D'ÉMISSION PAR OBLIGATION
1ᵉʳ Versement	30 fr. en souscrivant	30 fr. »
	60 fr. à la répartition (15 au 18 décembre 1888)	60 fr. »
2ᵐᵉ —	30 fr. du 5 au 10 Janvier 1889, sous déduction des intérêts acquis à raison de 4 0/0 l'an	29 fr. 80
3ᵐᵉ —	30 fr. du 5 au 10 Février 1889 — —	29 fr. 73
4ᵐᵉ —	30 fr. du 5 au 10 Mars 1889 — —	29 fr. 60
5ᵐᵉ —	30 fr. du 5 au 10 Avril 1889 — —	28 fr. 54
6ᵐᵉ —	30 fr. du 5 au 10 Mai 1889 — —	29 fr. 47
7ᵐᵉ —	30 fr. du 5 au 10 Juin 1889 — —	29 fr. 39
8ᵐᵉ —	30 fr. du 5 au 10 Juillet 1889 — —	29 fr. 28
9ᵐᵉ —	25 fr. du 5 au 10 Août 1889, sous déduction des intérêts acquis à raison de 4 0/0 l'an jusqu'au 1ᵉʳ Septembre 1889	23 fr. 38
	Total	320 fr. 33

Les coupons échus et ceux à échoir en Janvier 1889, de rentes françaises au porteur, d'actions et d'obligations des six grandes Compagnies de Chemins de fer français, d'obligations de la Ville de Paris, de valeurs de la Compagnie de Suez et de la Compagnie Universelle du Canal Interocéanique, seront acceptés en paiement.

La Souscription sera close le 12 Décembre 1888

A la Compagnie Universelle du Canal Interocéanique, 46, rue Caumartin.
A la Compagnie Universelle du Canal de Suez, 9, rue Charras.
Au Comptoir d'escompte de Paris, 14, rue Bergère.
A la Société Générale de Crédit Industriel et Commercial, 72, rue de la Victoire.
A la Société de Dépôts et de Comptes Courants, 2, place de l'Opéra.
A la Société Générale *pour favoriser le développement du Commerce et de l'Industrie en France*, 54, rue de Provence.
A la Banque de Paris et des Pays-Bas, 3, rue d'Antin.
Au Crédit Lyonnais, 19, boulevard des Italiens.
A la Banque d'Escompte de Paris, place Ventadour.
A la Banque Franco-Égyptienne, 3 et 5, rue Saint-Georges.

Et dans leurs bureaux de quartiers à leurs agences en province et à l'Étranger et chez leurs Correspondants en France et à l'Étranger

On peut souscrire, dès à présent, par correspondance.

To heighten the allure of their moribund corporation as a prospective borrower of 720,000,000 francs, the Panama Canal Company's directors made their last issue a lottery loan. This advertisement in *Le Figaro* listed the rich payoffs to winners at the quarterly drawings.

FRENCH HISTORY AS IT IS MADE.
[N. B. – The artist forgot to put in the kodak.]

When insults exchanged in the Chamber of Deputies provoked Georges Clemenceau's duel with Paul Deroulede, some observers professed to see a shootout at twenty-five paces as a perfectly safe pastime. *The New York World's* cartoon (above) registered this viewpoint nastily.

A view of Culebra cut from Harper's Weekly of July 4, 1885 bears out de Lesseps's statement to an American Naval intelligence officer that "it is a great and difficult work."

Clemenceau

Andrieux

Deroulede

Boulanger

Rouvier

de Reinach

Delahaye

Cornelius Herz, most detested and inveighed against of the multitude suspected of complicity in the Panama affair, was reputed to hold destructive information against many in power, which he never revealed.

Doux Pays
(LA COMMISSION CHEZ CORNÉLIUS HERZ)

— Le Patron n'y est pour personne !...
— Mais, mon ami, c'est la Commission d'enquête..... Nous lui rapportons son grand cordon...

The press declared open season on the Deputies left stranded by Herz's abrupt withdrawal of his offer to have them examine him at Bournemouth. In Figaro's jibe, when the butler tells them that "the boss isn't at home to anyone," they plead: "But, my friend, it's the investigating committee. We're bringing him back his Grand Cordon."

6

For defenders of the French Republic few
events could have been more untimely than the collapse of the
Panama Canal Company.

The reactionary Right and the futuristic Left had joined
forces in an election campaign from which their candidate,
General Georges Boulanger, the original Man on Horseback,
appeared likely to emerge as the dictator of France. Just when
the campaign reach its bitterest pitch, the canal company went
under, wrecking the meager security of hundreds of thousands
of citizens, each of whom had a vote and almost every one of
whom felt that the government was somehow to blame.

The government was thoroughly alert to the prevalent
state of mind and its very possible result—the Man on
Horseback had achieved immense popularity. He appeared to
be a favorite of the police and the *Garde Républicaine*; Paris
might rise for him, enabling him to exploit an impressive victory at the polls by marching on the Presidential palace and
declaring himself head of a provisional government, then mas-
tering the nation and obtaining a plebiscite to put himself on
the throne, as Napoleon III had done.

Republicans were painfully familiar with the evolution of
government-by-personage. They so feared to galvanize some
latent monarchial ambition that they refused to put a Presidential palace or even a museum on the site of the Tuileries palace,
which had been burned down by the Communards. Instead,
they housed their President in the Elysée Palace, the Second
Empire's guesthouse for royalty in transit.

The hundred years that followed the great Revolution of

1789 had been a kaleidoscope of political convulsions—the end
of absolutism, a brief flurry of constitutional monarchy, aboli-
tion of royalty, reign of terror, birth of a republic governed by
Directory and Consulate, Napoleon Bonaparte's seizure of the
crown, restoration of the Bourbons, Napoleon's return from
exile for his rule of One Hundred Days, resumption of Bourbon
rule, ascent of the Orleanist dynasty under Louis Philippe,
birth of the Second Republic under Napoleon's nephew, the
nephew's *coup d'état* that established the Second Empire and
put him on its throne as Napoleon III, and finally, the proclamation of the Third Republic after the disaster of Sedan in the
Franco-Prussian War.

Measured against the typical ministerial tenure under the
new Republic, the eight decades that preceded it seemed, in
retrospect, a golden age of political stability. Since 1871, cabinets had shuttled in and out of office like the alternating pla-
toons of a modern football team. Twenty-six had served in less
than eighteen years, some lasting only a few days.

From the beginning the Third Republic was never without
a strong party working openly and aggressively to overthrow it.
A republican form of government had been chosen in the first
place only because it appeared to be the system that divided
France the least. The constitutional formula that established it
had squeaked through the national legislature in 1875 by a one-
vote margin. The first President, Adolphe Thiers, headed a government full of royalists. The government continued to have a
predominantly monarchial cast until 1879, when Jules Grevy,
president of the newly created Chamber of Deputies, the real
seat of governmental power, succeeded Marshal MacMahon,
the monarchists' man, as President of France.

Under Sadi Carnot, who followed Grevy in 1887, the opposition still held about a third of the seats in the Chamber. Its
antipathy to the Republic was so acute that Theodore Stanton,
Paris correspondent of the Associated Press, was moved to
write: "When M. Carnot gives a reception at the Elysée Palace,
you never see a Deputy or Senator of the Right advancing to
salute the President or his wife, and when he offers a grand
state dinner to Parliament, he does not invite members outside
of the republican party because he would run the risk of receiving a curt regret."

The Panama Affair

The "republican party," a generic term, not a proper name, seldom presented a united front. It was a collection of splinter groups that frequently acted as though they despised one another although they shared the general political affections of the *Bloc Républicain.* The political technique known as opportunism was the "tent within which all republicans willing to adjust their ideals and hobbies to the necessities of the time took shelter." The farther left a republican deputy sat, the greater his outrage with this approach. After MacMahon's fall, Clemenceau, devouring cabinet after cabinet, formed a radical group that encompassed all political attitudes left of opportunism. In 1885 his radicals formed a separate group, detaching themselves from the extreme Left, which became a spectrum of every socialist hue.*

In this atmosphere the Man on Horseback emerged, General Boulanger, a seeming paragon of republicanism and, indeed, the political protégé of Clemenceau, the unshakable republican.

Boulanger was a soldier with an honorable record; wounded four times on fields of combat from Cochin China to the streets of Paris, the youngest General of Brigade, France's amiable representative at the Centennial of United States independence at Yorktown, an able Director of Infantry at the War Office.

At Clemenceau's insistence Boulanger was named Minister of War in Premier Charles de Freycinet's third cabinet, formed in January, 1886. He kept the post under Premier Rene Goblet, who came into office the next December.

As Director of Infantry, the reforms Boulanger instituted to ease the lot of the army conscript had made him the friend of households throughout France. As Minister of War, his denunciation of the political climate that had made a general of King Louis Philippe's twenty-one-year-old son, the Duc d'Aumale, on no other basis of merit than his father's exalted rank, brought Boulanger further fame, even though it became known later that he had fawned on the Duke while serving in his command.

An artistic crowd-pleaser, forty-nine years old, tall and trim, blue-eyed and brown-bearded, with an erotic preoccupa-

---

*see Notes

tion that became legendary, Boulanger stole the show at his first Bastille Day celebration as War Minister; for the holiday review he appeared at Longchamps in glittering uniform, astride a black charger that he high-schooled in front of the reviewing stand where the President, ministerial colleagues, and other Very Important Persons sat in somber civilian regalia. Cantering about Paris and taking his bows before an admiring public, he was a popular idol and perceptible political menace. His enjoyment of the fruits of his showmanship were readily apparent; "one could detect in him an anxiety to attract attention."

When his heavyhanded treatment of a border incident produced a threat of war with Germany, the government took advantage of a change of cabinets to get rid of him. Rouvier, succeeding Goblet as Premier in May, 1887, chose another Minister of War and rode out the storm of popular protest. For Boulanger, the bayonet-brandishing performance that had been the specific act that cost him the War Ministry was also the deed that riveted onto him the devotion of Frenchmen who yearned for vengeance on Germany for the defeat in 1870 and the seizure of Alsace-Lorraine.

For opponents of Rouvier's ministry, the exclusion provided a handy issue. They could attribute it to the government's fear of Germany; "this reproach could already be foreseen upon the lips of radicals and monarchists."

The new War Minister, General Ferron, assigned Boulanger to command of the Thirteenth Army Corps. It was not a demotion, since it was the highest command he had held, but it was, in effect, banishment. Thirteenth Corps was headquartered at Clermont-Ferrand, deep in the Auvergne, far from Paris and the German frontier as well.

The War Ministry made sure to get him out of town before the next Bastille Day, to deprive his admirers of the opportunity to turn the national anniversary into a Boulanger celebration. Instead, his departure became a triumph. Mobs lined the route of his carriage to the Gare de Lyon and blocked the tracks in front of his train, screaming, *"Partira pas!"* ("Don't go!"), and begging him to march on the Elysée Palace.

Suddenly the Presidency itself was spattered by a scandal that intensified the usual stress on the Republic's existence.

President Grevy's son-in-law, Daniel Wilson, who had "more effective power than was ever possessed by a Dauphin of France," was accused of selling the ribbons and rosettes of the Legion of Honor and other orders right out of the Elysée, where he and his wife lived as guests of her father. A newspaper of the time ran a price list, quoting the Legion of Honor at 50,000 to 100,000 francs and the *Mérite Agricole* at 10,000 to 20,000.

For attempting to get the Legion of Honor for a conniving citizen, Wilson was convicted of fraud and was sentenced to a two-year imprisonment, fined 3,000-franc, and deprived of civil rights for five years. The Court of Appeal reversed the conviction, however; it found his action repulsive but not fraudulent. Grounds for the reversal were that Wilson really had influence and really used it in his customer's behalf without making any guarantee of delivery, and that so far as the sale of decorations was concerned, there was no law against it. A bill outlawing the receipt or offer of gifts in exchange for decorations was introduced in the Senate at once, prompting a Right-wing legislator to remark: "Rather late."

While Parisians strolled the boulevards singing a ditty composed especially for the occasion, *"Ah, quel malheur d'avoir un gendre!"* ("Ah, what bad luck to have a son-in-law!"), Grevy stood by Wilson and kept him and Mme. Wilson on at the Elysée until they could move to the mansion they were building in the avenue d'Iena. But republican pressure on the President to resign was enormous, for the opposition used the family scandal to smear the whole republican regime.

Grevy did not give up without a struggle. He resigned only after Rouvier's ministry was overthrown in an attempt to get at the President, who then could find no one of any republican faith to form a Cabinet under his administration.

French Presidents at the time were elected by the National Assembly, comprising the Senate and Chamber of Deputies. For the far Right and Left alike, the possibility that the choice would be former Premier Jules Ferry, one of the country's most distinguished statesmen, intensified the agitation of the fortnight in which the country waited for Grevy to step down.

Ferry's accomplishments offered almost every special-interest group something to hate. His name was synonymous with the great extension of France's colonial empire; therefore Frenchmen, dedicated to reversal of the 1870 defeat and redemption of Alsace-Lorraine, despised him for employing the nation's military strength and treasure in southeast Asia instead of against the enemy right next door. He had been in charge of rationing during the siege of Paris; he was held responsible for the suffering the Parisians had endured. He had retired the Orléans princes from active military command, one of the reasons the monarchists loathed him. The clerical party detested him for expelling religious orders from control of education. His opponents attacked him constantly as "Tonkin Ferry," "Famine Ferry," "Bismarck's Valet."

While the politicians scurried about in search of a candidate who could beat him, some of them began to embrace the idea that it would be "better to retain Grevy in office with the help of Boulanger's sword" than to let Ferry win.

One of the most emotional proponents of this strategy was Paul Deroulede, a poet and playwright whose "hatred of the Germans blinded him to all other considerations of political ethics." In 1882, twelve years after the Prussian conquest, he organized the League of Patriots to foster the martial spirit among the French and provide physical training and moral guidance for future soldiers of the nation.

At the invitation of some of Ferry's most vehement republican opponents, Boulanger attended a series of Paris conferences at the end of November, 1887, which became known, pretentiously or ironically, as the Historic Nights. Clemenceau was among those present, along with several of his closest friends who were adamant against Grevy's retention, as well as Boulanger's most rabid supporters among the radicals.

The first meeting produced no solution. The next day Deroulede, who had been reviling Grevy for months for Boulanger's dismissal, went to the Elysée to entreat him to "remain the faithful and devoted guardian of the Republic and the country."

Both Deroulede and Boulanger were present at the second Historic Night meeting, held at the home of the radical Deputy, Georges Laguerre, one of Boulanger's most fervent champions. That day Grevy, now being courted, had laid down to Laguerre a condition for remaining in office: he would stay on only with a Premier of great authority. The Boulangist conferees, especially Deroulede, turned insistently to Clemenceau, one of the several leaders whom Grevy had beseeched in vain to form a government. As Clemenceau reported the proposition subsequently to his constituents in the Department of the Var, "the plan was simple; Boulanger—Minister of War."

"If I were overridden in the Chamber," he explained, "Deroulede would launch the League of Patriots against the Palais Bourbon, and the army would remain in its barracks. What do you think of that great patriot who would enroll his countrymen under the sacred flag of patriotism and who, having Frenchmen at his command for the defense of the nation, does not hesitate, in our country's state of affairs, to thrust them without their consent into an enterprise of civil war? My resistance put an end to these criminal aims."

In the middle of the meeting Boulanger was mysteriously called away. He was summoned to a conference with representatives of the Count of Paris, the Orleanist pretender, who offered him a deal: the royalists would support any ministry that gave the War Office to Boulanger, who would be the Cabinet's virtual head; in return, he would support a plebiscite in which the people could choose whatever form of government they wanted; thus, with the popular general in control of the armed forces, a well-managed nation might switch without bloodshed from a republic to a monarchy.

Returning from his meeting with the Right, he found his friends of the Left trying to slip him into power with another candidate for Premier, Louis Andrieux, the former Paris Prefect of Police who was one of Grevy's billiard-playing cronies at the Elysée Palace. But Andrieux, their last hope, turned Boulanger down for strategic reasons, saying: "Anything else, my dear general, you shall have, and in a few months probably you may have that also; but if you formed part of the Cabinet at first I could not conciliate the Chamber. You shall be Military Governor of Paris, the noblest military post in the world."

On December 1 Deroulede breathed the last gasp of the Boulanger leadership, addressing a crowd outside the Chamber of Deputies and shouting, *"Vive Grevy! Vive Boulanger!"*—to which the crowd shouted back, *"A bas Grevy! Vive la République!"*

Grevy resigned the next day, and the National Assembly, in thoroughly sedate proceedings, chose Carnot as the fourth President of the Third Republic. On the first ballot Ferry received 212 of the 849 votes cast, and thereupon withdrew in favor of Carnot, who had received 303.

Two months later the Minister of War inadvertently resuscitated Boulanger's political career by relieving him of command of Thirteenth Corps for breaches of discipline, such as coming up to Paris without orders. As had happened the year before with his banishment to Clermont-Ferrand, the disciplinary action against him only bloated his popular stature. He immediately became the hero of every out-of-power group in French politics except Clemenceau's radicals, who rallied to the government's support.

The junta of Right and Left extremists that gathered about the general ran him in by-elections for the Chamber in the Aisne Department and at Marseilles. He won in the Aisne by a 45,000-vote majority; but by running while still on active duty, he had violated army regulations. Once again the War Ministry advanced his political career; a court of inquiry ordered his compulsory retirement, thus leaving him free to be a candidate whenever he wished. A hybrid party that sprang up around him represented so many forms of opposition to the Republic that Boulanger came to be called the "main drain."

The ultra-Right looked to him as the instrument of restoration of the monarchy; the ultra-Left looked to him as the instrument for achieving its social program in a hurry. The revenge-seekers, sincere patriots and professional patriots alike, saw him as the leader of their conquest of Germany and their rescue of Alsace-Lorraine. The one political emotion all shared with him was antipathy for parliamentary government.

Multiple candidacies were legal, and his strategists decided to enter him in every forthcoming by-election; they looked to this plan to sample voter opinion under actual electoral conditions, and also to produce support that would snowball should he begin to win consistently—with the result that the general election for the National Assembly in 1889 might become, in effect, a plebiscite for Boulanger.

It became an "in" thing to be a Boulangist. In Paris drawing rooms, wrote Baron Pierre de Coubertin, the French authority on education who founded the modern Olympic Games, "the general reaped a harvest of smiles and also—as it was discovered later—subsidies for his cause."

The newspaper *La Cocarde* was started, he said, "with what money no one knew but with what intention everyone understood."

Boulanger campaign photographs and emblems began to flood the country; a photograph of him on his black horse even adorned the bamboo hut of a king in central Africa.

"With gaze impenetrable, with the peaceful manner of a man who feels himself not inferior to his destiny, however great it may be, he moved easily in the midst of the most eccentric party that ever was collected around a politician," said de Coubertin.

The Count of Paris contributed a monthly allowance of 55,000 francs to Boulanger and his campaign.

The Bonapartist pretender, Prince Napoleon Jerome, promised the general the sword Napoleon Bonaparte had worn at Marengo. The Duchesse d'Uzes, who could call herself the premier peeress of France* and was an heir to the champagne fortune of her great-grandmother, the Widow Cliquot, put 3,-000,000 francs into the Boulanger kitty. One of the Duchess's teammates was Louise Michel, the "Red Virgin" of the barricades in the days of the Commune, who was exiled to New Caledonia on its suppression. When she took up the Boulanger cause she was not long out of jail after serving a term in solitary confinement for participating in an anarchist demonstration in Paris.

Two of the general's staunchest supporters in the press were Arthur Meyer and Henri Rochefort. Meyer, born in Germany of a Jewish family and "now one of the pillars of Catholic Christianity," was publisher of *Le Gaulois,* the royalist newspaper. Rochefort, the Marquis of Luçay, was a Left-wing hero and one of the wildest pens in Paris journalism. The empire had jailed him for his assaults on the government; the early,

---

*The Duchess owned this claim because the coachman of her husband's seventeenth-century ancestor, the first Duc d'Uzes, was an intrepid rein; twelve ducal peerages had been created before his, but when Louis XIII ordered proof of title, he was first to comply, his coach overtaking the equipage of the Duc de Luynes near the Louvre and sideswiping it into the mud to win the race to the royal palace.

royalist-tinged rulers of the Third Republic, of which he was a founder, had exiled him to New Caledonia as a member of the Commune, and he was back in town between banishments. A sample of his prose was the attack of his paper, *L'Intransigeant,* on the Ferry ministry during the Tunisian campaign of 1881: "A cabinet of Natural History, a band of swindlers, imbeciles, impostors."

Clericals and anti-Semites flocked to Boulanger, while his chief speech writer and one of his most important managers, Senator Alfred Naquet, was a composite of anathema to all of them; he was a republican, a Jew, and author of the current French divorce law. The young novelist Maurice Barres, an anti-Semite, was one of Naquet's colleagues in Boulanger's high command. The campaign manager, Arthur-Marie Dillon, known as Count Dillon, was at St. Cyr, the French military academy, with Boulanger, but resigned his cavalry commission for trade, and eventually became an executive of the Commercial Cable Company. Finally, there was Deroulede, perhaps Boulanger's best front man because "it was his known integrity, his high idealism, and his devotion to his country which blinded many to the woeful shortcomings of his chief."

Indicators of the general's popularity shot up like a bamboo forest. Crowds cheered him wherever he went, even at such a solemn occasion as the funeral of President Carnot's father, the life-Senator Hippolyte Carnot, where they rushed Ferry's carriage screaming, *"A bas, Ferry! Vive Boulanger!"*

When a corn law pushed up the price of bread, the name of "Boulanger" itself, the French word for "baker," inspired a campaign slogan; "Boulanger will bring us cheap bread; long live our Boulanger!"

He ran in the old Bonapartist constituency of the Dordogne and won handily, but refused the seat on the plea that he had promised to represent the voters of the Nord, the coal-mining and manufacturing district bordering Belgium and the North Sea. He won in the Nord by a two-to-one majority over the combined votes of his radical and moderate republican opponents. He took his seat in the Chamber, proposed its dissolution, and demanded revision of the constitution. Both proposals came to nothing, and he resigned after an exchange of insults with Charles Floquet, then the Premier, with whom he thereupon fought a duel.

The general was lucky to get out of it alive. Floquet, who came from Bayonne near the Spanish frontier, had the "deftness of a toreador in handling a foil." Sprawled in a clump of bushes into which Boulanger's inept rush had backed him, he stuck out his weapon and managed to wound the general severely between the carotid artery and the jugular vein.

Fortified by hysterically uncritical support, Boulanger's public image was invulnerable even to this humiliation at the hands of a sixty-one-year-old civilian. During his convalescence he won by-elections in the Nord, in the Somme and Charente Inférieure by huge majorities, spending almost 700,000 francs in the three campaigns.

He could even disappear for two months at the height of his campaigns without damaging his position. Not until he returned for his daughter's wedding at the end of October, 1888, was it learned that he had slipped away to Tangiers with his mistress, Mme. Marguerite de Bonnemains, recently divorced from the son of General the Viscount de Bonnemains.

Boulanger demonstrations grew in frequency and bitterness. His partisans trotted after his carriage worshipfully and attacked his opponents with clubs. Each of his rallies was a sellout. Suddenly, an opportunity arose to demonstrate his magic in the nation's political show-window—Paris. A Parisian Deputy died, and an election to choose his successor was scheduled for Sunday, January 27, 1889. General Boulanger filed for the seat.

Various republican splinter groups united on a colorless candidate, a distiller name Jacques, president of the General Council of the Seine Department. He was a radical on whom the *Times* of London bestowed the accolade, "However extreme his views, he has affable manners."

The Boulangists opposed him with money and muscle. They spent 15 per cent of the Duchess's slush fund on this one election. Deroulede's League of Patriots, armed with prospect lists of various voting blocs, performed beaverishly as doorbell ringers. Mobs awaited the general's appearances in the doorway of his handsomely furnished house at 11 bis rue Dumont d'Urville, near the Arc de Triomphe.

Scarely six weeks before election day the Panama Canal Company fell apart, adding another sturdy plank to his all-purpose platform. Boulanger sent a message of sympathy to de

Lesseps at once, saying the rejection of the bill to grant the company the three-months moratorium for meeting its obligations was the Chamber's crowning sin. He denounced the government for letting honest people think the canal enterprise was sure of official patronage and then deserting it.

A particularly effective weapon was a pitiful letter from a peasant in Bergnac who said that when the lottery loan was authorized he had cashed his *rentes*, sold his father's watch, and mortgaged some land to raise 3,000 francs with which to buy bonds.

When a delegation of Panama bondholders called on Boulanger, he offered practical as well as moral support; he subscribed to twenty-five bonds to prove his interest. But when the bondholders' committee visited the Premier to thank him for the government's introduction of the moratorium bill, he could only express his sympathy, assure them of his undiminshed interest in the Panama company, as in all the nation's great undertakings, and take care to point out that he was speaking only for himself.

De Lesseps told his army to vote for Boulanger and gave a dinner for him. A *New York Tribune* editorial called Boulanger "the political patron" of the Panama company directors and said that "his triumph, they assume, will open the way for government intervention and financing support from the national treasury." The doorbell ringers of the League of Patriots added the Panama patients to their list of house calls.

The *Times* of London described the investors' view of the issue in these terms: "M. Floquet is in power, yet while sympathizing he either cannot or will not help us. Parliamentarianism is unwilling or unable to assist us. Our interest is therefore to promote a dictatorship."

On election day the Boulangist machine functioned with unbeatable efficiency. The election was the first in Paris in which contestants offered voters free transportation to the polls; and Boulanger carriages were the first on the streets, while his canvassers raced about the wards energetically, getting out the vote among the Panama investors and other special interest groups.

Cavalry detachments patrolled the streets, and a huge force of police was on the alert, their loyalties yet to be demonstrated. Crowds stood in the Place de la Bourse and the rue Montmartre all night, watching the illuminated returns on the façades of newspaper offices and promotion-minded stores. A mob packed the Place de la Madeleine in front of the general's command post at the Café Durand (on the site now occupied by the Thomas Cook & Sons building), waiting for him to come out and take over.

The election was a Boulanger landslide, and the shock it produced among French republicans made an unforgettable impression on a competent American observer who was living in Paris that winter, Dr. Albert Shaw, later editor of the *Review of Reviews* in New York. "Tried and dignified republican leaders gathered their families about them in uncontrollable tears," he recalled, and "such cool-headed and veteran statesmen as the late Senators de Pressense and Jules Simon admitted to me that they expected to be banished from France within six months."

The excitement mounted with the vote, which eventually reached 245,236 for Boulanger, 162,875 for Jacques. A few blocks from the Café Durand a popular demonstration was building up in the rue du Faubourg St. Honore, outside the Elysée Palace. The general's war council prodded him repeatedly to move out and let the mob lift him to their shoulders and carry him to the Presidential palace to oust Carnot.

At last, at midnight, he left the restaurant. He stepped into the midst of his screaming, singing partisans, made his way past them to his carriage, climbed in, and went home, leaving generations of second-guessers to speculate why he refused the opportunity thrust at him so ecstatically.

Nor did he show up at the Chamber the next day. He told the *London Daily Telegraph*: "I did not desire a demonstration. I will show the people that the government is the party of disorder, while I personate order. I shall wait and let the government act. Whatever they do is certain to help me. They are blind."

Not all of them were. Jean Constans, a hard-handed lawyer named to the post of Minister of the Interior in the new Cabinet formed after the election-night panic, took up his chores as a sort of ministerial bouncer.

"I had no conception before the Boulangist time that republicans could so resolutely throttle their Frankensteins," said W. F. Lonergan of the *Daily Telegraph*, who covered Paris for years.

The government dissolved the League of Patriots for illegal political action and unlawful association, set detectives to tailing Boulanger around the clock, and got across to him the idea that he was about to be arrested.

Boulanger slipped out of Paris with Mme. de Bonnemains, completely crossing up his good friend and faithful chronicler, Charles Chincholle, *Figaro's* famous "king of the reporters", who was left to explain away an article about a luncheon he was supposed to be having with the general at a moment when the general was en route to Brussels.

Dillon pursued him to Brussels, where he had put up at the Hotel Mengelle under the name of "Bruno," and fetched him back despite the tearful protests of Mme. de Bonnemains. The court order for the Panama company's liquidation, and a run on an important bank, the *Comptoir d'Escompte*, which had over-extended itself in support of an attempted corner on copper, produced a fortuitous climate for the Boulangist party's war on the existing government.

The feelings of the Panama investors, moreover, could scarcely have been assuaged by the enthusiasm for another lottery loan, consisting of 1,250,000 bonds at 25 francs each, that was being offered just then to finance the forthcoming Paris Exhibition. The Parliament had sanctioned an arrangement of the *Crédit Foncier* under which each bond carried not only a chance at eighty-one lottery prizes, including one of 100,000 francs, but also twenty-five tickets to the fair.

The resurrected Boulanger returned to the attack with a speech at Tours and a manifesto against the "pack of parliamentarians," but found the parliamentarians waiting with a bill of particulars charging him with conspiracy against the state and misappropriation of public funds while he was in the War Office. The indictment also charged Dillon and Rochefort with the conspiracy.

A tip-off enabled all three to evade arrest, and Boulanger returned to Brussels, where his presence and the lavish hospitality of his headquarters attracted so many demonstrative hangers-on that the Belgian Premier invited him to move his émigré court to another country.

The French Senate, sitting as a high court, convicted the three fugitives in April, 1889, and sentenced them to detention for life in a French fortress. By then, however, they were in London, safe from arrest, and a few years later Dillon and Rochefort returned to France under an amnesty.

The general never went home. His political career ended in the first summer of his exile. In an election of departmental and district councils, he was a candidate in 400 constituencies, but won only in twelve. In the general election soon afterward, the republicans won almost 65 per cent of the seats in the Chamber of Deputies, although Boulanger was the winner in the Clignancourt District of Paris despite his disqualification to serve.

The general and Mme. de Bonnemains retired to the Isle of Jersey, where she died of tuberculosis on July 16, 1891. She was buried in the cemetery at Ixelles, near Brussels, where he committed suicide eleven weeks later, firing a bullet into his head at her grave, on which he had just placed a wreath inscribed, *"Marguerite, à bientôt."*

Authorship of a pitiless epitaph, "Here lies General Boulanger; he died as he lived—a second lieutenant," was attributed to his old mentor, Clemenceau. At the general's political demise a famous English editor, W.T. Stead, of the British *Review of Reviews*, had composed a more charitable one: "It seems as if it were almost a libel to say of General Boulanger that he is a Boulangist."

The public soon forgot Boulanger, but Boulangism persisted as a haven for political extremists, battening on such issues as the Panama disaster, which the electorate had buried only shallowly beneath the habitually heaving surface of the Third Republic. Three years after the Boulangist rout at the polls, the Panama issue exploded with a force that jolted even so formidable a combatant as Clemenceau. Commenting on the involvement of one of his former associates, he said prophetically: "It is true that despite the pressing solicitations of General Boulanger, M. Cornelius Herz would not join in the Boulangist campaign. He is paying for that refusal now. As for me, I shall suffer for it in my turn. I accept my fate."

7

At 5 p.m. on Monday, November 21, 1892,
Jules Delahaye, the Deputy for Chinon, rose from his seat
among the benches on the Right, made his way down the semi-
circular tiers of the Chamber of Deputies, and mounted the
eight steps to the speaker's stand, as stragglers rushed from the
lobbies to hear what he had to say.

Delahaye was nearing the end of his first term in the
Chamber. In private life he was editor-in-chief of the monarchist *Journal d' Indre-et-Loire*. He was an ardent Boulangist.
During the 1889 campaign he had declared: "Civil and foreign
war is what Jules Ferry and his accomplices stand for. General
Boulanger stands for peace and order." Boulanger had replied
from his London refuge: "Your program is mine; you are the
only candidate of the nationalist party."

Delahaye was an athletic young man, with thick black hair
combed straight back, a closely trimmed beard, and a huge
mustache that looked like two four-inch parentheses placed
end to end, open side up. "His mouth and all the lower parts of
his face betoken inflexible cruelty," said the novelist Maurice
Barres, his colleague in Boulangism and also a freshmen
Deputy, representing Nancy.

"I detected at once what we call a good hater," Barres said,
"but his hate is not melancholy and somber; it has something
fierce, joyous, brilliant; it is the hate of a successful fighter who
neither asks nor gives quarter."

Delahaye stood at the lectern, pale and tense, took a long,
tough look at his colleagues in the most powerful governing
body in France, and told them that 150 of them had taken bribes

from the Panama Canal Company. At last the upheaval of the Panama canal scandal had begun, having followed the pattern of the great earthquakes in nature: more than forty months of increasingly violent and ominous tremors deep in the French political firmament had preceded the first major shock of Delahaye's charge, with investors thrashing about in desperate efforts to salvage their investments and legislators demanding juridical vengeance for their aggrieved constituents.

First, an engineering committee that the receivership sent to Panama to examine the prospects of finishing the canal reported that it would take eight more years and 900 million more francs. Bonaparte Wyse, at the liquidator's behest, returned to Colombia and negotiated a new concession that extended the construction period for ten years, until 1902, provided a new canal company was organized by February 28, 1893; but the investors could not get the man they wanted to lead the new enterprise. He was Albert Christophle, governor of the *Crédit Foncier*, who had taken no part in the de Lesseps company's financing. Christophle was the financier to whom "French thriftiness responds with the most eagerness and the greatest confidence." The investors put huge pressure on him to take up where de Lesseps had left off and finish the canal; a hundred thousand of them petitioned the Government to use its influence with him.

In June, 1890, the Chamber of Deputies voted overwhelmingly to refer the Panama question to the Minister of Justice. But action was slow in coming. On June 11, 1891, the first chamber of the Court of Appeal appointed Henri Prinet, one of its councilors, as *juge d'instruction*, or examining magistrate, to investigate the official acts of several members of the Panama company's administrative council. An ancient law exempting Grand Officers of the Legion of Honor and other important personages from trial before magistrates of summary jurisdiction placed the case directly before the Court of Appeal, because Ferdinand de Lesseps was a Grand Officer.

Prinet's first step was to summon him, his son Charles, and Henri Cottu, another member of the company's top management, to appear before him three days later. De Lesseps, now eighty-six, had at last become an aged man, increasingly withdrawn from the world; but when the summons was brought to him at his town house in the avenue Montaigne, he rose from bed, dressed, put on his Grand Cordon, and went to face his interrogator.

"What a terrible nightmare I have had," he told his wife next day. "I imagined I was summoned before the examining magistrate. It was atrocious."

On September 7 the police searched the homes and offices of several promoters of the canal, and of Gustave Eiffel, and seized documents.

On January 5, 1892, the Chamber of Deputies voted a demand for "resolute and speedy action against all those who have incurred responsibilities in the Panama affair."

Prinet's investigation continued intensively for another ten months. Not long before he completed his task, the newspaper *Libre Parole*, a newcomer to Paris journalism, published a series of letters under the title, "The Secrets of Panama," attacking the company's directors violently and accusing several present and former members of Parliament of trafficking in their mandates during the 1888 vote for the lottery loan bill. The author of the series, who signed himself "Micros," was Ferdinand Martin, a Nyons banker who had lobbied for the company but had left its service angrily because he thought he had not been paid enough.

Libre Parole, the newspaper Martin chose as his vehicle, was headed by Edouard Drumont, who had already found a profitable niche in France as a professional anti-Semite. The "Micros" series was not Drumont's first assault on the Panama venture. Two years earlier, in his book *La Derniere Bataille*, he had attacked Ferdinand de Lesseps as "this man who has lied so shamelessly, who has abused the public with false promises, who has squandered this money in the most disgraceful way, who used it in part to pay the newspapers told off to sing his praises."

He had referred to "the Great Frenchman" description of de Lesseps as "an anti-phrase in reality," saying that "except for Gambetta and Jules Ferry it may be said that no contemporary Frenchman was ever more systematically hostile to French interests nor ever did more harm to our institutions."

Drumont's new contributor, the disgruntled Martin, charged that legislators of all political shades had been involved in the Panama affair, and named Baron Jacques de Reinach, Henri Cottu, Emile Arton, an absconding executive of a dynamite company, and Irenee Blanc, of the editorial staff of *L' Economiste Pratique*, as the principal agents of corruption.

De Reinach, the canal company's financial agent in its last bond issues, was one of those the examining magistrate interrogated, seeking especially to unearth details of the multimillion-franc *publicité* expenditures. The transcript of his testimony, in the three-volume report of a subsequent legislative investigation of the Panama affair, was unsigned and undated and was thus unique among the depositions published.

"The Panama company has had to pay large sums to the newspapers," de Reinach told the investigator. "I advanced part of these sums, and the 3,015,000 francs to which you refer are merely my advances."

The questioning went on:

Question: "Are you in a position to prove that these advances were really made?"

Answer: "I did not make any advances to the company. I made them direct to the newspapers. The company reimbursed me. I could prove it at any given moment."

Q: "The moment has come. How can you make this proof? Have you any books?"

A: "No, I have not any books, but I can tell you, for instance, that I gave 1,000,000 francs to M. Arton and the rest to other newspapermen.

Q: "Arton is a fugitive and was not himself either a journalist or an advertising agent. He was a member of the Dynamite Company. For what purpose was this million paid to M. Arton?"

A: "M. Arton was in newspapers for he was a partner in *La Presse*. He had to meet the expenses of advertising preliminary to the issue, that is, with the object of preparing the public for the issue. I do not know if he was concerned with this advertising at the time of the issue."

Q: "Do you know upon what persons he distributed this million?"

A: "He never told me."

Q: "Are you sure that he gave the money only to newspapers and that he did not use part of it to subsidize certain politicians?"

A: "I utterly refused to receive any confidence as to the use to which he put the money."

At last the investigation by the magistrate drew to a close, and Jules Quesnay de Beaurepaire, the chief public prosecutor, presented his conclusions to his chiefs in the Cabinet. In September he recommended criminal prosecution, but reversed his position because he decided he could not prove a criminal motive.

On November 5 he reported directly to Premier Emile Loubet that "the affair, from the judicial point of view, was very simple: criminal proceedings more than doubtful, civil action excellent."

On November 13 he reported to the Minister of Justice, Louis Ricard, that "very honorable people, in great numbers, were ready to come forth to declare in court that the MM. de Lesseps had never been moved by the spirit of fraud, that they had always for their goal not the continuation of their rewards as administrators but the pursuit of a labor they believed in fanatically, and that if they had made gross mistakes they had never realized nor even sought a personal profit at the expense of others."

"In the face of these positive revelations of October, which I obviously had not been able to take into account in September, could one continue to hope to prove in court the fraudulent intent?" he asked. "My impression on this point was not isolated, for at the Palais [de Justice] the most competent did not hesitate to predict the negative outcome of the lawsuit."

Two days later the Cabinet held a momentous meeting, at which the Premier ceded the starring role to his Minister of Justice. The prosecutor, not only a lawyer but a professional word-painter, having written spicy stories for *La Vie Parisienne* under the name of "Lucie Herpin," and romantic novels as "Jules de Glouvet," regarded the Minister of Justice as a stuffed shirt who affected a majestic solemnity and fulfilled all the theater's specifications for the role of the heavy father.

"Without any doubt, his ambition was to replace not President Carnot but *le Roi Soleil*," the versatile prosecutor wrote.

He learned the details of the Cabinet meeting from one of the Ministers, whom he would not name.

"Loubet, who the night before was armed for war, appeared at the meeting with an olive branch in his hand," Quesnay de Beaurepaire related. "He came from a conference about the matter with the Minister of Justice and had abdicated in his favor.

" 'Let us settle the question of Panama,' he said by way of introduction. 'Since it is in the legal domain, its solution becomes the business of our colleagues in the Justice Department.'

"This sudden meekness and deference caused some surprise. M. Ricard spoke out at once: 'My decision is firm. I have already sent to the prosecuting attorney the order to bring criminal proceedings against de Lesseps, Eiffel, and others.'

"Two Ministers protested. The rest kept their silence."

On Monday morning, November 21, summonses were served on Ferdinand and Charles de Lesseps, Cottu, Eiffel, and the scholarly Marius Fontane, the old man's faithful assistant.

Ferdinand and Charles de Lesseps, Cottu and Fontane were charged with swindling and breach of trust, Eiffel with complicity in swindling and breach of trust.

The aged canal builder, who had been removed to his country home, La Chesnaye, where he spent most of his days reading, talking little, reclining in a bathchair in the sun or before the fire, was not even aware that a prosecution had begun.

The Minister of Justice disclosed that de Reinach would have been included in the prosecution, but at 6:45 o'clock on Sunday morning, when the Baron's valet went to wake him to ride with his hunt, he found his employer dead in bed in his palatial home at 20 rue Murillo, near the Parc Monceau.

The fifty-five-year-old banker was a member of a Frankfort family ennobled by Victor Emmanuel in 1866, its Barony being recognized by the King of Prussia the next year. Jacques de Reinach had come to Paris and joined an old and respected banking house founded early in the century by Baron Samuel Kohn, whose nephew, Edouard Kohn, became de Reinach's partner in Kohn, Reinach & Cie., and his brother-in-law.

DeReinach was not only a financier but an aspiring writer.

He had collaborated on a ballet, titled "Maladetta," with Pierre Gailhard, former co-director and principal *basso cantante* of the opera, whom he had notified that he would attend a rehearsal on Monday night.

His death, disclosed in the Monday morning newspapers, produced an enormous sensation, a deluge of rumors as to its cause—illness, suicide or murder—and such diagnoses as *Figaro*'s statement that he was full-blooded, had a short neck, and therefore was a likely subject for apoplexy. His family physician, Benoit de Martouret, attributed the Baron's death to a "cerebral congestion," the first incident of which he had suffered two years earlier.*

Several Deputies had notified the government earlier that they would ask questions about the Panama affair at the session that afternoon; among them was Delahaye, who added to the atmosphere of strained expectancy when he told a colleague on the way to the legislative chamber: "Do not leave the sitting. There will be a big explosion."

Even so, the session opened quietly with a question by the Boulangist Deputy for Corbeil, Jean-Baptiste Argelies, one of the most courteous debaters in the house. He said his object was to defend the interests of the investors. Rouvier, the Minister of Finance, put in a bland disclaimer of government responsibility, to which Argelies replied that since authority to float a lottery loan was a privilege, the government had assumed moral responsibility by granting it.

Then Delahaye climbed to the tribune, the speaker's stand of the Chamber. "My first concern is to appear in your eyes not as an informer but as a representative of the country who has a profound sense of the obligations incumbent on him," he said with delicacy.

"If you want names you will vote an inquiry" became his unvarying refrain as his recitation of a roster of unidentified malefactors provoked his colleagues to continuous shouts of "Name them! Name them!"

There was one name he was willing to disclose. "I can say that the medium of these transactions was a man named Arton, who has since fled the country to escape punishment for embez-

*see Notes

zling a large sum from a dynamite manufacturing company of which he was a director," Delahaye said.

"There was a sum of 3,000,000 francs distributed among 150 Deputies and a few Senators," he charged, "but the appetites thus excited grew greedier and the financier managing the matter was compelled to ask the administrators of the Panama company for more millions. A veritable pack of politicians hounded the administrators."

A reference to a pay-off in the form of Panama money, for expenses of an election held at a time when Floquet was the Minister responsible for its conduct, goaded the former Premier to angry protest. Looking down from the curule chair he occupied as President of the Chamber, Floquet proclaimed: "I am always ready to appear before all investigations."

When the uproar subsided, Delahaye plunged ahead: "Three hundred thousand francs were spent in buying three papers.

"A Minister now dead asked 400,000 francs, another 200,000 francs was paid for a journal of little value but behind which hidden influences were working. A foreign paper was bought for 500,000 francs, a check for which was signed at its office. I can name the person who acted as the messenger between the contracting parties. Now for the last scandal. The committee of this Chamber charged with the duty of examining into this lottery bond scheme comprised 5 favorable to it and 5 opposed. The eleventh member, before casting his vote, offered his services to the company for 200,000 francs. As the company refused his proposition, he formed a syndicate, being aided by a banker, and caused a fall in the shares and compelled the company to yield. The scheme was then approved by the committee, but the banker was not warned in time. The shares recovered and he was ruined.

"You ask me for proof. Although the authorities conceal evidence, there are a hundred here present who know where it can be found.

"There are two categories of Deputies—those who took money; those who did not."

At last Delahaye stepped down, having put in every mouth in France the question the *Spectator* of London paraphrased as "whether all the waste went into the pockets of engineers, contractors, and financiers, or whether any of it found its way to the bank accounts of journalists and politicians."

"It was a sitting not to be forgotten—the day of the accuser—as tragic, it may be, as the famous 'day of the first cartful,' " Barres said.

"So much disgraceful rough-and-tumble bandying of phrases, so much battledore and shuttlecock of insinuation and counter-recrimination, so much wild disorder and savage gesticulation," the *Times* of London man reported with disapproval.

It was the "beginning of a convulsion which was to end by making the Panama enterprise impossible for anybody, owing to the infamous character attached to it," Philippe Bunau-Varilla, a former acting chief engineer of the canal, said mournfully.

The Premier followed Delahaye to the tribune; when the noise died down, he said he would not reply to the charges because they were politically motivated, but the government had nothing to hide and would not refuse the inquiry.

The Chamber promptly voted to investigate, and the republicans caucused next day and set up a committee consisting of twenty-three of their own number, nine reactionists, and one Boulangist, Paul Deroulede, who refused to serve because he said his faction should have had four seats. The committee was created without subpoena power, the Premier contending that it had sufficient moral authority to compel cooperation. The caucus named former Premier Henri Brisson as chairman; he was an austere and able attorney of high repute, who had received twenty-six votes when the National Assembly in 1887 chose a new President of France to succeed Jules Grevy, the indulgent father-in-law.

The investigation was a fat harvest for newspapers throughout the world; a new crop of sensations ripened every day. *Le Gaulois*, the royalist paper, gave an account of de Reinach's death that was as detailed as if a reporter had sat in on the banker's last hours. *Libre Parole* published allegations of bribery against Antonin Proust, the Deputy for Deux-Sèvres, who was France's first Fine Arts Minister. Louis Andrieux, the former Prefect of Police, used the same paper as the forum for a charge that the Deputy for Corsica, Emmanuel Arene, a popular drama reviewer, took a 20,000-franc check from de Reinach.

The committee called *Libre Parole*'s managing editor to testify on the charges against Proust, but he said that only Drumont, the editor, could speak on the matter and that Drumont was in Ste. Pelagie Prison. He had been sentenced to serve three months in jail and pay the cost of eighty-nine retractions for libeling the Minister of Marine, August Burdeau, a young philosopher well-regarded by scholars for his translation of the works of Herbert Spencer.

Drumont refused to appear before the committee unless the rest of his sentence was remitted. Both Proust and the committee supported this deal in order to obtain his presence, but the government "did not see its way to release him from the effects of one libel so that he might attend to give evidence in another."

The press, in turn, was denounced for its handling of the Panama story over the years. The report of Auguste Flory, the examining magistrate's expert accountant, listed payments of 22 million francs for *publicité* for the company's eight issues of securities. Money went to prominent newspapers of almost every political persuasion and not all of it was in payment for advertising space. The largest press pay-off was to *Le Petit Journal*. In addition to the payments to general-circulation newspapers, there was an extensive distribution of cash tidbits to numerious special-audience periodicals: for example, *Wines and Alcohols Bulletin, 75 francs; Marriage Journal*, 100; *Choral Societies Echo*, 200; *Illustrated Theatrical Chronicle*, 200; *The Picturesque World*, 300; *The Poetic World*, 310; *Foresters Echo*, 775; *Art and Fashion*, 2,310.

Emily Crawford had described the Panama company's publicity arrangements years before in an article in the *New York Tribune* in which she said: "The papers were filled with puffs and advertisements. The latter were ostensibly paid for. The puffs expressed editorial conviction. The bonds were issued and taken up with enthusiasm by the smallest class of the bourgeoisie, which only affords *Le Petit Journal*, a miserable cent print which vegetates through the most opulent existence of all journals in France. M. Thomas Grimm, the sole leader writer, puffed Panama. He sometimes was carried above the concert pitch of the paper by the heat of his enthusiasm."

Clemenceau, discussing these practices in a campaign speech, told a pitiful tale of a Panama puff writer who possessed transcendent powers of persuasion. "There is a Paris journalist who wrote three pro-canal articles for 1,000 francs each," Clemenceau said. "By the time he had finished the third he had sold himself on it so thoroughly that he invested all his savings in it and lost everything he had."

The investigating committee, in its eventual report to the Chamber, denounced the "supreme imprudence" of the press and its almost unanimous cooperation with the canal company which "contributed to luring French savings into unprecedented disasters."

"It must be admitted that the financial press has blindly served companies that paid for it," the committee told the Deputies. "It has been deemed necessary to show you the organization of the financial press and to point out what is called the new morality."

The *Pall Mall Gazette* of London, commenting on the new morality, reported: "The greatest surprise is expressed by various editors that anybody should consider it reprehensible to have acted as they did." One editor even sued J. F. Rossignol, the liquidator's auditor, for understating the amount of the Panama company's pay-off to his paper.

Although the attack on the press provided diversion for a whole generation of public figures abused repeatedly in print, the big blows landed on the Government. A week after Delahaye's speech, the Loubet Cabinet fell, principally on the issue of its opposition to the investigating committee's demand to exhume de Reinach's body for an autopsy. Ricard, the Minister of Justice, said that an autopsy would be justified solely on suspicion of crime, that he had no such suspicion, and that even if the Baron had killed himself, suicide was not a legal offense. The Marquis de la Ferronaye, a royalist Deputy, said that the town was full of suspicions, including one that there was no cadaver in the coffin, and he insisted that the public interest demanded exhumation. An order of the day, which the Premier had accepted as a vote of confidence, was rejected 304-319, and the Chamber then voted 303-3 to investigate de Reinach's death.

President Carnot immediately sent for Brisson and asked

him to form a government. After Brisson tried and failed, Loubet's Foreign Minister, Alexandre Ribot, took up the task and succeeded.

Presently a huge detachment of physicians, assistants, public officials, and newspapermen went up to de Reinach's country place at Nivillers, where the banker had been mayor for ten years; they unearthed the coffin from the snow-covered rural cemetery and transported it to the *Mairie* for the autopsy. Dr. Alphonse Bertillon, head of the police department's anthropometric bureau—whose methods of identification were gaining acceptance by law enforcement agencies throughout the world—was an observer. The autopsy party took the vital organs back to Paris for toxicological examination, stopping on the way for lunch at nearby Beauvais.

The medical examiner's report, filed a month later with the prosecuting attorney, failed to satisfy the suspicious; it said that the toxicologists had found no trace of poison in de Reinach's body, but that decomposition was too far along when the autopsy was conducted to let death be attributed to natural causes.

At the end of its first week of digging, the investigating committee began to strike documentation. On November 30, Anthony Thierree, a securities dealer, volunteered testimony that de Reinach had once swapped a 3,400,000-franc Panama company check with him for twenty-six checks for various amounts made out to "Bearer." The transaction, he said, took place on July 17, 1888, exactly three weeks after the meagerly productive issue of the lottery bonds.

Thierree said he had the canceled checks in his safes, each bearing the endorsement of the person who had cashed it, but as banker in the deal he did not want to violate any professional confidences by disclosing these names unless he was compelled to. The wait for the committee to find a way to get at the canceled checks, in the absence of subpoena power, produced a torment of apprehension, made more painful by the testimony of other witnesses.

A member of the parliamentary committee that handled the 1888 lottery loan bill described the sudden, last-minute switch of the former Deputy for Ariège, Charles Sans-Leroy, to the support of the measure. Another committee member testified that someone claiming to represent Charles de Lesseps had offered him 100,000 francs to shift to the bill's support.

Martin, author of the "Micros" series, testified that Francois-Paul Barbe, former Minister of Agriculture who had since died, was one of seven Deputies who had promoted the lottery bill and that Barbe got 500,000 francs for it.

By Martin's testimony, his own services to the canal company had been thoroughly ineffective. When the lottery measure of 1886 was under consideration, he had sold the company the idea of promoting a favorable decision by organizing a huge petition to the government from Panama investors. He had also tried to persuade a dozen Deputies to support the bill, but with no success. He said he had received only 45,000 francs for this service. Asked why he wrote the "Micros" series, he said: "The Panama company and I, we are longtime enemies."

The public prosecutor devised a neat solution to the problem posed by Thierree's professed scruples: he simply arranged a friendly seizure. On December 3, Police Superintendent Julian Clement went to the broker's office at 22 rue de la Bourse and picked up the checks.

There were eighteen endorsements on twenty-six checks, two of them illegible, several by dummies or messengers, one of whom had since died; but the best known names, by far, were those of two Senators: Albert Grevy, on a 40,000-franc check, and Leon Renault, on two that totaled 25,000.

Albert Grevy was a brother of former President Grevy and had been Governor of Algeria in 1879-1881. Renault, a handsome, courtly man who had been Paris Prefect of Police in the Republic's early years, was one of the most eloquent orators and eminent lawyers in France.

Publication of the Thierree checks drove a throng of well-known Parisians to the hearing room to explain to the investigating committee why they had received money from de Reinach. Grevy said his "Bearer" check was in payment of legal fees and of his share in an underwriting syndicate. Renault said de Reinach had given him 25,000 francs out of the profits of a Panama syndicate to make up for his loss on another investment he had made at the Baron's advice.

Joseph Dugue de la Fauconnerie, a Bonapartist Deputy for the Department of Orne, revealed that he was the recipient of the proceeds of a 25,000-franc check endorsed by someone in a brokerage house. The signature on the endorsement of five checks totaling 550,000 francs proved to be that of a clerk of the Dynamite Company, the firm with which Arton and Barbe, the deceased former Minister, were associated. Antoine Vlasto, manager of the *Comptoir d'Escompte*, one of the nation's leading banks, testified that he had endorsed two checks cashed by the *Crédit Mobilier*, another important financial organization of which he had been the head. He said the checks represented partial payment of his share of the syndicate that handled the lottery loan.

No one came forward to identify the beneficiary of an 80,000-franc check endorsed with an illegible signature, and this voucher became the most obstreperous document in the dossier.

But the biggest checks by far were two for 1,000,000 francs each, endorsed by Dr. Cornelius Herz, who was the first to present his explanations to the investigating committee. On December 3, the day the police superintendent, Clement, picked up the checks at Thierree's office, Herz telegraphed to the investigators from London: "I am anxious to inform you that these two million francs were cashed in my behalf. I have to thank MM. Rothschild for their exceeding discretion, but I have no reason to profit by it, and I feel bound to let you know the facts. I was a creditor of M. de Reinach to the extent of more than two million francs in consequence of numerous and various transactions in which he had been associated with me: amongst others, dealings with telephones, electric light, the use of electricity as a motive force, the business of Marcel Deprez, etc. M. de Reinach in July, 1888, in this manner paid me a large part of his debt to me. It was not my affair to ask him where he got the money. I left this money with MM. Rothschild of Frankfort, as their books will show."

For a man of such impressive affairs, Herz was so little known by the public at large that when his name was first mentioned, New York and London editors were unable to dredge up more than the vaguest descriptions of him, such as the *New York Herald*'s on December 4:

"Two checks for 1,000,000 each bear the name of Cornelius Herz, the electrician. He is mixed up in all sorts of enterprises. He is an American citizen, and a good friend of politicians, to some of whom it is believed he lent his name."

Until that moment there had been only scarce mention of Cornelius Herz in the New York and London newspaper indexes. The first had come a dozen years earlier, a paragraph on page 1 of the *New York Tribune* of August 15, 1880, under the headline, "Submarine Telephone Experiments": "In the telephone experiments made on the submarine cable from Brest to Penzance, the Bell, Phelps, Grover, and Edison telephone systems were all applied and failed to work satisfactorily over the circuit. The new invention of Dr. Herz for telephone communication over submarine wires proved a success."

Herz's best press notice had been two lines buried deep in a long feature story about the Legion of Honor that *The New York Times* had run during the Wilson decoration-vending scandal: "Dr. Cornelius Herz, the eminent electrician, is the only American who has ever made Grand Officer."

The clerical journal, *Le Monde*, defamed him in 1886, calling him a bankrupt, a spy, a Prussian, a fugitive; but two days later it printed an abject retraction, after Herz sent around his seconds, two distinguished officers on duty at the War Ministry, to demand satisfaction.

In 1889 Henri Rochefort, the inventive master of journalistic abuse, subjected him to some of the colorful vituperation with which Rochefort's *L'Intransigeant* habitually slandered the best known names in France. To this the Paris correspondent of the *Times* of London responded with almost a full column of eulogy that must have assuaged Herz's wounds—even though the piece spelled his name "Hertz" throughout.

Then suddenly, in just the last three weeks of 1892, this slender file of press clippings swelled to a massive narration of such worldwide notoriety that Cornelius Herz and his family could look back with longing on the relatively tranquil days of Rochefort's diatribes and the libels of *Le Monde*.

Herz's catapult to infamy was a news story in *Figaro* on December 12; it supplied, at last, part of the answer to one of the most obvious questions prompted by the suspicion-laden circumstances of Baron de Reinach's death twenty-three days earlier: Who was the last person to see him alive? *Figaro* did not pinpoint the identification, but it related some of the Baron's desperate activities on the last night of his life.

The *Figaro* story, describing Herz as a man who had amassed a fortune through the help of powerful political connections, said that de Reinach had visited him in his final hours, accompanied by Maurice Rouvier and Georges Clemenceau. The disclosure produced the most violent shock yet registered in the Panama upheaval.

Rouvier, the perennial Finance Minister, who had floated a huge loan successfully, worked *rentes* up to par and prevented financial panic by firm action when the *Comptoir d'Escompte* was trapped in the collapse of the copper corner, called on President Carnot at once and resigned. Then he mounted the tribune in the Chamber and told his colleagues that he had accompanied de Reinach out of pity. The banker was being driven mad by attacks in the scandal sheets, he said, and hoped to stop them through the influence of Herz and of former Interior Minister Jean Constans.

Rouvier said he had asked Clemenceau to accompany him as a witness whose "loyalty" no one could distrust. Herz had told de Reinach that it was too late, the Finance Minister said, and Constans had denied furiously that he had any influence to stop the press campaign.

Suddenly, Paul Deroulede, the emotional Boulangist, leaped to his feet, pointed a lean finger at the compromised Minister, and cried out: "You, too, must go before the high court!"

"It conjured up in every brain the blood-red picture of the Convention, with Saint Just pointing his finger of fate at Danton," *The New York Times* reporter wrote.

Clemenceau testified before the investigating committee the next day. He had been sitting on a banquette in the Chamber's Salle Casimir-Perier, he said, when Rouvier walked by, paused, and turned back to speak to him of the newspaper attacks on de Reinach and the banker's "extraordinary state of mind, which called for the gravest solutions." Clemenceau had agreed to go with de Reinach and Rouvier to see Herz.

The visit was brief. De Reinach, "very flushed, his eyes popping out of his head, and expressing himself with great difficulty," saw at once that Herz "did not have the power to do anything for him," Clemenceau told the deputies. Grasping for straws, the banker turned to Clemenceau and said: "I beg of you, you cannot refuse me this. Come with me to see M. Constans."

"I told him that he could go alone," Clemenceau testified. "He replied: 'No, it is not the same thing! Come with me.'"

They hailed a carriage and rode to Constans's house in complete silence, de Reinach's obvious state of mind repelling any conversation. Clemenceau had arrived at Herz's residence just ahead of Rouvier and de Reinach, leaving no time to discuss the banker's reasons for his hope that Herz could stop the attacks in the press, nor did de Reinach tell him now how he thought Constans might help; but Clemenceau understood the reason for the visit to the former Minister.

"According to the newspapers, M. Constans had influence with certain people who were directing the press campaign," Clemenceau testified.

His statement referred to an extraordinary rumor going around Paris: de Reinach, who was Jewish, supplied Panama secrets to the anti-Semitic *Libre Parole* in exchange for immunity from its allegations; Constans, Boulanger's conquerer, kicked upstairs to the Senate after slapping the face of an infuriating Boulangist Deputy during a session of the Chamber, was feeding Panama dirt to the notorious Boulangist paper, *La Cocarde*, in a bid to regain power.

During the ride to Constans's home, de Reinach had undergone a complete transformation, Clemenceau testified. "At M. Cornelius Herz's we had had a man very much aroused, very tough," Clemenceau said. "At M. Constans's we had to deal with a man very lethargic, very resigned."

There the banker had dropped onto the sofa, saying nothing, leaving Clemenceau to introduce the reason for their visit. Clemenceau told Constans that he must know about the rumor as to the inspiration of the campaign.

"M. Constans received this statement with the most violent protests," Clemenceau testified. "I can even say that he was downright furious. He had the attitude of a man very wounded that someone could say this to him, and, I say again, he protested with the greatest vigor. Then M. de Reinach, who was sitting on a sofa, lifted his eyes to the ceiling in the manner of a man coming out of a dream, and told him what brought him there."

"This attack must stop; I can't take it; I have come to ask you to make it stop!" the Baron cried out.

Constans replied: "It's impossible. I do not know. I agree to look into it and try, but don't count on me. I won't succeed. I can't."

"M. Constans repeated this statement once or twice," Clemenceau said. "You know what these conversations are where someone asks for something and the other one won't or can't do it. It's always the same phrase repeated a couple of times. I don't think the visit lasted more than five minutes. M. de Reinach stood up without a word and walked out."

At the door he discovered he had no money with him and borrowed five francs for carriage fare from Constans, who said, with an attempt at humor: "I'm fixed well enough to lend five francs to a millionaire."

As de Reinach was about to climb into his fiacre, he gripped Clemenceau's hand and said: "I am lost."

"I saw a man who was beaten to death," Clemenceau testified, "but I did not know why he was lost."

Then Ferdinand de Ramel, a royalist member of the investigating committee, asked about Clemenceau's relations with Cornelius Herz.

Herz had been a stockholder in *La Justice*, a radical newspaper Clemenceau founded in 1880 with a platform he once described as follows: "To promote universal suffrage, to increase its efficacy by spreading education widely, to relieve the individual of the old obstacles—debris of the monarchy—which hemmed him in; as to the Church, common liberty of conscience, and the secularization of the state; in the economic and social domain, to seek the principle in which the whole republican program is summed up—*la justice*; and finally, to remake conquered France and not waste her blood and gold in profitless expeditions."

Clemenceau's second in command at *La Justice* was Camille Pelletan, known in the Chamber of Deputies for his apoplectic declamations; he was a son of Eugene Pelletan, one of the most strenuous foes of the Second Empire. Stephen Pichon, an up-and-coming young legislator, was an editor. Charges Longuet, Karl Marx's son-in-law, was one of its leader writers. Despite its dedicated staff and its proprietor's political force and personal dynamism, *La Justice* had only a tiny circulation, about 15,000, and could never make ends meet.

Clemenceau, needing money, had sold some shares to Herz.

"Can you tell us for what price?" de Ramel asked.

"I answer because it is a colleague who asks, but I hold that the question has nothing to do with Panama," Clemenceau said. "I bought back these shares for 50,000 francs. M. Cornelius Herz lost more than 200,000 francs in the transaction."

The timetable for the transaction was contained in a note published in *La Justice* on November 3, 1886: "M. Herz is not a sleeping partner of *La Justice*. He was a stockholder from February 26, 1883, until April 5, 1885. M. Clemenceau transferred some of his paid-up shares to him on February 26, 1883, in payment of sums put in by him from March 31, 1881, to June 16, 1883. On April 15, 1885, M. Clemenceau bought M. Herz's shares."

The attack on Herz began the next day in the Chamber of Deputies when Louis le Prevost de Launay, a Bonapartist Deputy and partisan of Boulanger, demanded to know why "this man, who is a foreigner, of German origin, has risen so far and so fast in the grades of the Legion of Honor, to Knight, to Officer, to Commander, to Grand Officer, in scarcely seven years between 1879 and 1886."

Paul de Cassagnac, a violent young Bonapartist who could "never find words too sharp or too strong to throw at the republicans," interrupted to say: "General Dodds has not been so rapid," referring to the commander of France's expeditionary force then struggling to put down the slave-raiding King of its Dahomey territory.

Le Prevost de Launay wanted to know why Charles de Freycinet, as Minister of Foreign Affairs in 1886, had granted the nation's highest honor, the Grand Cross of the Legion, to a foreigner who was not yet forty years old and had rendered no service to France.

Clemenceau interrupted to say: "I never recommended him

for a decoration. There are official papers, and the Ministers, you can ask the Ministers and you can inspect the papers and you will not find a word or a signature of mine in the papers nor a single Minister to say that I have recommended M. Cornelius Herz to him by word of mouth."

The badgered de Freycinet, four times the Premier, got in a word at last and said that the decoration had been conferred on Herz at the recommendation of the scientific fraternity as a reward for his support of the pioneer experiments by Marcel Deprez, the French electrical engineer, in the transmission of electrical power over a long distance. Deprez was elected to the Academy of Sciences in recognition of these experiments, de Freycinet explained, and several of the savants asked that some honor be conferred on Herz.

The session grew violent, fights broke out all over the Chamber, Deputies exchanged challenges to duels, and Baudry d'Asson, a royalist representing a Breton constituency, was ushered off the floor screaming and waving his arms. At last the new Premier, Alexandre Ribot, managed to rally the republicans to the government's support; he was still in office when adjournment was voted. Immediately on leaving the Chamber, he and his Minister of Justice, Leon Bourgeois, ordered Celestin-Louis Tanon, the new public prosecutor, who had succeeded Quesnay de Beaurepaire, to bring bribery charges against Charles de Lesseps, Cottu, Fontane, and Charles Sans-Leroy, the former Deputy whose switch in committee had brought the lottery loan bill to the floor in 1888.

Charles de Lesseps, a black-bearded, patient man with a withdrawn look and nothing of his forceful father's flair and drama, was about to leave for work at 8 o'clock the next morning when Police Superintendent Clement showed up at his sumptuous fifth-floor apartments at 51 avenue Montaigne and arrested him. Charles's brougham, waiting to take him to his office in the Suez Canal building at 9 rue Charras, just around the corner from the old Panama company headquarters, took them instead to the Palais de Justice.

Fontane, who had faithfully served the de Lesseps family for years, was arrested at the same moment at his flat in nearby rue Pierre Charron. Years earlier he had moved to Paris from southern France, worked as a free-lance contributor to *La Pa-*

trie and other newspapers, and finally become Ferdinand de Lesseps's private secretary and the Suez Canal Company's corporate secretary. He held the same post in the Panama Canal Company, and for a time had been its press liaison officer. He was a learned man and a voluminous writer; his arrest interrupted his work on his ten-volume *Histoire Universelle*, published over eighteen years, from 1881 to 1899.

Sans-Leroy, who had left the Chamber to represent the interests of the great Paris sugar refiners in England, where a storm was blowing up against the bounty-sustained competition of the French product, had come to town to testify before the investigating committee, and the police picked him up at his lodgings in the chaussée de la Muette.

Cottu, the dandy of the Panama directorate, a provincial banker who became one of the youngest members of the canal company's board, could not be found at his home in the avenue du Bois de Boulogne, a luxurious villa that a rich English peer had built for the famous comedienne, Mlle. Hortense Schneider. A warrant was issued for his arrest, but he had only gone to Vienna on a brief trip, and as soon as he learned he was wanted, he returned to surrender.

The prisoners were lodged in the great metropolitan jail opposite the Gare de Lyon in the boulevard Diderot. The street had formerly been named boulevard Mazas, in honor of the heroic commander of the thirty-fourth Brigade who was killed while leading his troops at the battle of Austerlitz. The jail was still called Mazas Prison, an unfortunate monument to the heroic soldier. At the time the Panama prisoners were lodged there, it was considered the crowning insult to say a man was "worthy of Mazas."

Ferdinand de Lesseps's age saved him from the disgrace of incarceration on a fraud charge, and he was not even aware of the plight of his son and his old colleagues.

Initial reports of harsh handling of the accused men promptly gave way to detailed accounts of the consideration they received in jail. "Their cells are well warmed and their beds are almost luxurious," the *New York Tribune* reported. "The prison authorities have allowed them to obtain toilet articles not included in the prison rules, and they get their meals from a restaurant outside and drink good Bordeaux wine and mocha coffee with brandy from their own cellars." Cottu, for example, had dined the day before on veal chops with potatoes, duck with peas, cheese and fruit, a bottle of Bordeaux, and a glass of Chartreuse.

Incredible as the imprisonment of Charles de Lesseps and his codefendants seemed, it was only a herald of more ominous events. On December 20 the president of the Chamber, Floquet, and the Senate's president, Philippe Le Royer, read out letters from the public prosecutor asking their respective houses of the National Assembly to suspend the parliamentary immunity of ten of their colleagues so that they might be prosecuted on the same charges of corruption that hung over the four men in Mazas. The accused legislators, five in each house, were among the best known politicians in France.

The Deputies were Rouvier, Proust, Jules Roche, former Minister of Commerce, Arene, the Corsica-born chronicler of the boulevards, and Dugue de la Fauconnerie, a shrewd Norman who, although a Bonapartist, had been one of Gambetta's courtiers at the Palais Bourbon. The accused Senators were Renault, Albert Grevy, Eloi-Bernard Beral, Marius Thevenet, former Minister of Justice under whose administration at the Palais de Justice the Boulanger prosecution took place, and Paul Deves, former Minister of Justice and of Agriculture, a politician of such talents for conciliation that he was often called "the Newfoundland retriever" for the numerous Ministers he had tried to save after Clemenceau had pushed them overboard. The government had moved with such complete secrecy that even the adept Rouvier, exactly one week out of office, knew nothing of its plans.

"With his sanguine complexion, his broad shoulders, that nearsighted glance of his that does not condescend to rest on anyone; that singular mien of an Armenian suddenly transported to Paris from the wharves of Marseilles; that wonderful loud and authoritative voice of his that for four years had subdued and controlled his set, he went from group to group, asking everywhere, 'Whom do they mention as connected with the checks?' " Barres said. "A quarter of an hour later, in the very same place, now boiling over with excitement, Rouvier was again to be seen; but how changed! His hands in those of two or three intimates, his face convulsed with an expression that I can compare only to that seen on the features of a murdered man; his anguish was painful to see. He was motionless, but his flushed face, his staring eyes, and rigid mouth were like those of one in a nightmare."

The two houses were "aghast at the demands," *The Spectator* said, but "granted them with impetuosity and absence of delay which make parliamentary proceedings in France so startling to Englishmen, and at the same time so exciting."

The Senate, acting with upper-house gravity, actually did not give its consent to the prosecution until a day had elapsed. The volatile Chamber proceeded at once, recessing for three hours while the Deputies met in committee of the whole, then reconvening and voting unanimously to permit prosecution of its members.

The accused Deputies, one by one, climbed to the tribune to deny their guilt, furious at the men who had turned them over to the processes of criminal prosecution. Many of them were friends and colleagues in the republican cause since their student days in the 1860's, when they had gathered around Gambetta at the Café Procope in the rue de l'Ancienne Comédie—at the same tables at which Danton, Marat, Camille Desmoulins, and other revolutionaries had sat seventy years earlier.

Arene, a journalist who wrote habitually on the deadline, this time took advantage of the three-hour adjournment to prepare his address. He was the first to speak, and his colleagues applauded warmly as he exclaimed: "Everywhere where it is sought to take me, I will go with my head erect. I have always served my party and my chiefs. I have nothing for which to reproach myself. Were I for sale, I might have prostituted my journalist's pen. I shall go in triumph through this ordeal."

Then came Rouvier, whose initials, it had just been reported, were on the stub of one of the Thierree checks. Rouvier reminded the Chamber of his long and useful service, and denied emphatically that he had accepted any Panama checks or had any disreputable connection with the enterprise. When he became Premier, he said, he found the Secret Service fund entirely inadequate for defense of the Republic and turned to friends for emergency support. This statement provoked an outburst of hoots and jeers, to which he shouted: "What I have done all politicians worthy of the name have done, and if I had

not been able to act as I have acted, many Deputies who inter-
rupt me today would not be on these benches. These are matters
which I should have wished to say only before the magistrate.
I have been obliged to bring them before the Chamber, and I
have finished. I will submit to any jurisdiction whatever. There
is nothing to fear, for never have I derived any personal benefit,
either direct or indirect, from a company whose interests I
have never defended."

Jules Roche, a founder of the republican *Petit Parisien*,
later director of Gambetta's newspaper, *La Republique Française*, looked at the ministerial bench in outrage and shouted:
"Oh, you hypocrites and scoundrels!"

An attack of gout had kept Dugue de la Fauconnerie away
from the Chamber earlier in the day. As he was limping across
the Pont de la Concorde on his way to the Palais Bourbon, he
met a newspaperman, who told him what was taking place. He
turned around and walked away.

Only the evening before, Proust, for years an ornament of
the Opportunist party, had left the Chamber arm in arm with
Leon Bourgeois, the Minister of Justice; now he said he would
never recognize him again.

Proust, who had owned a piece of the syndicate that handled the lottery bond issue, had resigned two weeks earlier as
director of the French participation in the forthcoming World's
Columbian Exposition at Chicago, saying he wanted no government appointments until it was recognized that his good faith
could not be challenged.

His inclusion in the prosecution was the second blow he
had suffered at the hands of his legislative colleagues in only
three years. In 1889 he thought he had won Millet's famous
painting, the "Angelus," for the Louvre in one of the most spectacular art auctions of the time; instead, it went to the American Art Association, the second highest bidder, when the
Chamber adjourned for the summer without appropriating
funds Proust had counted on as part of the purchase price.*

Momentous as was the Chamber's decision to expose some
of its most illustrious members to the ordeal of criminal investigation, the day's sensations had scarcely begun.

*see Notes

8

The Salle des Séances of the Palais Bourbon was still rank with the air of accusation and recrimination let in by the Chamber's vote to permit criminal prosecution of some of its leading lights, when Paul Deroulede, the voluble patriot, added a charge of treason to the Panama convulsions.

He had put the Chamber on notice that he intended to question the government about Cornelius Herz—to ask whether it did not intend to strip him of his Legion of Honor Grand Cross. But the thrust at Herz was only a diversion; Deroulede's real target was vastly more important.

Many crushing disappointments had overtaken the poet since the night Clemenceau had exploded his dream of a government sustained by Boulanger's martial façade and by the muscle of the League of Patriots. Boulanger had refused to seize power right on the threshold of it; Boulanger had fled; Boulanger had committed suicide; Paris had welcomed "Lohengrin" despite Deroulede's pledge, "While I live there shall be no German music heard in Paris." Finally, the government had suppressed his League of Patriots.

But he had achieved one all-important, offsetting victory: the right to speak with Parliamentary immunity. In the face of a government landslide in the election of September 22, 1889, Deroulede the vehement Boulangist had won the seat for the Angoulême constituency of Charente.

Clamorous and intense, a strangely somber figure in a tall, straight-brimmed stovepipe hat and a long coat of Robespierre cut that emphasized his lankiness, Deroulede already was widely known in Paris for his noisy demonstrations of patriotic fervor, his warm poems, and his plays on patriotic themes. By dint of uproarious questioning of the government and interruptions of debate, he became quickly one of the most conspicuous members of the Chamber, a Deputy "for whom no parliamentary rules are sufficiently stringent."

The government, recognizing his eminence among the handful of Boulangist Deputies, offered him a place on the committee investigating the Panama affair, but he turned it down; "he preferred a *coup de théâtre*, a thundering and unexpected outburst in the most public place in France, and provocations which will not end in verbal battle."

No charge had been filed against Herz when Deroulede demanded that the Legion of Honor disown him. The investigating committee had summoned Herz to testify on December 13; but the day before his scheduled appearance he had responded from the Burlington Hotel in London's West End, pleading that he was too ill to return to France just then and submitting certificates from some of the foremost medical men in England to support his plea.

It was Herz's political influence that outraged Deroulede. He wanted to know why it was that "at a decisive moment, under most critical circumstances, which wrested from the hands of M.Rouvier the portfolio of Finance and which cost M. de Reinach his life, the man who was the arbiter of their fate, at whose feet they fell, from whom they sought mercy, whose silence they strove to obtain, was not the President of the Republic, nor the president of a Court of law, nor the head of the Cabinet, but was Dr. Cornelius Herz." It was to "bring him down a little from these threatening altitudes" and "because of the strangeness, the inexplicable mystery of his selection," that Deroulede asked the government to take back the Grand Cross it had given Herz. But it was no mystery to him, Deroulede said, just how Herz had come to be so honored.

"Without patronage or patron," he said, "this little German Jew could not have made such strides along the path to honors, could not in so few years have risen so completely, so brilliantly from the bottom of the ladder. I repeat, he must have had someone to represent him, an ambassador to open to him every door and every circle, especially political circles. He must have had a most obliging and a most devoted friend to enable him to meet, on equal terms, as hail fellow well met, at one time Ministers of State, at another the directors of newspapers, at another even, I admit, General Boulanger himself.

"Now you all know who was this obliging, devoted, indefatigable intermediary, so active, so dangerous.

"His name is on the lips of all of you, but none of you will name him for you fear three things about him—his sword, his pistol, and his tongue.

"Well, I shall brave them all, and name him.

"He is------------M. Clemenceau!"

It was Clemenceau who silenced the storm that Deroulede's declaration set loose, cheers from the Right and shouts of glee from several benches on the far Left.

"I ask that M. Deroulede be permitted to finish," he said.

"I thank you, in fact I have not yet finished," Deroulede acknowledged, and went ahead to accuse Clemenceau of selling out his country.

What he wanted to know specifically was what Herz had received for the 200,000 francs that Clemenceau said he had lost in *La Justice*. "Since it is not only affirmed by M. Clemenceau but appears on examination of the paper that *La Justice* has never sold anything publicly to M. Herz, what did he sell him secretly?" Deroulede demanded. "What passed between this foreigner and this politician for there to be no trace of any interchange of good offices?

"What, did one give all and the other nothing? Would this German without interest, without an object, without a view to gain something, have piled up all these repeated and redoubled payments? Whom will you get to believe that, M. Clemenceau?"

He implied that Herz had called the tune by which Clemenceau had worked his great political talents so destructively. "We have to ask ourselves," Deroulede said, "whether what he expected, if not demanded of you, was not the overthrow of all these ministries, these attacks on all men in power, all the confusion caused by your great talent in all the affairs of Parliament and of this country. For your efforts have been devoted to destruction.

"How many things, how many men have you crushed?

"Your career is over ruins.

"Here Gambetta, there another, and another, and another,

all devoured by you. I am, it is true, opposed to the parliamentary system, but I do not think any man in France has given it ruder shocks or severer wounds than this self-styled parliamentarian. How Dr. Cornelius Herz must rejoice over this ever-recurring spectacle."

Another Boulangist Deputy, Lucien Millevoye, leaped up in his place and shouted: "Cornelius Herz is a foreign emissary!"

"Yes, Cornelius Herz is a foreign agent, and it is because he is so that everyone who acts under his inspiration does great harm to France," Deroulede went on, expressing outrage that Herz should be at liberty across the Channel, "unpunished, happy, mocking."

"Let us mark for public vengeance," he demanded, "the ablest, the most dreaded, the most guilty of his supporters, whose evil and baneful policy the majority of this house have deplored, without daring to treat it as a crime, or even as ground of reproach. That reproach I now have been bold enough to cast upon him to relieve my conscience and enlighten my country."

"There was no laughing at Deroulede, however melodramatic he may have been in his utterances and gestures," said W.F.Lonergan, the *London Daily Telegraph*'s reporter, who witnessed the confrontation. "There were many of his opponents there who secretly applauded his attack on the masterful man who was feared and hated. I saw Clemenceau pulling himself together and trying to assume an air of calmness to bluff the gallery, or rather the galleries. It was with suppressed rage that he uttered the words, '*Monsieur Paul Deroulede, vous en avez menti.*"

Standing flat-footed in the tribune, arms folded across his chest, speaking with the quiet emphasis and stubbornly preserved calm that were a hallmark of his delivery, he began his reply with the age-old cogitation of the wrongfully accused—how to supply documentary proof of innocent motive.

"It is easy to bring such accusations," Clemenceau said, "because they leave the man against whom they are brought totally disarmed and reduced to calling as witnesses his conscience and his intentions. I cannot bring here papers showing that I have only been influenced in my politics by the best interests of France."

He gave Deroulede carte blanche to dissect his political life and to discuss and condemn every word or action of it. "One thing he has no right to do," he said, "and that is, in a spirit of Boulangist malice to pour out on me the most hateful calumnies; that is, to hurl at me the greatest insult one Frenchman can offer to another. This insult you who utter it know is undeserved, you know it is a disgraceful calumny, an abominable lie."

Herz had been a stockholder in *La Justice* along with several eminent men, Clemenceau said, taking up Deroulede's charges one by one. Herz was not a German, but "so good a citizen of the United States that he was the official delegate of the American government to the Electrical Congress at Paris"; Clemenceau said he had seen the letter of appointment signed by James G.Blaine, Secretary of State of the United States. Herz had served as a surgeon in the French army of the Loire in the Franco-Prussian War. Herz was a friend and one-time financial supporter of Boulanger. Clemenceau had never supported any of Herz's projects and voted against him when Herz asked the Budget Committee of the Chamber for authority to form a telephone company. Nor had he ever recommended Herz for any grade of the Legion of Honor.

"Is there anything else left to deal with, any calumnies or imputations unanswered?" he asked. "I find none except that supreme insult, which I swear to you, gentlemen, I do not think I have deserved from my most implacable opponent; that I have betrayed French interests; that I have betrayed my country; that I have introduced into this Chamber a foreign influence, of which I have been the agent; that I have been a traitor to my country, to the land that gave me birth; that under the direction and guidance of this foreign influence, enslaved and subjected by it, I have sought to injure my country; that by my parliamentary action I have sought to bring trouble and disorder to my native land.

"That is the charge you have made from the tribune. I have answered every point as calmly and cooly as I could. To this last charge, there is but one answer.

"Monsieur Paul Deroulede, you have lied!"

No one in the Chamber, legislator or casual visitor, doubted the accuracy of the prediction in next day's *Journal des Débats* that Deroulede's "thundering and unexpected outburst in the most public place in France" had constituted "provocations which will not end in verbal battle." Clemenceau's and Deroulede's seconds met at once.

The French were a dueling people, and since the beginnings of their legislative institutions the "reparation at arms" had been as much a part of parliamentary procedure as caucuses and quorum calls. Thus, when Constans, the Minister of the Interior, slapped Deputy Francis Laur, a badgering Boulangist, for aggravation beyond endurance at the opening of the 1892 session of the Chamber, his conduct was condemned severely as "startlingly illustrating the decadence of political manners in France." The blow was an act "for which M.Laur could obtain no reparation," the *Times* of London correspondent explained, not explaining what had prevented M.Laur from taking a swing at M. Constans in return.

Although the insistence on duels as the only honorable amends continued, over the years they brought progressively less lethal results, with an "almost invariable absence of an intention on the part of the principals to do grievous injury." As long ago as 1848 Adolphe Thiers, who became first President of the Third Republic, and Alessandro Bixio, the Garibaldian's brother, engaged in a bloodless shoot-out and then returned to Paris to have breakfast together.

But Paris had heard that the meeting of Clemenceau and Deroulede would be no charade. "Friends of each say they intend a duel to the death, and will be satisfied with nothing less," the *New York World* reported.

Although the left-handed Clemenceau was renowned as a dangerous duelist both with pistol and sword, their seconds struggled grimly to determine which was the offended party—on whom the code of the duel traditionally bestowed the choice of weapons. For example, when a royalist asked Danton, who had declined a challenge by the Duc d'Antin, whether he preferred to be kicked like a poltroon or shot like a dog, he replied that as the offended party he would choose the guillotine's knife, which he employed on his tormentor before the week was out.

Clemenceau's seconds were Paul Menard-Dorian, a Deputy of the extreme Left who was one of France's richest men, and

Gaston Thomson, the perennial Opportunist Deputy for Constantine in Algeria. Maurice Barres, the youngest novelist who had been one of Boulanger's high command, and Jean-Marie Dumontiel, a Boulangist Deputy for the Aisne, represented Deroulede.

The problem they labored with was whether Deroulede had been the offender for calling Clemenceau a traitor, or Clemenceau for calling Deroulede a liar. When the poet's seconds refused to let the point be arbitrated, Clemenceau's representatives told their principal they considered their mission ended. Clemenceau replied with a sarcastic comment on Deroulede's display of courage in the Chamber and expressed the hope that the poet, on reflection would "make up his mind."

Deroulede's seconds then agreed to arbitration.* After General Felix Gustave Saussier, the much respected Military Governor of Paris, refused the mission because of his official position, Fery d'Esclands, a distinguished gentleman whose life's work was the adjudication of difficult questions arising in affairs of honor, was named umpire. Then Deroulede settled the question himself by conceding the choice of weapons to Clemenceau, who selected pistols.

On form, no greater mismatch could have been arranged than Deroulede vs. Clemenceau. In temperament, manner, nature, and philosophy no two men could have been more unlike or pursued in public life more dissimilar courses than those that brought them face to face across pistol sights in the paddock of the St. Ouen racetrack, just north of Paris, on the cold and foggy afternoon of December 22, 1892.

Clemenceau was persistently self-contained; Deroulede was volatile. Clemenceau was spare in manner; Deroulede was dramatic. Deroulede aroused the sympathy of the kindly disposed; Clemenceau won the respect of adversaries.

Deroulede was a Parisian, member of a family with a rich literary tradition. His great-grandfather was the novelist who wrote under the name of "Pigault-Lebrun" and was sometimes called the "Fielding of France." His uncle was Emile Augier, the celebrated dramatist who died only a month after Deroulede's election to the Chamber.

*see Notes

Like his uncle, Deroulede began the study of law, but he left it to undertake the grand tour. As a young lieutenant in the war with Germany, he was captured, escaped, fought with distinction in the Loire and Est campaigns, and was wounded severely at Paris while raising a barricade against the Commune. After the war his patriotic plays and poems brought him considerable notice, and he "threatened at one time to become the French Kipling." One of his works, " *Vive la France!*" which he wrote for the Paris exposition of 1878, was a patriotic cantata that Gounod set to music.

Deroulede's career was full of ironies. Jules Ferry, the statesman he detested for fostering colonial expansion instead of seeking *revanche* against Germany, boosted the sale of Deroulede's "*Chants du Soldat*" enormously by ordering the distribution of 20,000 copies to French schoolchildren. In Ferry's department, the Ministry of Public Instruction, Deroulede and his friends, Henri-Martin and Edouard Detaille, the painters, were named to a commission on military education, and from this post Deroulede went on to found the League of Patriots, which he turned into a private army to use against Ferry.

With Deroulede's concurrence the League's weekly newspaper, *Le Drapeau* (*The Flag*), published warm congratulations to Cornelius Herz and praised his service to France when he was made Commander of the Legion of Honor in 1884.

Deroulede and Henri Rochefort, the uproarious editor, faced each other across the barricades in the uprising of the Commune, and Rochefort was Deroulede's most strenuous collaborator in the Boulanger campaign.

It was in company with Georges Laguerre, one of the extreme Left politicians in Boulanger's high command—that he was evicted from the Chamber for creating a disturbance; and it was with Laguerre that he fought a duel after calling him an informer and turncoat for spilling the secrets of the Boulangist movement to a writer.

It was with the most vital champion of *revanche* in the entire National Assembly, Clemenceau, that he was about to trade bullets.

In a moment of mildness generated by the unlikely comradeship among Boulangists, Rochefort called Deroulede "Don Quixote in an Inverness cape." An anonymous correspondent of

The New York Times surveyed him more comprehensively: "He has never managed to acquire real popularity. His songs for soldiers are sung by regiments on the march, but mostly in the form of parodies of questionable taste. In the House of Deputies his oratory, though poetic and high flown, is marred by a sputtering lisp and is so rapid that even the shorthand writers are unable to follow him. In spite of real literary talent and an undoubted dramatic sense, he overloads his plays with patriotic declamation to such an extent that no audience can sit them out. All his political dreams have been shattered even before they began to materialize."

To Baron de Coubertin, the French educator, a devoted admirer of Jules Ferry, Deroulede was a "valiant soldier and distinguished poet, who had not received from Heaven the gift of wisdom as his heritage, and whose pranks and excesses of language came near, more than once, causing the country serious harm."

Of Clemenceau, contemporary analysts spoke less in sorrow than in anger. "Men are most often moved by the ardent desire to surpass, to supplant each other; this man was not anxious to win himself, it sufficed him to prevent others from winning," the scholarly de Coubertin said. "He desired only a negative power, and loved to express it unexpectedly; his morbid dilettantism impelled him to analyze undertakings, to discourage sincere efforts, to sow distrust, to raise obstacles, to arouse hatreds, to utilize grudges; the qualities of his mind rendered his action formidable, for pure logic seemed to guide his mind, and the precision of his language redoubled its force; thus he succeeded in imposing his rule upon groups formed by chance, which afterwards disbanded, rather confused at having taken part in the unlucky work."

Maurice Barres was annoyed by Clemenceau's "arrogance, often amounting to insolence." Across the English Channel the crisply-written *Pall Mall Gazette*, which had "no liking for the 'Wrecker of Cabinets,'" found in him a man "soured by the innumerable crosses his ambition has had to bear," who would "abandon any principle with a more than Gladstonian alacrity if haply he may win votes thereby."

Nevertheless, "there was a respect for M. Clemenceau in the Chamber," said *The Spectator*, "a great fear of him in the official departments, and a liking for him among some Englishmen, who, even when radicals themselves, are habitually impatient of the continental extremists" whom they consider "apt, like English peers, to live in a balloon."

Clemenceau had his first contact with political action at the age of ten, when his father, a Nantes physician with outspoken Jacobin beliefs, was arrested as a menace to the new imperial government of Napoleon III.

He made his own debut in protest against monarchial government in 1862 as a twenty-one-year-old medical student in Paris, where he had become a part of the circle of young Latin Quarter radicals who gathered around Gambetta. He was arrested for celebrating the fourteenth anniversary of the February 24 revolution that pulled down Louis Philippe's throne, and was sent to Mazas Prison for seventy-three days, which he remembered forever as a period of incredible boredom.

He won immense popularity as a physician in the turbulent Montmartre district, where he settled after returning from a sojourn in the United States. When the Third Republic was proclaimed after the fall of Sedan, he was appointed Mayor of Montmartre and served his apprenticeship in government under actual combat conditions—the five-months siege of Paris began exactly two months after he took office. He also was elected to the 630-man National Assembly convened to act on the peace terms imposed by Bismarck, and was one of 107 delegates to vote against accepting them and ceding Alsace-Lorraine to the Germans.

When he tried to reconcile the city, starved and embittered by the siege, and the National Government, operating beyond the siege ring, he lost both his popularity and his authority. He could not save the lives of Generals Clement Thomas and Claude Martin Lecompte, who fell into the hands of rioters and were murdered, nor could his efforts and those of the other Paris mayors prevent the hostility from escalating into the uprising of the Commune. "It is perhaps the only time that he tried to conciliate anything," said an anonymous biographer in the lengthy sketch of Clemenceau in the *Dictionnaire des Parlementaires*, 1789-1889.

This period of Clemenceau's life was subjected to the most minute scrutiny; "but even his most bitter enemies have never succeeded in throwing a shadow on his character," *The New York Times* reported years later.

When Gambetta embraced Opportunism and accepted the post of President of the Chamber after the fall of Marshal MacMahon as President of France and the end of royalist domination of the Republic's government, Clemenceau became the acknowledged leader of the radical party. The immediate springboard to this eminence was a speech on March 3, 1879, attacking the Minister of the Interior, Emile de Marcere, for the existence of corruption and abuse of power in the Paris Prefecture of Police. "It began very calmly, almost disappointingly tame," *The New York Times* said, "but before Clemenceau had reached the middle of the speech, de Marcere rose from his seat, pale as death, and left the house."

In the position he now assumed, "he did not exactly lead a party in the parliamentary sense," the *Spectator* commented, "but whenever there was an opportunity for making a radical coup, up rose M. Clemenceau and amidst breathless silence made a speech which either overthrew or seriously damaged the existing ministry."

Clemenceau's oratory, because of its spectacular impact, was one of the most studiously examined tools of modern political weaponry. To his famous socialist adversary, the murdered Jean Jaures, his words were "darts flung by a dextrous and ever youthful hand." To W.F. Lonergan, the *London Daily Telegraph* reporter who covered Clemenceau for years, his ideas were frequently commonplace, but "uttered with an intensity and a vivacity of expression which was purely personal and has never been equaled." Clear and methodical in argument, he spoke in an intense but quiet tone, and his relative understatement was an oratorical breakthrough in an age of gesture and grandiloquence.

The *Spectator*'s analyst found him "frequently too bitter for English ideas" and discerned in his speeches a "flavor of personal disappointment" that "sometimes gave an impression of that pitilessness not unfrequently seen in men who are very sure of their own motives, and especially of their own disinterestedness."

To Gambetta's loyal follower, Joseph Reinach, editor of the Opportunist newspaper, *La République Française*, Clemenceau was two distinct individuals; "one of them detestable, a demagogue"; the other "a republican as capable of courage as of coolness, with whom I am always charmed to be in accord, especially when he hunts down the quondam demagogue in order to correct the latter's stupidities."

For the most part, inquisitive contemporaries attempting to analyze the man found little help from their subject; "even when he appeared the most open there has been the impression that the true man was shut up and the door double-locked."

Yet, once, in an election speech that became a classic of French campaign eloquence, he opened the door for a bitter instant, in which he met the rumors of millions in handouts from Cornelius Herz: "I am accused of having arranged my youthful debts with a loan made with a notary of Nantes. Anyone can go there and ascertain that the debt still remains. Where are the millions?

"I married my daughter without a *dot*. Where are the millions?

"I have been six years in my present home. The furniture dealer and the upholsterer have been paid slowly in installments, and the debt is not yet canceled. Where are the millions?

"It is to such confessions as this that the disinterested servants of the republic are reduced. Let the shame of this humiliation be on those who have rendered this confession necessary!"

In this revealing moment he also replied to "some more or less disinterested persons" who reproached him for the numerous ministerial upheavals he had caused, protesting: "What is not said is that whenever they have encountered a radical Cabinet the moderates have thought it no crime to unite with the Right to overturn it."

A cigar-smoking teetotaler, always dapper, alert, and in training, Clemenceau prepared for his duel with Deroulede as conscientiously as he gathered facts for his battles in the Chamber. The day before, at the shooting range of the gunsmith Gastinne-Renette, in the rue d'Antin, he scored twenty successive bull's-eyes from twenty paces.

He went to the duel from the offices of *La Justice* in the rue Montmartre; the last to say goodby to him were members of his staff. He tried to dispel their tearful concern with the reminder:

"I have stood on the field of honor too often to have any apprehension now."

His American-born wife, from whom he had been estranged for years, was back in the United States, recuperating from a serious illness at the home of her uncle, James Stickner, president of the West Side Street Railway Company in Rockford, Illinois.

Mme. Clemenceau, whose maiden name was Mary E. Plummer, was a daughter of William K. Plummer, a Bristol, New Hampshire, dentist who had moved to Skinner Prairie, Wisconsin. She had been one of Clemenceau's pupils at the Catherine Aiken Seminary at Stamford, Connecticut, where he had taught French and horsemanship during a sojourn in the United States after graduating from medical school in Paris. They were married in the Governor's Room of New York's City Hall in a ceremony performed by Mayor A.Oakey Hall. Clemenceau and his twenty-year-old bride were scarcely settled in Paris before he was plunged into his own mayoral nightmare in Montmartre.

"His personal morality and his devotion to his beautiful wife had always been regarded with amazement, if not admiration, by the gilded society of the capital," the *New York World* related. But suddenly their marriage fell apart, and Mme. Clemenceau returned to the United States, leaving him to a well-publicized career of reputed liaisons with spectacular Parisiennes. They were later divorced.

Deroulede's leave-taking was, characteristically, far more demonstrative than Clemenceau's. He said farewell to his friends at the Hotel St. James, embraced them repeatedly and permitted them to divide a few locks of his hair as keepsakes. He expected to be killed, he said, but assured them that he would die with honor.

His carriage was first through the racetrack turnstile, followed almost immediately by Clemenceau's landau, which a procession of reporters' cabs had trailed from the offices of *La Justice*. Their arrival brought a crowd of inquisitive neighbors to the racetrack gates, and the faces of curious spectators filled every window overlooking the course. Preliminaries took an hour, during which Clemenceau remained in his carriage, whereas Deroulede slowly paced the alley beside the park wall.

Fery d'Esclands, the arbitrator, had ruled that the duelists would fire three rounds, starting from twenty-five paces, with permission to advance three steps during the firing, and the first one hit would have the privilege of stating, if he could, whether his honor was satisfied. D' Esclands rejected a proposal that the combatants advance until they were only five paces apart; he said it was too murderous and contrary to the French dueling traditions.

At 3:05 p.m. Deroulede, bareheaded, and Clemenceau, still wearing his hat, took their places, raised their weapons, and fired *au commandement*, a convention under which each of them had to get off a shot during a one-two-three count by one of the seconds.

As the first shots sounded, almost simultaneously, a railbird hopped down from his perch on the paddock fence and scampered to safety. The seconds and witnesses also backed off slightly before the combatants, still untouched, could blaze away a second time. Again they missed, and this time one of the witnesses rushed forward and pleaded with them to consider their honor satisfied and leave off trying to kill one another. They insisted on another shot, however, and their good Samaritan scurried out of range.

The pistols cracked a third time, and Deroulede reached for his coattail and examined it apprehensively, but found it intact. Clemenceau did not budge. Their seconds rushed in and assured them that they had conducted themselves heroically and vindicated fully any outrage of honor. The two principals accepted this decision and started back to town, each escorted by a throng of partisans.

The bloodless outcome caused eyebrows to be raised around the world.

There was "considerable surprise on the boulevards," the *New York Herald*'s Paris correspondent said, "for Clemenceau at any rate is known to be an excellent marksman, and both are men who have 'been out before.' " Edmond Goncourt, recorder of the minutiae of life in Paris, heard from Barres that "if Deroulede had been killed or wounded, Clemenceau would have been cut to bits by the mob that awaited the result of the duel at the racetrack's gate." The *San Francisco Evening Bulletin* dismissed the St. Ouen shootout with a disdainful voice from the Old West: "The men were placed twenty-five paces apart. To do a great deal of harm with a dueling pistol at that distance was out of the question. The American dueling code generally called for ten paces. In fact, only forty paces were allowed when the fight was to be with rifles." But the Paris reporter for the *San Francisco Chronicle*, the *Bulletin*'s competitor, attributed Deroulede's escape to Clemenceau's magnanimity, adding: "He simply yielded to the solicitation of Ministers and Deputies and spared Deroulede's life."

Deroulede attributed his escape to higher authority. "I feel that I owe my life to the interposition of the Supreme Power," he said. "I know that M. Clemenceau meant to kill me, and only Providential protection saved me, so I thank God. I can now go on in the pathway marked out for myself toward the establishment of a Republic ruled by God."

His chosen course allowed no forgiveness for Clemenceau. Before they had taken their places on the firing line, he had instructed his seconds to tell Clemenceau that if he survived he would continue to attack him in the Chamber. When the duel ended, he refused to shake hands.

The inevitability of a return bout was apparent.

9

*L*ouis Andrieux, a shrewd Lyonnais lawyer
who had been the Paris Prefect of Police in the early 1880's,
owed whatever notoriety he enjoyed to his zeal in enforcing the
government decrees, aimed chiefly at the Jesuits, that barred
unauthorized religious bodies from teaching in public schools.
Since then he had won some attention as President Grevy's
cuestick companion at the Elysée Palace billiard tables and as
a willing candidate for Premier when no one else would have
the job; but he had been out of public office since the Boulanger
campaigns of 1889, when he was beaten soundly in his quest for
re-election to the Chamber of Deputies. Suddenly, after all
those years, he was the most fearsome man in Paris.

It was simply the convergence of moment and man that
shot the old police chief into this frightening eminence. In a
nation "grown wild with 'preternatural suspicion,'" as a British
essayist described the mood of France, borrowing a phrase
from Carlyle, Andrieux was the chattering oracle of Panama
corruption, a perpetually replenished reservoir of allegations—
some of which he made as hearsay evidence, others that he
merely hinted at but never elucidated, pleading that fuller disclosures would violate confidences.

According to the editorial verdict of the season, Andrieux
was the prime mover of the Panama scandals, but the anomal-
ies of his career made his motives as bewildering as were his
true political convictions. Long identified with the republican
Left, he had acquired *La Petite République Française* as the
instrument of a violent campaign in 1889 against the prime
ministry of Charles Floquet, a model of a radical republican.

Former Commerce Minister Jules Roche was Andrieux's old-time colleague at the Lyon bar and his collaborator in launching the republican *Petit Parisien* in 1876; and Roche was one of the first he mentioned as a recipient of de Reinach cash.

Andrieux was also a salaried confidential adviser of Cornelius Herz, whose innocence he appeared to be protesting loyally; and Herz had become the most defamed performer among the whole Panama cast.

To the *Times* of London Andrieux was a "semi-Boulangist." To *The New York Times* he was "more or less of a monarchist" and "supposititiously a royalist agent" who was "supplying evidence piecemeal day by day against new victims" but "lopping off heads on his own side quite as freely as on the other." To London's *Pall Mall Gazette* he was merely "a disappointed place-hunter" who had "his own ends in view." To the *London Daily Chronicle* he was a man "bent on torturing his victims and worrying the committee."

In the eyes of Emile Zola's close friend, Yves Guyot, a former Public Works Minister and director of the anti-clerical newspaper *Le Siècle*, Andrieux was the manager of a campaign that embodied " the fine Boulangist revenge" and had behind him "those dark and mysterious men who were also behind Boulanger and who are called Jesuits."

Ironically, it was Guyot's sensational newspaper exposures of police practices years earlier that helped set the stage for the speech by Clemenceau that routed the Interior Minister and brought Andrieux to the Paris police prefecture and the action against the Jesuits.

The lavender gloves he wore when he went to evict the Jesuits from their schools brought him a reputation as a dandy. He was also known as something of a wit.

The night after his first appearance before the Panama investigating committee, he granted an interview to a *San Francisco Chronicle* correspondent, after stipulating that it was for publication only outside of Europe. "My aim," he told the *Chronicle*, "is to secure a revision of the constitution of France and to stamp out opportunism in French politics. I well know what will happen to me now that I have openly begun my campaign. I shall be vilified and abused, and attempts will probably be made on my life. I have been falsely accused before now. I shall have my revenge, and it will be terrific."

Then, switching to excellent English, he said with a grin: "Now that I have uncovered my batteries, don't shoot me down."

By his own assessment, given in a campaign speech in 1889, he was not a Boulangist "in the strict sense of the word" because he had held his opinions a long time before they became the basis of Boulanger's program.

Throughout the inquiry he was a constant source of copy for newspapers of all camps. In the *Libre Parole* he accused Arene, the Deputy for Corsica, of taking 20,000 francs from de Reinach. He "used the *Cocarde* and such of the *Cocarde* gang as happened not to be in prison for libel as a means of discrediting parliamentary government." He told the radical *Matin* that the unnamed beneficiary of a bribe, whom he had mentioned in testimony, was a member of Parliament, explaining with manifest conscientiousness, "I prefer to say so to prevent public opinion from being misled"; but when the reporter wanted to know whether the alleged bribetaker was a Minister, he replied: "Ah, now you are asking too much." When a *Figaro* reporter asked if he was about to involve the Presidency of the Republic, he kept the ball in play by saying: "Each name comes in its own time."

He told the nationalist *L'Eclair* that the government was scheming to silence him by implicating him in a royalist or Boulangist plot and putting him in jail; but the government neither arrested him nor prevented him from leaving France to visit Herz.

Andrieux's principal contribution to the investigation was a document with a hole in it. He said he had cut out a name he was honor-bound to protect. The document was a photograph of a note Andrieux said Herz told him he had received from de Reinach in 1890 as a token of the Baron's good faith, offered in an attempt to heal a quarrel that had grown so bitter that de Reinach had tried to have Herz poisoned. The note was not dated and not in the banker's handwriting, but Andrieux insisted that in view of its sensational contents de Reinach must have dictated it to someone in whom he had the highest trust and who should therefore be easy to identify.

The note, he said, named the individuals who were the

actual recipients of the "Bearer" checks for which de Reinach was said to have exchanged the 3,400,000-franc check the Panama company handed him soon after it issued its lottery bonds in 1888. Most of the names had already been revealed by the endorsements on the canceled checks; but the note did not mention Herz, who had received two checks for one million francs each. Andrieux had a ready explanation for the omission; he said it would have been superfluous to name Herz to Herz.

The hole appeared in a reference to a check "for 80,000 francs, received by Cloetta, employee of Cahen d'Anvers, for the account of Monsieur [   ] and four Deputies whose names can be found among the records of an influential person."

To the public the cutout became a manhole through which "the most monstrous calumnies could pass." One day a person close to the head of State would be hinted at, the next an Ambassador accredited to France; "sovereigns felt themselves in peril of being insulted in the persons of their representatives, and the German press insinuated in high glee that henceforth it would be sufficient to send plain *chargés d'affaires* to the Republic."

When newspapers published unmistakable hints of ambassadorial identities, Premier Ribot apologized in person to the Italian and Russian embassies, and his government kicked out the correspondents of the *Berliner Tageblatt*, *Budapesti Hirlap*, and Milan's *Corriere della Sera* for dispatches they had sent home.

Andrieux insisted he would fill in the hole only if compelled to by judicial authority, which the committee did not have. He told the committee's president: "It is useless to insist; for me it is a question of scruple and honor." Yet when he testified subsequently in the Assize court at the trial of the legislators and Panama company officers indicted on bribery charges, he would not reveal the name.

The role he played in the Panama investigation cost him some personal discomfort. While the bribery trial was still in progress, he appeared in another part of the Assize court to prosecute a charge of criminal libel he had brought against a former Communard journalist. The old Communard had accused him of getting a considerable bribe for his brother in the sale of a provincial canal to the government. When defense counsel taunted Andrieux, asking how he, of all people, could be so thin-skinned, the judge would not let him reply to this line of attack, and the jury brought in a verdict of not guilty.

Jules Delahaye, the Deputy whose charge of wholesale graft-taking by Parliament had touched off the investigation, was as adamant as Andrieux in refusing to make full disclosures to the inquiry committee. He said that a trustworthy, well qualified person, whose name he was pledged to protect, had shown him a list of compromised officials, that he had held the list in his hands, had read it, had complete faith in it, and felt it justified him completely in assuming his role of "revealer, not accuser"; consequently, he would not tell the investigators where they might find the list or corroboration of it. His refusal earned him a sharp rebuke a few days later when he interrupted a speech in the Chamber by Premier Ribot to accuse the government of remissness in its duty to find the fugitive Arton, whom he had named as one of the bagmen. "When you, sir, have done yours, it will be time for you to accuse others of failure in theirs," the Premier retorted.

The Panama investigating committee assumed the posture of the country's most powerful political body, despite its lack of subpoena power.

"Examine what is going on in this committee, the too faithful image of the Chamber," *Le Temps*, one of France's most respected newspapers, protested. "There is no doubt a majority which might seize on the inquiry and direct it to the profit of the Republic. But in reality the majority as well as the ministry obeys and does not command. It is at the mercy of the minority, which is trying to exploit this inquiry only against the Republic. This minority, sometimes even one or two rather resolute members, have only to accuse with loud voices their republican colleagues of wishing to smother the light in order to terrorize them immediately, and to make them take a road they would not wish to travel. Thus one needs no magnifying glass to see what we shall call the most effective of tyrannies of the minority over the general policy of the country. The minority, indeed, drags with it the entire committee, which in turn drags the Chamber, which drags the ministry. Where can such a government and such a majority, bound hand and foot by their most dreadful foes, be said to be going?"

The committee's hearings became the most spectacular shows in Paris. Each session brought such a mob of celebrity-hunters to the main entrance of the Palais Bourbon that the celebrities took to using a side door on the rue Bourgogne as an escape hatch. There elegant carriages waited for such witnesses as Baron Hely l'Oissel, director of the *Société Générale*, and Henri Germain, head of *Crédit Lyonnais*, who came to explain to their fellow Deputies that their price of supporting the desperate canal company in 1888 had not constituted interest at the rate of 85 per cent. Another was the director of the *Banque d'Escompte*, Deputy the Baron de Soubeyran, who gave evidence about his participation in almost all the syndicates handling the canal issues.

By the end of 1892 the entire French Republic, government and governed alike, was a multitude transfixed by the unending flow of smears, disclosures, and assaults on public confidence brought forth by the Panama investigation.

"An archbishop who had taken a Panama check would not now be believed upon his oath of innocence," the *Spectator* said, congratulating the Republic on its good fortune in harboring "no Bourbon and no Bonaparte who just now attracts the masses, and no general who has the full confidence even of the army."

The state of affairs grew so deranged that Paul de Cassagnac, the violent Bonapartist who edited *Le Pays*, thought he saw the Chamber taking on the role of the Convention, whereas the radical republican newspaper *La Nation* predicted gloomily that a splendid opportunity awaited a pretender who was prepared to take up the inheritance of the Republic.

Anarchists covered the walls of Paris with blood-red posters summoning the masses to arise. Marxian socialists charged that "all great banks and industrial enterprises are in much the same condition, only the turpitude is hidden more deeply." Anti-Semites found nutriment in the fact that Baron de Reinach, Herz, and Arton were Jews; the *Libre Parole* sponsored an anti-Semitic meeting that ended in a riot. Newspapers reported that royalist money and influence were behind the revolutionary activity in Paris.

Rumors of imminent revolt in the provinces in outrage at

the disclosures of the Panama scandal grew so insistent that they drove the government to issue a tranquilizing communiqué citing reassuring reports from provincial Prefects.

Friends of the Republic found comfort in the incorruptibility of General Saussier, the Military Governor of Paris who was no ardent champion of republicanism but a soldier of unshakable loyalty to his civilian commanders. The Paris garrison stopped granting leaves and furloughs, and deployed its batteries to bring the entire city under the gun. *The New York Times* correspondent saw security in the garrison's personnel: "young peasants from Brittany, Normandy, and Picardy who are untouched by socialist notions and whose terrible Lebel rifles itch to teach the blouses of Montmartre and Belleville a lesson to last them into the twentieth century."

Scandal sheets increased their runs, and the entire press discovered a gold mine of ridicule in each new phase of the affair. A new word, *chéquard*, rich in connotation of graft, evolved from revelations of high-level distribution of canal company checks. Comedians built whole routines around the word "check." Caran d'Ache, a popular cartoonist, put out an album entitled *Chic et le Chèque*. "Panamist" became Paris vernacular for those involved. A headline writer across the Atlantic on the copy desk of the *New York World* chipped in with the word "Panamiteur."

Camelots, or sidewalk peddlers, hawked song sheets with such titles as "Who Hasn't Had His Little Check?" and "Mind You Get the Real Check." A toy called Question of Panama, consisting of a cardboard head on which a convict's cap replaced a Panama hat when a string was pulled, became a best seller.

One of the Panama gags produced an international incident. The French demanded and received an apology from the Swiss government after a group representing France in an international cavalcade at the Basel carnival depicted gendarmes leading away a handcuffed head of State and his Ministers.

Eventually the constant bombardment of accusations, true and false, became as punishing for the friends of the French as for the French themselves. George W. Smalley, head of the *New York Tribune*'s London bureau, cabled protestingly to his paper on New Year's Day: "Their history is not to be read in the dismal narrative of these last ignoble weeks. That is not the real France. The real France is the France of M. Pasteur to whom on Tuesday the whole civilized and enlightened world offered a just homage.* It is the France of Baron Alphonse de Rothschild, who makes the new year welcome to the poor by his gift of a million in charity. It is the France not of Panama but of the French who rejoice to think themselves the friends of America and the one great republic of Europe."

The *Saturday Review of Politics, Literature, Science, and Art*, a thorny London biweekly magazine, blamed much of the turmoil in France on the taste of Deputies of modest means for high life in expensive Paris. Deputies then received scarcely 9,000 francs a year in salary, plus railroad transportation, free lunch at the Palais Bourbon bar, and a reduced price on a special brand of cigar called the *cigare des députés*, useful in electioneering.

"We entertained the same suspicions as the French and were every whit as credulous," the *Saturday Review* said, "in the days when, according to the old seventeenth-century jest, a secretary who wished to go to Heaven might make £2,000 a year, a secretary who was prepared to endure some purgatory could make £5,000, but there were no limits to the gains of a secretary who would risk the greater punishment."

The New York Times updated these thoughts on Christmas Day with the following comment: "No door can be opened without a glimpse of the whisking gauze of a ballet girl's dress. Whatever name is mentioned, it is recalled at once that its owner needed a great deal of money to live as he did in the *coulisses* of the Opera and the supper rooms of Montmartre. To this very day one may see a grave, white-haired man who has been more than once Premier and who expects to be President and who holds the most powerful portfolio in ministry after ministry dining almost nightly at Foyot's in the company of well known courtesans."

Zola, whose novel, *L'Argent*, had been inspired by the collapse of the *Union Générale* bank ten years earlier, dictated a cynical statement to Rene de la Villoyo, a young Breton writer

---

*Pasteur's seventieth birthday was December 27, 1892.

who pursued him to his home in the rue de Bruxelles for an interview. "With regard to the waste of money, the corruption, the bribes that were given, do you fancy that there wasn't just as much of all that sort of thing over the Suez Canal scheme?" Zola asked. "When a speculation of that kind succeeds, all these preliminary traffickings pass unnoticed, or at least are forgotten with all speed, because the profits realized allow the shareholders being reimbursed and with increase. When the enterprise doesn't succeed, then everybody cries out, and really I for one can't blame them. Suez created 'the Great Frenchman' and Panama has left this poor M. de Lesseps reviled, pointed at, a man overboard."

On January 10 the action shifted a mile down the Seine from the Palais Bourbon to the Palais de Justice, behind whose massive iron gates the First Chamber of the Court of Appeal convened to try Ferdinand de Lesseps, Grand Officer of the Legion of Honor and member of the Academy, and his son and their associates on swindling and breach of trust charges. It was a work still scarcely imaginable to many who remembered the triumph of Suez.

The clerk of the court read out the name of "the Great Frenchman" in the midst of a profound silence. His lawyer responded with medical certificates attesting that the principal defendant, now eighty-seven, was too ill and enfeebled to stand trial. The court promptly granted the prosecutor's application to permit the trial to proceed without his presence and to accept a judgment by default.

Charles de Lesseps, the first of the defendants to be questioned, told a story of the education of an innocent in the ways of corporate finance, late nineteenth-century style. When the canal company was organized in 1879, he said, and its shares offered to the public the first time, they learned that his father's name was not enough to put the issue across. Then they had arranged for a banker, Marc Levy-Cremieux, to be their man at the Bourse, and had learned how to buy support in the press. In testimony of the effectiveness of the instruction, *Le Petit Journal*, which had attacked the canal project so furiously that the first issue failed, praised it to the skies the second time around, and the company was launched triumphantly.

"A number of persons offered assistance to Baron de Reinach and M. Levy-Cremieux, who was first charged with the distribution of the money," he said, and when the court asked the purpose of the huge handouts, he replied: "In remunerating financiers and without doubt Senators and Ministers."

"That is, you gave them the dirty job which you preferred not to do yourself but provided them with the means of doing," said Judge Samuel Perivier, who salted the record with uncomfortable observations.

The beleaguered de Lesseps testified that when the company had asked the government the first time, in 1885, for permission to float a lottery loan, the Public Works Minister, Charles Baïhaut, had extorted 375,000 francs from him to let the measure come up for consideration.

Justifying company expenditures that the court considered extraordinary, he testified that the assistance of the so-called American committee, at whose disposal he said 12,000,000 had been placed, had been valuable and "would have warranted the expenditure of a still larger sum."

"The members of syndicates run a risk of loss and we had to allow them 8 or 9 per cent," he said in justification of the costs of the 1888 lottery bond issue. "The experts are mistaken in speaking of 14 per cent. The *Société Générale* and *Crédit Lyonnais* furnished us with 30,000,000, which at the time prevented suspension of payment, and they stipulated for a commission of 2,000,000 each. M. Hugo Oberndoerffer received 3,000,000 because he devised the idea of a lottery scheme, and as a large speculator on the Bourse his hostility would have been mischievous. I myself wished to give him a large sum. Baron de Reinach for the various loans received at least 6,-000,000 as a member of the syndicate. He never refused his assistance and succeeded to the role of M. Levy-Cremieux. Neither of them ever received more than 1 or 1½ per cent. We were flooded with offers of help, and being unable to judge of them, left the task to Baron de Reinach. I took care not to ask him what he did with the money.

"I considered that it was necessary at any price to finish the canal. Reinach asked for ten or twelve millions on the occasion when he received only five for expenses of publicity. Nearly all the papers were holding out their hands."

At last, after three weeks of testimony and days of summations, the court rendered its judgment on February 9, moved neither by the chief defendant's age nor the professed innocence of his son and associates.

The two de Lessepses, Cottu and Fontane were found guilty of having acted in concert to use fraudulent means to raise hopes for the realization of a chimerical event in the bond issue of June 26, 1888 and thus swindling subscribers, of attempting similarly to swindle subscribers in the bond issue of December, 1888, and of misappropriating or dissipating funds entrusted to them for a specified purpose. Eiffel was acquitted of the charge of complicity in swindling but found guilty of the last charge.

Ferdinand and Charles de Lesseps were sentenced to five years in prison and fined 3,000 francs each. Cottu and Fontane each got two years and 3,000 francs, Eiffel two years and 20,000 francs.

The newspapers, including the *Libre Parole*, whose editor, Drumont, had excoriated Ferdinand de Lesseps a few years earlier in his book, *La Derniere Bataille,* now inundated the old man in waves of pity.

Other segments of the public reacted less tenderly. Residents of the rue Panama, a new street in the Eighteenth Arrondissement, named a few years earlier when the canal venture looked like a bonanza, petitioned unsuccessfully to change its name. The Eiffel company met to consider changing its name, which still adorns the most prominent landmark on the Paris skyline. The municipality of Rouen renamed the Quai de Lesseps the Quai de Bois Guilbert, honoring a local celebrity. Only seven years earlier, the Rouen Mayor had said to de Lesseps in bestowing his name on the bit of Seine embankment: "Though still living, you already belong to history, and, as to Victor Hugo, so to you, we can unreservedly do an honor which is usually granted only to the illustrious dead." In 1892 the Mayor, Louis Ricard, now Minister of Justice of France, ordered the prosecution of the fraud charge.

The sentence on the aged de Lesseps was not executed. Languishing at his country home, La Chesnaye, falling asleep continually while trying to read the same old copy of the *Revue des Deux Mondes* over and over again, he seemed scarely aware of what had taken place, or that his son and his devoted assistant, Fontane, still had to undergo the ordeal of the bribery trial, along with seven other defendants.

In the bribery case the examining magistrate, Tiburce

Franqueville, a cynical, scholarly man, learned in Latin as well as the law, determined that there was no cause of action against three of the ten members of Parliament who had come before him. They were the former Minister of Justice, Senator Thevenet, the former Minister of Commerce, Deputy Jules Roche, and Arene, the drama reviewer.

To the seven who remained, he added three new defendants: former Public Works Minister Baïhaut, Baïhaut's one-time private secretary Leopold Blondin, who was accused of having been the intermediary in Charles de Lesseps's 375,000-franc bribe, and Gustave Gobron, a former Deputy who was Jules Ferry's brother-in-law.

Franqueville's interrogation of Baïhaut went on all day, while the minister's beautiful, rich wife waited for him in the examining magistrate's anteroom. When at last she saw him emerge in the custody of detectives, she threw herself at his feet in hysterics and clung to him so piteously that Police Superintendent Clement let them share a farewell dinner in his office before sending Baïhaut off to Mazas Prison.

The second stop on the route to the Assize court, the *Chambre des Mises en Accusation*, or Chamber of Indictments, whose functions approximate those of a grand jury's, threw out the cases Franqueville had sent up against former Premier Rouvier, Henri Cottu, and Senators Deves, Albert Grevy, and Renault. Its findings left Senator Beral and Deputies Proust and Dugue de la Fauconnerie to go to trial with Charles de Lesseps, Fontane, Baïhaut, Blondin, and former Deputies Gobron and Sans-Leroy. But before they could be brought to trial, the name of Cornelius Herz was formally added to the list of "Panamist" accused.

News of his arrest in his sickbed at a hotel in Bournemouth, England, at midnight on January 19, overshadowed every other aspect of the case, thanks to his terrifying dossier of incriminating data that Andrieux's testimony had conjured up.

"Prospect of his return to France and revelations of evidence he holds against conspicuous politicians and financiers produced feelings near panic in all but royalist and socialist circles," a Paris correspondent cabled to the *New York Tribune* the next day.

Herz was charged specifically with complicity in the

Panama frauds and blackmail of Baron de Reinach; but the extent and depth of the evil that rumor imputed to him made his formal indictment seem, in comparison, like a letter of recommendation for a position of trust. "Fiend," "Werewolf," "Cagliostro," "Evil Genius of the Politicians of the Third Republic," "Engineer of the Panama Briberies" were some of the epithets that pelted him. In London there were newspaper reports that he was an agent of the German Chancellor and the Premier of Italy. In Paris the story got around that he was a British spy.

"Of all the persons connected with the Panama scandal, he is the most hated and despised," the *Tribune* correspondent wrote. "He seems to be without a friend so far as public expressions give indication, and it would be difficult for him to secure an entirely impartial trial."

The Legion of Honor promptly struck his name off its rolls on the ground that his secret departure was a presumption of the suspicious character of his relations with Baron de Reinach and that the acts of which he was accused constituted an offense against honor.

When the bribery trial started early in March, Herz was still in British custody and there seemed little likelihood that he would face his accusers either in France or in England. The foremost British medical authorities certified that he was too ill to attend an extradition hearing, and the British Foreign Office informed the French Ambassador to the Court of St. James's that an accused foreigner could not be subjected to judicial examination in England by his own government while under arrest on an extradition warrant.

The bribery trial was conducted in an atmosphere of continuous disorder, attracting crowds of young lawyers who, "being avowedly clericals and monarchists, felt free to groan and boo at radical witnesses, cheer every insult to the Republic, and several times to break up a session by their turbulent behavior."

Among the radical witnesses paraded before them were Clemenceau and the former Premiers Floquet and de Freycinet. Charles de Lesseps had testified that de Reinach, under relentless financial pressure from Herz, had in turn demanded huge payments from the canal company, which he had refused. As a result, word had spread that the Baron was about to sue the company. Thereupon, he said, the radical leaders had urged him to keep de Reinach satisfied and prevent the suit. They testified in their turn, that they had urged this course because such a lawsuit would damage the company and the opposition would seize upon its difficulties as a stick with which to beat the Republic at a time of intense political anxiety.

Spectators at the bribery trial immediately became aware that a sharp change had taken place in the courtroom demeanor of Charles de Lesseps. At the fraud trial in the Court of Appeal he had appeared pale and haggard, testifying with extreme caution, speaking in a voice frequently so low it was difficult to hear. Having been found guilty there and drawn a stiff sentence, he brought to his next trial the air of a man with little to lose. He spoke out in a firm and lively manner, and impressed the jurors of the Assize court with his fearlessness and apparent candor.

Once more he lamented the financiers' practice of levying tribute on company promoters, and when the presiding judge, Pilet Desjardins, admonished him to "cut it short," he replied cooly: "No, I have time enough. All this is necessary for my defense. Great financiers cannot force people to subscribe, but they can prevent their doing so; for if there is no agreement between the financier and the promoters, an applicant who goes to the former is told, 'Do not subscribe just now, but wait.' Hence the cooperation of financiers is indispensable, and must be paid for."

In the earlier trial, in explaining that the first time the company had sought government approval of the lottery device it had given Herz a 600,000-franc payoff by discounting notes for him and then returning the notes, de Lesseps had said only: "Everybody knows what his influence was, and we had much trouble to escape giving him more."

Now he spelled out the motives for his beneficence. "Herz came to my father and me and told us that he had great influence with the government," he said. "The statement hardly surprised us as his relations to those in power had already become apparent through his rapid promotion in the Legion of Honor. His proposals greatly embarrassed us, but we did not feel that we could afford to ignore or offend him. He was much too powerful. He had supporters in the government and was moreover a secret partner in *La Justice*, the organ of M. Clemenceau, who was then considered likely to become Premier. He was not the kind of man likely to neglect any of the opportunities afforded to him. We would have preferred that he had not come to us, but after he had come and made his proposals, it was better to do that which would make him our ally than that which would make him our enemy. He talked very freely at the time, boasted of the services that he had rendered to the government, and invited me to accompany him to Mont-sous-Vaudrey to see evidence of his friendship with M. Jules Grevy. I went with him and found evidence that M. Herz was received as a friend of the family. I was then convinced that he was a man we must reckon with."

Clemenceau, when his turn came, retorted from the witness box: "When de Lesseps was discounting bills for Herz, the latter did not own a single share of *La Justice*."

At the time of the 1888 lottery loan, Charles de Lesseps said, de Reinach told him Herz was pressing him for 10 or 12 million francs and "you must extricate me"; but de Lesseps did not tell the court from what the Baron yearned to be extricated.

"I replied that I had not seen M. Herz for a long time, but that I had nothing to do with his affairs." de Lesseps testified. "De Reinach seemed desperate. I added: 'He is insatiable. After you have given him ten or twelve millions he will demand your whole fortune, and when he has got this he will take your overcoat and shirt and will then tell you to stand on your head and walk from the Bastille to the Madeleine.'"

He said he offered de Reinach 5,000,000 francs as his share of the syndicate handling the lottery issue, and he "had no knowledge how de Reinach disposed of the money except that he has given M. Herz 2,000,000 to quiet him."

Three of the members of Parliament accused of receiving bribes from de Reinach—Proust, Gobron, and Dugue de la Fauconnerie—protested that the payments represented their profits on legitimate business deals in which they had engaged with the Baron. Senator Beral accounted for his check to "Bearer" as his fee for engineering services performed for de Reinach. Sans-Leroy said a large sum of money traced to his account at the time of the lottery votes was the return on reinvestment of part of his wife's dowry. He said he had documentary proof of this contention but had not submitted it to the examining magistrate because he preferred acquittal after a trial to mere avoidance of indictment.

When Baïhaut was called to testify he collapsed in tears and readily confessed acceptance of 375,000 francs from Charles de Lesseps as the price of his support for the first lottery loan measure. De Lesseps protested that the money did not constitute a bribe but was a down payment on blackmail exacted by the Minister, who demanded 1,000,000 francs in installments. When the bill was withdrawn, de Lesseps said, he refused to pay the balance.

The jury returned verdicts of not guilty for the five legislators and Fontane, but convicted Baïhaut, Blondin, and de Lesseps. The former Minister was sentenced to five years in prison and fines totaling twice the amount of the bribe. Blondin was sentenced to two years, and de Lesseps to one. The court ordered the three convicted men to repay the bribe money to the liquidator of the canal company and held de Lesseps jointly responsible with Baïhaut for payment of the fine.

Mme. Baïhaut, managing to function fiscally though overwhelmed with grief by her husband's arrest, applied at once for a decree of separation of their property, which the court granted, reserving to the canal company's liquidator the right of intervention in the investors' behalf.

One of the Panama payments that Charles de Lesseps had disclosed in his testimony, the 12,000,000 francs to the so-called American committee, prompted an investigation by a special committee of the United States House of Representatives. Under a House resolution adopted January 28, 1893, a five-member committee inquired into activities in the United States on behalf of the canal company and also into various commercial relationships of companies engaged in transportation across the Isthmus of Panama. The Congressional investigators filed their report on March 3, the last day of the life of the 52nd Congress, devoting the larger portion of it to the operations and purposes of the American committee—in which three eminent New York investment banking houses had had a hand.

The "perfectly clear" object of the formation of the American committee, the Congressmen said, was the creation of widespread public impression that "American capital, in the persons of some of its most respectable agencies," was supporting the canal enterprise. When former President Ulysses S. Grant turned down the job of chairman, the investigators said, the canal committee looked for the "next best thing," a widely known public figure, "if possible one whose orthodoxy in the past in relation to the Monroe Doctrine would make his support of the canal project all the stronger in the eyes of the American people."

At the suggestion of the canal company's financial agents in Paris, said the Congressional report, the American committee was composed of representatives of the houses of J.&W. Seligman, Drexel, Morgan & Co., and Winslow, Lanier & Co.. Unable to get General Grant as chairman, they recruited R.W. Thompson of Terre Haute, Indiana, from his post as Secretary of the Navy in President Hayes's administration—the "whole tone" of which had been "suspicious of and hostile towards the enterprise." To the investigating Congressmen it was "perfectly clear" that had Thompson not been in the administration, "no controlling reason existed for his selection."

Representative Josiah Patterson of Tennessee, one of the members of the investigating committee, questioned Jesse Seligman, of J.&W. Seligman, specifically on this point at a hearing on February 15. The *New York Tribune* published their colloquy the next day:

Patterson: "He [referring to Thompson] was not a great financier and used to handling vast sums, was he?"
Seligman: "No, but he was a great statesman and lawyer."
Patterson: "But you offered the place to General Grant. Now he was a great soldier, a popular idol, but he was not a great lawyer, or financier, or a great statesman, was he?"
Seligman (smilingly): "Well, General Grant was a bosom friend of mine and I always look out for my friends."

Seligman testified that the member houses of the American committee received compensation totaling 6,000,000 francs, one fourth of it on formation of the canal company and the balance in six annual installments, a reward of $50,000 per firm per year over eight years. This was independent of any other canal funds handled by his firm, which processed payments for more that $40,000,000 worth of matériel the de Lesseps company's purchasing agents bought in the United States for the canal job. The other 6,000,000 francs of the 12,000,000 Charles de Lesseps mentioned remained in Europe, Seligman testified, for distribution to a group whose membership, he said, he did not know.

The $50,000 a year the New York bankers received, said the investigating Congressmen, was "apparently for the loan of their names and for nothing else to this enterprise," and was paid "without the knowledge of the chairman of that committee, who all the time supposed that he was the important factor in this enterprise and was himself receiving only half of that sum annually."

"In fact," the report stated, "two years before the canal company went into liquidation it is in evidence that Mr. Thompson voluntarily reduced his salary by one half—that is, to $12,500, remaining in complete ignorance that the other members of the committee, of which he was still chairman, were still receiving $50,000."

The Congressmen reported that "the only specific matter the three banking members of the American committee seem to have had in charge and to have accomplished was the purchase of the stock of the Panama Railroad Company by the canal company at a price more that double what it had been quoted in the market for two or three years previous to the beginning of these negotiations."

"This stock," said the Congressional investigators, "had been selling from $140 to $150, and the result of the negotiations and contract of sale was that the Panama Canal Company purchased 68,500 out of 70,000 shares of stock, at a price of $291—$250 a share for the stock, $41 and some cents on each share for certain 'assets' of the railroad company, the nature of which is not very clear."

Jesse Seligman explained in his testimony: "The canal company was satisfied that unless they had control of the Panama Railroad the canal could never by built."

The investigating committee, composed of Representatives John R. Fellows of New York, chairman, T.J. Geary of California, H. Henry Powers of Vermont, Bellamy Storer of Ohio, and Patterson, reported to the Congress: "It has been unable thus far to trace directly or indirectly the expenditure of any money whatever in a corrupt way to influence the legislative or executive action of the United States government. It may be that no investigation, however prolonged after this lapse of time, could be efficient in making such discovery, even if such corrupt use of money was made, but this is the subject of which your committee does not desire authoritatively to express its opinion that further investigation would be entirely fruitless."

The Chamber of Deputies investigation of the Panama affair came to a close on June 23 with the filing of a 1947-page report that called the charges of wholesale corruption of legislators false in every detail. "We have studied and weighed them one by one, and we have shown how little founded they were," the Deputies' report said, but the committee considered it regrettable that some politicians had solicited or accepted participations in risk-free financial syndicates organized by a company that had to deal with public officials.

"It can be said that they thus exposed themselves to alienation of their independence and imprudently involved themselves in conflicts of interests," the inquiry committee said, spelling out its regret.

From the financial standpoint the "Panama enterprise was carried on in the most deplorable fashion," the report stated. "It was always with the help of deliberately erroneous statements that it launched its issues, the total of which rose to no less that 1,335,565,000 francs," the investigators charged. "This enormous capital did not even approach its true destination, and in the use made of it the company engaged in inexcusable prodigalities."

Chief beneficiaries of these prodigalities, they said, were the contractors, the financiers, and the press. "Thanks to badly arranged contracts, endlessly shuffled around and obtained for the most part with the help of fat commissions, the contractors made fat profits," they explained.

"The financial world took considerable sums, out of all proportions to the services rendered. It preyed on the Panama company and was not content to receive legitimate compensation for which it might pretend to have given support; it demanded much more, so much so that, to satisfy it, recourse had to be taken to unprecedented financial arrangements, especially the fictitious syndicates that were for the Panama direc-

157

tors an opportunity to remunerate ill-defined cooperation and for certain financiers a means of reaping absolutely unjustifiable bonuses."

The report cleared of all blame the Premiers mentioned in the testimony of Charles de Lesseps, but disapproved of the use of funds obtained through private channels for governmental uses—as Rouvier said he had used a loan from friends in the fight against Boulanger.

Those who had tried to compromise the regime by dishonoring its leaders and its distinguished servants failed, the report said, because they used "a tactic too old and shopworn to succeed in a country as clearsighted and deeply honest as ours." The Government, tossing aside all political considerations, let the courts judge the charges against accused public officials, the investigators said, and "those supposed to be guilty were acquitted by the jury, that is to say, by popular justice."

Baïhaut, the grafting Public Works Minister, got his just deserts, his former colleagues agreed, but they insisted it would be as unjust to blame the Republic for his skullduggery as it would to blame royalty for the public works scandals that had helped bring about the downfall of Louis Philippe.

Only a week before the investigating deputies filed their report, the *Cour de Cassation*, the country's supreme court of appeal, reversed the convictions in the earlier trial on the grounds that the statute of limitations had outlawed the charges. Of those defendants only Charles de Lesseps had been in custody, serving the bribery sentence; the others had been free pending decision on their appeal.

Charles de Lesseps continued a prisoner until September 12, though he had spent most of his time in custody at the Hospital Saint-Louis as he was suffering of dyspepsia. Held jointly responsible for the huge fine imposed on Baïhaut, and unable to pay, he fled to London and lived in exile for several years in Thurloe Square, handy to the Victoria and Albert Museum. Finally the French fiscal authorities accepted a compromise payment and let him come home.

Blondin, whose physicians had protested his imprisonment from the start on the ground that he had incipient paralysis and should be in a private asylum, was freed on October 7.

Baïhaut, alone of all those implicated in crimes, was kept

in a penal institution—the rugged, solitary-confinement prison of Etampes, with so strict a system that a prisoner being taken out of his cell was masked or hooded to prevent recognition by any other inmate. Nor would the government even let him go to the bedside of his dying daughter in 1893. But three years later, when he was brought from his cell to testify in a trial of Emile Arton, "his general bearing and the painful simplicity of his evidence moved all present" so profoundly that the government pardoned him. Since he could not pay his fine, he was returned to prison, this time, however, to Ste. Pelagie, "a Riviera for prisoners" in comparison to his former jail.

Herz, too, was a prisoner, although he had not been tried. His cell was his bedroom at the Tankerville Hotel in the English Channel resort town of Bournemouth, where he was held in custody on the extradition warrant for forty months; his case a *cause célèbre* that plagued France and Britain until the day he died.

The decrepitude of Ferdinand de Lesseps spared his presence in the protracted juridic melodrama in which he was the central character, but whether he was spared the knowledge of the calamity that had befallen him was a matter of dispute. Newspapers reported that he had no awareness of the ordeal his son and his associates were undergoing, and one of Edmond Goncourt's pitiless gossip items in his journal said that M. de Lesseps had "become gaga"; but Anatole France told the French Academy he understood that the aged canal builder was completely lucid and "conscious of his extreme misfortune."

"In the tragic hour for his name and glory, alone amid his family, in the rustic dwelling of La Chesnaye where almost half a century previously he had drawn on the map the small line which was to unite two worlds, now infirm, helpless, and saddened, putting his traveling rug over his chilly knees, the great traveler was dying in silence," Anatole France said. "But one by one, tears were seen running down his wasted cheeks."

Withdrawn though he had become, whatever took place with Ferdinand de Lesseps remained a topic of worldwide interest, and at the very moment he died at La Chesnaye on the afternoon of December 6, 1894, a telegram from the *Times* of London was delivered, inquiring about his state of health.

His prosecution, two years earlier, had set in motion a public autopsy on his role and motives in the Panama undertaking and the causes of its failure, and his death reactivated it throughout the world. The judgment finally arrived at was almost unanimously sympathetic to the old man's memory.

Editorial analyzers in Europe and America agreed that it was not avarice that had powered his drive. He had little left to show for his works. The Suez Canal Company came to the aid of his family, voting a pension of 60,000 francs a year to Mme. de Lesseps and a similar amount to their numerous progeny. De Lesseps had put his wife's *dot* of 100,000 francs into Suez stock the day of their marriage, and in less than twenty years his shares were worth 2,000,000 francs. Then he had put all his wife's savings, his children's, and his own into Panama bonds. His last share of Suez Canal founders' stock was sold to help pay the Panama company's liquidator 675,000 francs.

"M. de Lesseps is not a man of bad faith," said the President of France, Sadi Carnot, himself an engineer. "I should rather consider him punctilious. Only his natural vehemence carries him away; he is a bad reasoner, and has no power of calculation. Hence many regrettable acts on his part, done without any intention of injuring anybody. I knew him well, having seen him very close, when his imagination suggested to him the scheme for excavating an inland sea in Africa. A commission of engineers, of whom I was one, was appointed to hear him and study his proposal. We had no difficulty in showing him that the whole thing was a pure chimera. He seemed very much astonished, and we saw that we had not convinced him. Take it from me that as a certainty he would have spent millions upon millions to create his sea, and that with the best faith in the world."

Anatole France told the French Academy when he succeeded to de Lesseps's chair: "He had too much confidence in himself and in his long good fortune, but generous, great, full of kindliness, strength, and courage, in sympathy with mankind, capable everywhere of action and inspiring action, he labored all his life at vast and pacific undertakings, and gained by toil his place among the elite of useful men. What he effected is immense and benefical. For the west fettered by too narrow bonds, he opened an outlet, he opened a new highway for energy, and afforded opportunities for action in concord and harmony. Such a man has but one judge—the universe."

Similarly the London *Pall Mall Gazette*, whose former editor, Frederick Greenwood, had brought Disraeli's Foreign Secretary the tip that enabled Britain to buy the Egyptian Khedive's 44 per cent share of the Suez Canal Company's equity in 1875, esteemed de Lesseps as a man who "worked for the world with the highest intentions" and believed that "even the Panama scheme would be for the greatness of France and her increase among nations."

"He did not realize its difficulties because he had grown old and was enfeebled in his intellects," the *Gazette* said. "He had lost his memory and his perception. There can be no harm now in saying that once, while he was still asking for more money, he dined at the British Embassy and dined in the belief that Lord Lytton and his staff were Lord Lyons and his staff.

"As many a great commander is reckless of lives, Lesseps was always reckless of details and the expenditure their conquest involves. He knew his mind, he was one of those men who do what they intend to do, whatever the cost. He failed to make the Panama canal, for the reasons we have stated, but in him the failure will be seen only to have half eclipsed a shining record. For it must always be included to him for honor that in spite of overwhelming difficulties, although the idea was not his own, he began and finished the Suez Canal, which is one of the world's wonders."

The *Times* of London, assiduous chronicler of the Panama enterprise from start to finish, insisted that much of the blame for its failure had to be borne "by the crowds that acclaimed him without knowing why, by the press which wrote him up, by the investors who positively invited him to lead them to their ruin." Public opinion, it prophesied, would one day accept this appreciation of de Lesseps: "He was neither an impostor nor a swindler. He was a man of great originality, of indomitable perseverance, of boundless faith in himself, and of singular powers of fascination over others."

Henry Mitchell, of Nantucket, Massachusetts, had substantial professional qualifications for appraising the works of Ferdinand de Lesseps. He was an engineer. He had inspected the Suez works in 1868 with de Lesseps's permission. In 1874 President Grant had appointed him to represent the Coast and Geodetic Survey on the board of engineers for the improvement of the Mississippi River mouth. He had specialized knowledge of ocean currents. After de Lesseps's death he began to prepare a monograph on the canal builder for publication in the proceedings of the American Academy of Arts and Sciences.

In the case of the Suez Canal, he wrote, "its opening was an easement to all the world," and "its construction was sure because it was the next legitimate step forward under the pressure of an enormous demand." It was not an experiment, he said; the ground had been profiled and bored, the climate tested and found healthy, and an ample manpower pool was near at hand. But the Panama project "was highborn, and burst into life a full-blown scheme."

"What the scheme lacked from first to last was justification in immediate necessity," he said. "It had an illegitimate and premature birth, and its sponsors limited their risks to brokers' charges, except M. Lesseps, who gave all. He gave his past earnings, the best service of our age, and he gave his fair name as endowment enough for the whole credit of the company, at the start.

"For the Panama project the almost unprecedented depth of the cut, the peculiarly obdurate ledges, the great rainfall interrupting labor and causing sloughing of the banks, the necessity for turning the Chagres River were difficulties weighed and discounted at the start by able engineers and by a very large and very intelligent company in France. But the 'bodily slipping of the hills' in the excavations near the summit was a frightful disappointment. It necessitated postponement of a sea–level cut, and the adoption of a scheme of locks which involved the ponding of the Chagres River. This *change of pace* was fatal and the company broke."

The enormous price of the failure gave rise to an anecdote he related: "The King of Spain, looking from his chamber window, shaded his eyes and said: 'I am looking for the walls of Panama, they have cost enough to be seen from here.' "

In Egypt, Mitchell said, de Lesseps had been the actual manager-in-chief; but a quarter of a century later, at Panama, he had to depend more and more on others, and no longer verified the statements of the engineers by adequate inspection and exploitation.

"His old attitude of control and command continued,"

Mitchell said, "but he merely endorsed the reports of the chiefs of division—*whose figures, we now know, were correct*—without discovering their misleading limitations. His famous promise that the canal would be open to the passage of vessels in 1889 was based, as he stated, upon the unanimous acquiescence of his chiefs of division. Moreover, if we plot on profile paper the amount of work done from date to date, the curve of increments, projected, seems to justify the prediction. His own belief in it is enthusiastically stated in his *Recollections of Forty Years*, and he adds: 'I am an octogenarian. Old age foresees, and youth acts.' This last *mot* was lost upon the public, who saw him now only as the figurehead of a brave ship given over to pirates."

Mitchell did not send his monograph to the academy at once, because he feared his "very much foreshortened view" might be inadequate. He withheld it until Nathan Appleton, of Boston, one of de Lesseps's earliest employees in the Panama venture, sent him "the last word spoken on the subject by a *competent* witness." It was a biographical sketch of de Lesseps by the geographer, Gabriel Gravier, that Mme. de Lesseps had sent to Appleton with her autograph endorsement.

Gravier wrote: "The work was marching to a certain success, the original estimate had proved very nearly sufficient. Whence came the cyclone which swept away the company and its 400,000 shareholders? From Paris, the distracted brain of France!"

"With some personal and professional knowledge of the American isthmus, and from reading the recent reports of Kimball, Rogers, and others," Mitchell commented, "we distinctly see that the difficulties in the scheme were really intrinsic, although not insurmountable, and we have let our account stand."

Of all the post-mortems on the fiasco at Panama, the most purposeful one was performed by an international board of fourteen distinguished engineers, who were recruited to re-examine the entire project in order to assure complete objectivity in the decisions that would be made by a new company formed to try to complete the canal.

Reporting four years after the death of de Lesseps and ten years after the collapse of his undertaking, these professionals said: "An impartial examination of the financial failure of the company founded by M. de Lesseps disclosed a number of cases which had more or less grave consequences, speaking either from a financial or technical point of view, but all relate to an initial or fundamental cause—that is, from its beginnings, there was an omission to make careful and thorough surveys to determine the character and cost of the work, as well as the time necessary to complete it. It would be unjust, however, to underestimate the importance of the work accomplished, and the results obtained by the old company."

While completed surveys on the Isthmus of Panama demonstrated undeniably that de Lesseps's vision of a sea-level canal was "now practically susceptible of realization," they reported "Mr. de Lesseps was entirely mistaken concerning the conditions of execution in the first attempt he made."

Citing the repeated reductions of the early estimates of time and money that would be needed to complete the canal, the investigators said: "It was under these conditions that the work was commenced in 1881. After employing two or three years in making more careful and thorough surveys and in preparatory work, the real difficulties of the undertaking began to be understood."

10

Paris in the Spring of 1893 expanded its vocabulary to embrace two new epithets, both forged of Panama irony.

"The Comedy of Bournemouth" became the standard designation for the extradition proceedings against Cornelius Herz, defaming by implication everyone connected with the case. It imputed insincerity to the French government in its attempt to gain custody of Herz. It accused world-renowned British and French medical authorities of venality or stupidity for certifying that Herz was too ill to be moved from his Bournemouth sickbed. It charged connivance between British diplomats and physicians to thwart honest French attempts to bring a fugitive to justice.

Mention of "the Invalid of Bournemouth" conjured up a vision of a master malingerer laughing satanically at frustrated French justice while he luxuriated in a pleasant Channel resort under the protection of a perfidious nation for which he had spied on France.

The name "Cornelius Herz" became synonymous with so much evil that Paul Deroulede, just a month after surviving a duel with Clemenceau, had to fight another one with Stephen Pichon, a young editor of *La Justice,* for calling Pichon a secret partner of Herz.

Since the duel between Deroulede and Clemenceau their feud had only simmered. The emotional Deroulede had been maintaining an air of calm that he himself was moved to comment on; whereas Clemenceau had been plainly damaged by the association with Herz. Clemenceau was "under a cloud of increasing density," *The New York Times* reported; and Emily Crawford informed the *Tribune:* "Clemenceau's position is now weaker than I have ever known it to be since he set out to be the rival of Gambetta."

The lull ended flashily on Monday evening, June 19. As Clemenceau climbed to the tribune of the Chamber to debate a proposed change in the term of office for Deputies, Deroulede shouted suddenly from the back benches: "Ah, now the Invalid of Bournemouth is going to speak! Let him speak in English!"

"I am ready to have an explanation with M. Deroulede whenever he likes," Clemenceau retorted, although the meaning and magnitude of the poet's insult was clear to everyone. "Today I might remind him of the night when he proposed to me to march against the Chamber of Deputies to break it up, and the categorical refusal I then gave him."

"I did not then know you were a foreign agent," Deroulede replied, accusing and confessing in the same breath.

The President of the Chamber was Jean Casimir-Perier, a rich, frosty, conservative republican blue blood who had been chosen at the start of the 1893 session when Floquet withdrew his candidacy for re-election because of his connection with the Panama affair.

When the presiding officer could not control Deroulede and maintain order, Clemenceau took up his own defense with a threat of a settlement at arms.

"I hold you responsible!" he warned Deroulede.

"No, you won't hold me responsible for anything any longer," Deroulede retorted.

Deroulede's Boulangist colleague, Lucien Millevoye, jumped in, shouting at Clemenceau: "Fulfill your own responsibilities first!"

"When a man refuses to fight, it is easy enough to keep on talking," Clemenceau answered.

Millevoye persisted: "First explain your relations with Cornelius Herz."

Clemenceau struggled to resume his speech, constantly drowned out by the two Boulangists screaming: "Cornelius Herz!" "You are an agent of a foreign power!" "Universal suffrage will throw you out!"

He managed to get out half a sentence: "If there is in this

country a feeling, deep-rooted and inveterate . . . "

" . . . it is scorn for you," Deroulede finished for him.

"Neither of you wishes to fight," Clemenceau repeated. "It is easy to insult in that case."

Millevoye replied: "I am at your disposal when you'd like to accept. Pistol or sword."

Casimir-Perier managed to control the Chamber long enough to pronounce a closure. A vote was taken on the almost forgotten election bill, and it was defeated, 323 to 214.

As Clemenceau returned to his seat, Deroulede began the descent from his bench. A fist fight in the well of the Chamber appeared so likely that a questor quickly slid into the place beside Clemenceau. But Deroulede was only going to the tribune.

> Deroulede: "There is, at this moment, beyond the sea, a friend of the previous speaker, a foreign agent, whose person and papers are in the hands of the English. Over there is a state secret."
>
> Clemenceau: "You know well that you lie."
>
> Deroulede: "Oh, do not talk any longer." [To the Chamber] "I must apologize to the Chamber for the scandal that I have aroused, but this scandal was the last act of justice. Do not think that I joyfully abandoned the calm attitude I have been maintaining of late. [Picking up the thread of his speech] But who has these papers of his, Cornelius Herz's? It is upon this question that hangs the appointment of our Ambassador to England, and you wish me to let this man quietly ascend the tribune who introduced this person into France?"
>
> Clemenceau: "That is not true."
>
> Deroulede: "It is not for you to deny any longer. There are some people who cannot do that, and you are one of them. You have seen the Chamber's attitude. It is the conscience of those who hear me which has interrupted you."
>
> Clemenceau: "You are a liar and a coward."
>
> Deroulede: "I said you can no longer deny. You can no longer insult. I am not making a party question of this matter, I have been silent when one after another of the guilty members of this Chamber has risen to this

167

tribune, silent because after all they belong to us. But this man in not of us. I only regret one thing, that I had not oratorical power or personal force enough to stigmatize him still more."

Clemenceau: I have already told you that you are a liar. I add now that you are a charlatan of patriotism."

Deroulede shrugged off this new characterization and vacated the tribune for Millevoye, who said only that he would explain his charges on Thursday, by which time he would have decided how he would respond to Clemenceau's challenge.

"It is clear that you will turn tail," Clemenceau told him.

Immediately after adjournment Clemenceau sent his seconds to Deroulede and Millevoye. Deroulede refused the challenge on the ground he had stated in the Chamber. Millevoye insisted he was the injured party and named two combative aristocrats, the Count de Dion and the Marquis de Mores, as his own seconds to resolve his latest crisis of honor with Clemenceau.

Both Millevoye's seconds brought ripe, practical qualifications to their mission. De Dion could display among his press notices the following item from *The New York Times* of January 10, 1884: "Paris, Jan. 9: A duel with swords between M. Aurelien Scholl, the journalist, and Count Albert de Dion was fought today in consequence of an article printed in the *Evénement.* M. Scholl was wounded in the side, Count de Dion's sword breaking in the thrust and a fragment being left in the person of the former."

De Mores had achieved a far more lurid career than his associate, building it on the wastage of substantial advantages —good looks, money, an old Sardinian title, an education at France's military academy at St. Cyr and the cavalry school at Saumur. He had attempted to create a beef-raising enterprise in the United States, but had failed with heavy losses. He had tried to promote a railroad in the French colony of Cochin China and had been frustrated by politics. He had consorted with anarchists, agitated for the Orleanists, and was presently striving to qualify as a professional anti-Semite.

A year before, acting as voluntary gladiator for his friend Edouard Drumont, the anti-Semite editor, de Mores had killed Captain Armand Mayer, a French army officer who was a Jew, in a duel de Mores and Drumont had provoked with insults of Jewish officers. De Mores was tried on a manslaughter charge, his seconds and Mayer's as accessories, and all were acquitted.

In Dakota Territory, where de Mores had built a ranch after marrying an heiress from Stapleton, Staten Island, he and three other men were tried and acquitted three times for the murder of Riley Luffsey, a Badlands bravo who was shot to death while resisting arrest for a drunken threat against de Mores's life. In Toulouse, during a Chamber of Deputies election campaign, he was fined 100 francs for carrying prohibited arms while opposing the candidacy of Jean Constans, who, as the Governor General of Cochin China, had kept de Mores from getting the railroad franchise. In Paris in 1890 he was sentenced to three months in jail after being arrested during a roundup of anarchists ordered by Constans, then Minister of the Interior, to forestall May Day uprisings.

At the moment he received the invitation to be Millevoye's second, de Mores was in court again, this time in a suit brought by his father, the Duke of Vallombrosa, to deprive him of the management of his property.

De Mores and his colleague, de Dion, weighed Millevoye's cause and certified its rectitude. "We are very glad to be your seconds," they told him, "but after having taken note of your communication we declare on our honor that there is no reason why you should demand reparation or afford reparation to M. Clemenceau. This all depends on the justice of the people and public scorn."*

Two days before Millevoye's promised revelations in the Chamber, *La Cocarde,* the Boulangist scandal sheet, prepared the nation for the shock by publishing a statement signed by its editor, Edouard Ducret, which said: "We have abstracted or caused to be abstracted (we will speak precisely later on, when an explanation is called for, either before the Assize court or the committee of inquiry) from a strongbox in the British Embassy at Paris some diplomatic documents of the greatest moment. These papers prove that very important documents

---

*De Dion, in turn, was outraged that Clemenceau did not challenge him to a duel for saying that Clemenceau was disqualified from challenging Millevoye. He insisted that Clemenceau, in all honor, had to consider himself insulted and demand satisfaction. Clemenceau ignored these intricate ratiocinations.

which were in the possession of the French government were stolen, and after being copied, were communicated to the British government by French political personages in British pay. The documents, which, alas! were stolen, contain many other matters of interest, some of which are of a very painful nature. One is sometimes called upon to make heavy sacrifices to meet the necessity of serving one's country, but let those who desire that the truth and the whole truth should be known be sure that it will be."

When Millevoye showed up in the lobbies of the Chamber the next day, he was much less coy than Ducret about the cards he held. He said he had possession of state secrets that might affect so many persons and were so grave that he wanted to act entirely in accord with the government; consequently he would consult with Premier Charles Dupuy that night. He said he might even withhold the questions on the Herz extradition that he had notified the government he would ask; but if Clemenceau should challenge him to an explanation, he would speak out.

The matter had nothing to do with the Panama affair, he said, but it was no exaggeration to say that charges of high treason were involved. When asked if he would seek an investigation by a committee of the Chamber, he said: "I will accept any form of inquiry, legal or other, and am prepared to take responsibility both for my words and acts. If it should turn out later that I have made a mistake and have calumniated M. Clemenceau, the latter will have the right to demand full reparation."

Examining the outburst against their own country and its supposed agents, the London press attributed it to the fermenting residue of Boulangism; but the motives for it baffled some of Britain's most distinguished pundits, and the turn it took was startling to them.

"For some months these sorry remnants of Boulangism have been calumniating, denouncing, agitating, but for whose sake?" the *Times* of London asked. "Who is behind them? Who incites them to prove that France is made up only of robbers, swindlers, and traitors, and that she has become the receptacle of the worst men and the worst things? For whom are these people working?"

The *Spectator* explained it readily, up to a point: Clemenceau was suspect because he opposed an alliance with Russia to counterbalance the menace to France of the Austrian-German-Italian alliance, but he was accused of a sellout to the wrong master.

"M. Clemenceau—who is, as we say, an old radical—has excited suspicion as to his patriotism by denouncing the Russian alliance in his paper, *La Justice*," the *Spectator* said. "It is quite natural that he should denounce it, for the old policy of France, and the steady policy of her radicals, is to protect Poland; but Paris had got a definite prepossession into its head. It was that M. Herz—who, whether guilty or not of the Panama scandals, has almost certainly been fighting for his own hand—was a secret agent of the Triple Alliance, and that he had used his hold over M. Clemenceau to make him resist the alliance which the Central Powers feared. It was expected, therefore, that the 'documents' would show that M. Clemenceau had taken money to denounce Russia; but, lo and behold, the Boulangists accused him of servility to England."

In the view of the old Boulangist partisan, the novelist, Maurice Barres, it was the Chamber's republican majority that was about to do Clemenceau in. "For weeks his colleagues had been combined against him; now they meant to crush him," Barres wrote. " 'Let us have done with him,' you heard them say; or, 'Clemenceau is in a bad fix.'

"Was it because of the sums he had received from Cornelius Herz that they thus forsook him? By no means. My word for it, there was hate, but no sentiment of justice, in the atmosphere of the House. The very genuine hostility to Clemenceau, felt by the majority, was caused by his arrogance, often amounting to insolence. However, to execute him they needed a specific charge; hence their delight when they learned he had been appointed 'English spy.' "

Barres said he heard that the Premier had said, the night before Millevoye's scheduled event: "If M. Clemenceau were a different man, I would have sent for him and advised him to commit suicide."

When the reporters arrived at the Palais Bourbon on Thursday afternoon, they had to fight their way to the Chamber through huge crowds clamoring for seats in the visitors gallery and willing to wait in the sweltering *Salle des Séances* for hours until the session began. The session opened quietly, with terse questioning by Millevoye: "One, where is Cornelius Herz today? Two, what is the state of his health? Three, what is the attitude of the English government toward him?"

Premier Dupuy replied as briskly: Herz was at Bournemouth; two French physicians had endorsed the reports of the English doctors; they had been sent to Bournemouth at the British Foreign Office's request to satisfy the French government as to Herz's condition. The French physicians were Dr. Paul Brouardel, the autopsist in the death of Baron de Reinach, and Dr. J. M. Charcot, the renowned neurologist. (One of Charcot's students at Salpêtrière Hospital in Paris, Dr. Sigmund Freud, of Vienna, was beginning to win fame of his own for his work with hypnosis in the treatment of hysteria.)

Millevoye, carrying a large portfolio, followed the Premier to the tribune. He extracted a paper and began to read, although he was habitually an extemporaneous speaker. "We sat around as if for a 'Judgment of God,'" said Barres, himself a Deputy, "and like the classic chorus, which both participates in events and judges them, we, in remarks that are not all published in the official record, expressed our commentaries on the leading actors."

When the paper Millevoye had read proved to be only a biography of Clemenceau, the presiding officer told him the obituary data was irrelevant and ordered him to put questions to the government if he wanted to keep the floor. He asked promptly what steps were being taken to extradite Herz and to find the fugitive Arton, accused as a bagman in Panama company bribes, and what the government intended to do about the documents stolen from the British Embassy. The Premier climbed back to the tribune to answer him.

Premier: "The government knows its duty in international matters. It is keenly alive to the fact that it cannot take official cognizance of documents of this nature whose origin is suspicious. The government of the Republic cannot think of giving the representatives of foreign powers in this country a feeling of doubt, uncertainty, and insecurity by proposing to bring to this tribune documents which are merely thefts if indeed they are authentic."

Clemenceau: "I ask to speak."

Millevoye (simultaneously): "I accept the entire responsibility."

Premier (continuing): "But we are nonetheless French Ministers, and it was our duty to find out how the papers in question can be examined and sifted. It seemed to us there was but one authority which had the right of examination—namely, the judiciary. The Attorney General this morning opened an inquiry."

Clemenceau: "Some papers have been stolen. And the government has chosen not to accept custody of them. But in France there is a place where we put the products of thefts as well as thieves, and that is the police station. Those who have stolen should answer for their act. But there is a personal question. I am surprised that after having spread the news of the great treason of M. Clemenceau, no one has dared to bring this allegation to the tribune."

Millevoye: "Yes, I have, and I am going to do so."

Clemenceau: "You began a long, written dissertation which has nothing to do with the present question, which is whether or not I have sold my country. If you have any proof of this, bring it forward. I take note of that pledge, and when you have kept it I shall leave this Chamber knowing what I have to do. Meanwhile, I challenge you to prove it. I know your trick. You will be reticent, pretending that patriotism demands it. But that cannot be. You have made definite statements. Explain them. I not only invite M. Millevoye, I challenge him to make good his words."

Millevoye marched down the steps again, his coattail brushing Clemenceau's shoulder as he passed his seat on the way back to the tribune.

Millevoye: "I shall proceed with my indictment. I have written what I have to say, so I will not reply to any interruptions. M. Clemenceau has taken in hand a traitor, a convicted spy, and brought him to the pinnacle of honor. The sense of revenge of a patriot from the Island of Mauritius, not against M. Clemenceau but against England, has placed me in possession of other proofs. The Mauritius and Canada have forgotten nothing."

Presiding Officer: "You must not indulge in such language against a friendly nation, and you are the more inexcusable seeing that your speech is written."

Millevoye (plunging ahead): "This man copied from day to day letters addressed by M. Lister to A. Lee.* The dossier concerns various men and various interests."

Clemenceau: "Give the names!"

Millevoye: "You shall have them before the Assize court."

Clemenceau: "Liar, liar, liar!"

Presiding Officer: "It will not escape M. Millevoye that if he is bound to respect the sentiments of international propriety it is also necessary, and that is why I have left him great latitude, that he should offend neither by omission nor reticence."

Millevoye began to read his purloined letters: " 'Herz has caused us much annoyance. He wishes by all means to leave Bournemouth because Waddington* gave the assurance that the sponge has been passed across Panama. . . .'

" 'The alter ego of Clemenceau has given us copies of all the correspondence that took place between M. Ribot* and M. de Reverseaux*, between M. Ribot and his Ambassadors to Petersburg and Constantinople, between M. de Reverseaux and the Khedive. . . .'

" 'I do not think I have to say that M. Clemenceau is completely rehabilitated in our eyes. We did not suppose that he would be of any further use after the discredit into which he had fallen. But we will keep him on our list. . . .'

" 'You ought not to let the Netherlands out of your sight.' "

The Chamber, a body of men with some knowledge of affairs of state, sat for a moment in astonished silence, digesting the first of these commentaries.

*see Notes

Then a Seine Department Deputy, Camille Dreyfus, called out: "What was the date of that letter?"

"It's the eighteenth of April," Millevoye replied obligingly.

"Isn't it rather the first of April?" Georges Trouillot, a Jura legislator, asked, bringing down the house.

Cutting through the uproar, Millevoye turned in desperation to the Minister of Foreign Affairs to corroborate his interview with the Premier.

The Minister, Jules Develle, replied angrily: "Since, contrary to the promise you gave, you have not kept silent about the interview, you compel me to say that in the Council of Ministers this morning I told my colleagues that you have, in all good faith, been the victim of an abominable hoax."

"No, not the victim! the author!" Clemenceau shouted.

With this, Deroulede bolted from his seat and strode down the tiered incline, clearing his way with powerful breaststrokes and shouting: "I leave this Assembly! I resign as Deputy! I have nothing more to do with politics here!"

"Do the same! There's a good example to follow," a chorus of Deputies urged Millevoye.

Deserted, Millevoye kept stubbornly to his chore, unfolding an official-looking blue paper and reading a few words in English: "These documents have been sent by the bag." Then he began to read from a list of purported disbursements from secret funds—£2,000 each to the *Journal des Débats* and *Le Temps,* and various sums to individuals, among them £20,000 to Clemenceau, £3,600 to Henri Rochefort, the irrepressible editor who had fled to London after his conviction in the Boulanger conspiracy, and £2,000 to Auguste Burdeau, the former Minister of Marine.

These allegations of perfidy were the hardest of all to swallow. Of the *Journal des Débats,* the *Times* of London's leader writer said next morning: "This inheritor of the Anglophobe tradition of John Lemoinne has appeared to be for many years past the sharpest and the most sleepless critic of English policy in Egypt, of English views and ways in general." Of Rochefort, a longtime champion of Irish anarchists, he supposed "they will next suggest that he lives in the Regent's Park because he loves us and not because he is a fugitive from the sentence of the High Court of Justice."

"Very stupidly M. Millevoye took these documents to the tribune of the Chamber and read them," Baron de Coubertin commented in *The Evolution of France under the Third Republic;* "his communication was greeted with tremendous laughter, so plainly did the ridiculous exaggeration of the language and the absurdity of the ideas bespeak the falsity of their origin."

The Chamber's shorthand reporters struggled to record the tumult of the session. Their verbatim account looked like a play script bristling with stage directions: "Lively cheering on a great number of benches," "Protests," "Repeated bravos and cheers from the Left and Center," "Exclamations," "Prolonged din," "Uproar on various benches from the Left and Center."

As Millevoye rode out his recitation on a wave of ironic applause, Burdeau declared: "This list shall not go out from here before having undergone examination by the Chamber. And you, sir, who are reading here documents to which you hope to attribute some calumnious significance, without having the courage to take the responsibility yourself, you shall not leave this house until you have explained yourself as to the sense attached by you to the lines that you have just read, and without declaring whether on your conscience the colleague who stands before you has sold his country for the sum that you have named."

"If this paper is authentic, it is indisputable that I owe no reparation to M. Burdeau, who is then a traitor," Millevoye replied.

"I shall not ask you for it, I won't pay you the honor," Burdeau retorted. "You, sir, have now gone too far not to finish what you have begun, and I am happy to have forced you to unmask all the infamies accumulated in this portfolio. We will finish this business today. You are delivering up to publicity papers which concern not only the ordinary honor but the patriotism of colleagues. You are the accomplice of a thief and perhaps a forger."

A freshman Deputy for the Seine, Adolphe Maujan, proposed a resolution of censure: "The Chamber, stigmatizing the odious and ridiculous calumnies brought forward at the tribune, and regretting that it has wasted the time of the country for a whole sitting, passes to the order of the day." The Chamber adopted it, 384–2, with the Right abstaining.*

Millevoye followed Deroulede's lead and resigned his seat, saying he wanted to be entirely free when he appeared before the judicial inquiry the Government had initiated.

At 6:45 o'clock that night a reporter saw Clemenceau, "radiant and justly so," crossing the Champs Elysées on his way to join some English friends at dinner. A few hours later Millevoye was hissed and denounced at a mass meeting of 1,500 Boulangists. He had disregarded the instructions of his associates. Deroulede, according to Barres, had cautioned Millevoye: "Attend to Clemenceau; read the payments that concern him, in your documents, and those only."

"Had he [Clemenceau] been the only one aimed at, I believe he would have fallen," Barres said ruefully, but with the help of Millevoye's clumsiness, "this little enervated Kalmuck, grown old in one week, but still unbroken in his energy and resourcefulness," managed to triumph.

The Attorney General began his investigation at once and traced the Millevoye-*La Cocarde* disclosures to the penmanship of a grifter known around Paris as "Norton." The records of Alphonse Bertillon's anthropometric bureau showed him to be Louis Alfred Veron, not a Mauritian patriot, as Millevoye had said, but an Algiers-born forger and swindler who had been convicted three times in France.

Ducret, the editor of *La Cocarde,* told the examining magistrate that Norton, professing to be a translator at the British Embassy, had offered him documents written in English and that Millevoye's seconds, the Marquis de Mores and de Dion, who spoke English well, believed they had been written by an educated, intelligent man, in elegant yet colloquial style beyond Norton's capacity. He said the de Mores children's English teacher had translated the letters.

Norton insisted he had acted on instructions from Ducret, who had sent for him in January. He said he understood the editor was acting as agent for certain politicians. Norton said he had demanded a 100,000-franc fee to forge the documents, but settled for 85,000—70,000 down and the rest later—of which

*Opposed, Admiral d'Hornoy, reactionist, and August Engerand, Boulangist.

he received only 10,000. He confessed when he learned that an agent of the Marquis de Mores and Millevoye had gotten the 10,000 back from Mme. Norton.

When the investigators examined Millevoye's documents and checked the reference books, they found that the manufacturers of the documents had used the wrong middle initial in the signature, original sin for editors, fatal for forgers. There was no "Sir Thomas W. Lister" in the British foreign service; the gentleman in Whitehall was Sir Thomas Villiers Lister.

The case against Norton, charged with forgeries, and Ducret, with complicity in them, went to trial at 10:30 o'clock on Saturday morning, August 5. Clemenceau applied successfully to be made a party to the prosecution and claimed damages of 1 franc. Rochefort made a smiliar application from London, but it was denied on the ground that he was in contempt of court, being a fugitive from justice for four years.

Expert witnesses testified that the documents had been written first in French and then translated into English. Millevoye, wreathed in parliamentary immunity, appeared only as a witness. He refused to answer questions put to him by Clemenceau, who commented, "It is better not to answer than to tell lies," and called him and Deroulede "patriots by profession." Norton testified that he had been offered a job on the staff of *Le Petit Journal* if the plot succeeded. Clemenceau told the jurors that *Le Petit Journal,* in its coverage of the affair, had not even mentioned the Chamber's resolution of censure, and charged that Marinoni, then the paper's proprietor, had given Norton 5,000 francs. "It was this money that has brought Norton and Ducret to the dock," he said.

At 2 o'clock on Sunday morning the case went to the jury, which took a half hour to arrive at a verdict of guilty with extenuating circumstances and to award Clemenceau the 1 franc he had asked for. Norton was sentenced to three years in prision, Ducret to a year; and each was fined 100 francs. *The New York Times* pondered whether Ducret's sentence meant that "the editor was aware that he had circulated forgeries or that an editor who believed the forgeries to be genuine was such a fool that he ought to be shut up for a season." It reached the conclusion that "either proposition appears to be plausible."

Although Ducret and Norton were the men accused, the court became the arena for a violent encounter between Clemenceau and the Marquis de Mores, who came to the trial from a crushing judical defeat of his own, which the *Times* of London had described in painful detail in a dispatch the week before: "Paris, July 25: The Marquis de Mores, son of the Duke of Vallombrosa, and one of the persons concerned in the Norton affair, has today at the instance of his father been deprived of the management of his property. The judgment of the court states that he had led a life of costly and foolish adventures, that on coming of age he possessed 1,800,000 francs, that at his marriage with an American heiress was heavily in debt, that he borrowed 217,000 francs of his mother-in-law, that he went to America to start cooperative butcher shops, that in 1885 his scheme collapsed and that he is still trying to borrow money at high interest. Mme. de Mores's application for a separation of property was rejected."*

Clemenceau's interrogation of de Mores degenerated quickly into an exchange of insults and challenges, with de Mores shouting that he had known for two years that Clemenceau was a British agent and would tell him so anywhere.

"Would it be indiscreet to demand upon what information he founds that opinion?" Clemenceau prodded him.

"A year ago the Russian Ambassador sent for me," de Mores began, when the judge cut him off and ordered him from the witness rail. He strode away shaking his fist at Clemenceau and screaming, "You are in the pay of a foreign government! We shall meet again in the Var"—a threat that referred to Clemenceau's candidacy in the forthcoming general election.

Addressing the court, Clemenceau said: "MM. de Mores and de Dion came today to insult me. Why? I do not know them. M. de Mores accuses me of treason. Why?" Suddenly he asked with ostensible casualness: "How does he formulate these accusations, the man who recently borrowed money from Cornelius Herz, the man whose brother-in-law recently was German ambassador to Madrid?"

To a student of Clemenceau's forensic tactics, the disclosure of de Mores's debt to Herz in this manner was a character-

*see Notes

istic ploy. A *Times* of London correspondent described it admiringly, saying: "He speaks only when it is necessary, and than tells only so much of the truth as can serve his purpose at the time. The usual result is that the person attacked loses all self-control and in replying betrays confidences which it was just M. Clemenceau's intention to avoid revealing himself but which he counted on his opponent to reveal."

Humiliated to be shown up as a man under obligation to a Jew at the moment he was striving to make his mark as an anti-Semite, de Mores took the bait and rushed into print with a melancholy explanation in which he blurted out that his mentor, Drumont, one of France's most vicious anti-Semites, had gone along to Herz to help get the loan.

"At the end of the 1889 campaign," de Mores explained in *Le Figaro,* having no newspaper of his own, "I was arrested the first of May, condemned by M. Constans to three months in prison, deprived of my civil rights for five years, abandoned and persecuted by my own. Moreover, I fell gravely ill; because of this illness I was obliged to ask a reprieve from the completion of my sentence. On leaving prison, in consequence of the sacrifices I made and the impossibility of taking care of my affairs during my imprisonment, I found myself in a very difficult situation. In the spring of 1891 I had to pay the sum of 20,000 francs in a hurry. I tried some friends. I was defeated. I found all doors shut. Finally I came to the house of M. Andrieux, with whom I was on good terms, and I disclosed my situation to him. He replied, 'I'll take care of it. Come back tomorrow.'

"Next day he told me, 'Only one man in Paris will lend you this money, but for this he wants Drumont to make the request.'"

The one man who would lend de Mores money was the inscrutable Andrieux's client, Cornelius Herz. He lent the Marquis 20,000 francs for a year. "Herz told Drumont," de Mores said, "that the interest on his loan was the presence of Drumont in his, Herz's, home."

The Marquis said he had to ask for an extension, but eventually paid off, remitting the principal plus interest to Andrieux.

Drumont, exasperated that his protégé had talked, exclaimed in his own newspaper: "What I find extraordinary is that Mores thought he had to bring in my name, which Clemenceau had the good taste not to mention."

Nourished by Drumont's pique, Clemenceau's small slip burgeoned with still gaudier revelations. "In the spring of 1891," Drumont wrote in the *Libre Parole,* " Mores had lost a big amount of money at the Rue Royale Club and he couldn't pay. He was going to be posted and this is very grave in those places. He talked about blowing his brains out. He spoke first with Andrieux. Father of a family, Andrieux could not furnish the necessary 20,000."

Nor did Drumont have either the desire or the means to "throw 20,000 francs down the pit of baccarat," he said, but he wanted to be useful to de Mores, who "with patrician prodigality consumed a fortune in the charming life of a young cavalry officer"; thus he was willing to endure "a boring visit" to Herz's home.

"In discussing the visit publicly, without being under any compulsion to do so," Drumont said reprovingly, "Mores knew perfectly well that he was causing me, on the other hand, if not chagrin, at least an annoyance. The most elementary delicacy would have compelled him to ask, before writing anything, whether it would be disagreeable for me to have my name mixed up in this story.

"A child of the people would have had the tact, which does not come from education but from natural character, breeding, and refinement, to have said 'I do not want to cause any embarrassment to a friend who has tried to get me out of a jam.' "

Scorched by his friend's rebuke, the Marquis hurried to the Var to help organize a violent campaign against Clemenceau, with the generous support of *Le Petit Journal.* Hired gangs of hecklers followed Clemenceau about, screaming continuously with lynch-mob levity, "Ow yes" and "Rosbif," which they seemed to believe indicative of the English language and of Clemenceau's attachments to Britain.

The election, the first since the outbreak of the Panama scandal, brought the republicans a tremendous victory. They gained sixty seats. Of the Deputies accused in the affair, only Proust and Dugue de la Fauconnerie, who was a Bonapartist, were defeated. Delahaye, whose charge of wholesale bribery of the National Assembly detonated the explosion, lost his seat in the Chamber, as did Naquet and Barres, "waifs of Boulangism." Andrieux, trying to get back in office, lost in the Seventh Arrondissement of Paris. The voters also turned down Drumont, who was running for Millevoye's seat at Amiens.

Six candidates opposed Clemenceau for the seat for Draguignan. On election day, May 20, he was high man on the ballot with a plurality of more than 1,600 votes; but he did not win a majority and a run-off was necessary. In the run-off the socialists and reactionaries formed a coalition to defeat him; they gave the seat to Joseph Jourdan, the conservative candidate.

By the time Clemenceau returned to office, in 1902, as a member of the Senate, most of the old Panama cast, principals and extras alike, were gone from the script and production of the epic transferred to new management. Ferdinand de Lesseps was dead at eighty-nine, de Mores murdered by Touareg tribesmen in North Africa, Deroulede banished to Spain for trying to foment an uprising, the canal company's concession and property peddled to the United States.

"Clemenceau's exact role in the story is not yet fully revealed," says his biographical sketch in the *Dictionnaire des Parlementaires Français, 1889-1940,* compiled under the direction of Jean Jolly, archivist of the National Assembly. "Has he been very kind to the crook Cornelius Herz, who was one of the secret partners of his newspaper *La Justice?* Or does he let himself be taken in by him?"

When Clemenceau was an aged man, he said: "Cornelius Herz was a bad lot; unfortunately this wasn't written on the tip of his nose."

11

This is the story of Cornelius Herz, a man who craved renown and achieved dishonor.

Herz was an obscure young physician who moved from San Francisco to Paris in 1877 with a head full of gamy schemes for getting rich in a hurry.

In less than fifteen years he had a lot of money, fine houses, close associations with some of the most important men in Europe, and the Grand Cross of the Legion of Honor, France's highest honor; and he managed his affairs so discreetly that scarcely a faint glimmer of them showed beyond the upper reaches of politics and finance.

But on the morning of November 20, 1892, his closest associate, Baron de Reinach, under attack in the scandal press and facing prosecution in the Panama affair, was found dead in his bed only a few hours after he had turned to Herz in a desperate plea for help, having taken along Clemenceau and Rouvier to reinforce his appeal.

The revelation of the rich, important banker grabbing at Herz's coattails for salvation, feeling he needed the presence of two of France's most powerful politicians to bolster his plea, stalled Herz's surge and tripped him into an endless spin toward ruin. It became the vehicle that carried him to world-wide notoriety as the reputed possessor of demonic powers over the government, and made him the man most detested and inveighed against of the multitude suspected of complicity in the Panama affair.

Herz's predilection for dwelling in the company of power, in an atmosphere of intrigue, colored him such a dark shade of mystery that speculation on his true stature in France swelled into a matter for parliamentary debate.

"I am astonished that protests should be raised when I say in this Chamber that M. Cornelius Herz has been one of the chief men in France," Paul Deroulede shouted to his fellow Deputies in the speech that provoked his duel with Clemenceau.

"Certainly not, you're kidding people!" the Count of Douville-Maillefeu retorted. "To say that M. Cornelius Herz has been one of the important personages of the French nation is an insanity!"

Even so eminently briefed a Paris observer as Emily Crawford, of the *New York Tribune* and the *London Daily News,* professed surprise at the influence attributed to Herz. "It has dawned on those who were in the inner circles of French and indeed European politics," she wrote, "that Herz was a man who held some very strong cards and who knew how to play them. But few who knew the wire-pulling world of Paris had any idea that he played so great and underhand a part in public affairs."

Such readily verifiable details as his birthplace, his early education and his citizenship turned into items of wild conjecture. Some of his detractors said his first business venture was a small banking house in Bucharest, which had failed, that he was born in a Frankfort slum, that he did not become a United States citizen until the 1870's, making him a German subject at the time he was in the French army in the Franco-Prussian War.

Some of his staunchest advocates were no more accurate. One of his most eminent defenders, both in the British Parliament and in print, was Sir Edward J. Reed, a renowned naval architect who left the admiralty for politics and became a perennial champion of controversial causes.

Reed, briefed on Herz's life and affairs in sufficient minutiae to write a 9,000-word panegyric about him for a respected London magazine, was permitted to say that Herz was graduated with honors from the College of the City of New York, was a lieutenant in the United States Army at the age of sixteen, became Chief Medical Officer of Mount Sinai Hospital, New York, and founded "the great California Electrical Works"—all not quite correct.

The Panama Affair

Cornelius Herz was born at 32 rue des Granges in Besançon, the principal city of the Franche-Comté region of eastern France, at 6 p.m. on September 3, 1845. His parents were Leopold Herz, a native of Rheinburckheim in the Grand Duchy of Hesse, and Adelaide Friedmann Herz, a Bavarian. The Herz family emigrated to the United States in 1849, and Leopold Herz became a packing box manufacturer in New York. He was admitted to United States citizenship on May 8, 1854, in the Court of Common Pleas of the City and County of New York; under the Federal laws then in force, his family derived United States citizenship through his naturalization.*

In July, 1859, Cornelius Herz, along with 375 other boys, took the entrance examination for the College of the City of New York, then the Free Academy, a school with rigid standards of scholarship and deportment. He was one of 324 accepted. The average age of the students was fifteen years, four months, fifteen days; Herz was not quite fourteen.

At sixteen he was not a lieutenant in the United States Army, but was dutifully attending classes on Manhattan Island in the three-story Gothic edifice at Lexington Avenue and Twenty-third Street which James Renwick, architect of New York's Grace Church and of St. Patrick's Cathedral, had designed for the Free Academy. Herz lived a quarter of a mile away, at 216 East Eighteenth Street.

In those days the school offered a five-year curriculum, the first year comprising an introductory period. Herz had six semesters each of English, French, mathematics, and philosophy, five of Spanish, four each of German and drawing, three each of chemistry and history, and two each of engineering and mixed mathematics, which consisted of natural philosophy and astronomy.

Students were graded "highest," "high," "good," and "low." Herz had grades of "high" every semester until the last two, when he dropped to "good." Instead of being graduated with the honors Reed attributed to him, he was thirty-first in a class that had shrunk to 39.

He was graduated in 1864, went back to Europe and studied medicine, or at least found out enough about it to become an assistant surgeon major in the French army of the Loire in the

*see Notes

Franco-Prussian War. According to Reed, he attended the Universities of Heidelberg, Munich, Vienna, and Paris, and took lectures at the Sorbonne and the College of France.

While he was in Europe his family moved from New York to Chicago, and he went there on his return from France, arriving just in time to see the city destroyed by the fire of 1871. Soon afterward he moved back to New York, where Mount Sinai took him on, but not as Chief Medical Officer, the rank Reed assigned to him.

Herz was house physician and surgeon at Mount Sinai for a brief period in 1873. The one reference to his service that survives in the hospital's archives almost a century after his residency is there only because in 1939 Miss Carrie Pollitzer, of 5 Pitt Street, Charleston, S.C., wrote on behalf of her mother, Mrs. Clara Guinzburg Pollitzer, to ask for some information about the old days at the institution. Dr. Joseph Turner, the superintendent of the hospital, recalling that Mrs. Pollitzer was a niece of Dr. Seligman Teller, house physician in 1860-1872, instructed an assistant to dig up information on which to base a reply. The investigator, recounting the succession of residents, put the following note in the files: "Dr. Cornelius Hertz [sic] held the position for three months and was then asked to resign. He had very ingeniously avoided taking the examination for house physician and surgeon, and it was suspected— later proven that his supposed graduation from the University of Paris was fictitious. When asked for his diploma he always insisted that it had been burned in the Chicago fire."

While the Mount Sinai records do not disclose the name of his sponsor, Reed identified him as "the great Dr. Brown-Sequard," whom Herz may have known. He may even have been influenced by Dr. Charles Edouard Brown-Sequard, a Mauritius-born neurologist whose description of the technique of Faradic induction, published in his first volume of *Animal Electricity* in 1848, led to its wide use as a new method of stimulation. After serving as professor of neuropathology at Harvard's medical school in 1865-1867, he lived in Paris at the same time Herz was supposedly studying there and he was living at 18 East Twenty-ninth Street, New York, not far from Herz's old home, when the young man returned from Europe with a hunger for high living and a conviction that the newly emerging electricity industry was a sure way to satisfy it.

When Herz turned up in San Francisco in 1874, after his Mount Sinai adventure, he proclaimed himself an "electrical doctor" and presented a new modality for some of the accepted quackery of the day. One of the innovations he proposed was a caloric engine that would heat a delicate platinum-tipped instrument for use in treating insomnia. It was to supplant the old-fashioned searing iron that some practitioners were applying to the backs of sleepless patients to eliminate tension on the nerves deploying from the spinal column. Herz said his instrument retained and conducted heat more effectively.

When James W. Marshall found gold at Sutter's Mill in 1848, San Francisco was a village of scarcely 800 residents; by the time Herz arrived there, only a quarter of a century later, its population had exploded to nearly 200,000. In a town for which the reception of a throng of strangers from every part of the world had become a daily habit, Herz found ready friendship and hospitality.

He was a short, pudgy man with a big, round face, a high forehead and dun-colored hair, inconspicuous-looking except when he spoke of his accomplishments and his aspirations, and then his eyes shone with a sharp intelligence and he became a man who enticed belief.

"He told of marvelous cures abroad and talked of kings, queens, and princes as if they had been his favorite friends," an anonymous reporter for the *San Francisco Evening Bulletin* recalled, "yet he was not boastful, nor was his egotism ever offensive. He was a man of the world, apparently well-equipped for his profession, yet with a sanguine, sky-scraping temperament that made him soar above men and to seek wonderful and world-stripping achievements. A dozen valuable inventions were his—a hundred marvelous scientific processes were to be worked out by his genius. His application of electricity differed from that of his medical associates. Electricity is life, was his argument. It flows from the generator, the brain. Any lessening of the vivifying influences must be renewed by artificial means. Disease is simply a break in the circuit or a diversion of the life power from its proper channel."

His practice grew sensationally, and three years after his arrival in San Francisco he tiptoed out of it, his pockets filled with money from patients, friends, and associates who were scarcely aware that he had tapped them for it or that he had no intention of coming back.

He headed straight for Paris, a city 1900 years older than the one he had just left, but a wide-open town for a young man with ideas and a well-bankrolled audacity. The whole country, in paying off the huge tribute Bismarck had exacted in the Franco-Prussian War, had worked itself into a high state of prosperity. Several summers of fine weather had produced abundant harvests. Savings bank deposits had almost doubled since the disaster at Sedan. Railways, canals, and harbors were being built. The relatively bright glare of electric light illuminated an enormous potential in a brand new industry in which Herz demonstrated a shrewd sense of the consumer wants of heliocentric man.

"In electricity as in all other things," he said, "the principal thing is to be able to create mass markets. This simple reflection led me to this observation: the production of light should be one of the most productive enterprises, because if one came to manufacture good light there would be no limit to its sale because the world in the past has lived half the time deprived of the light of the sun.

"From this fact we can proceed to turn from supplying an ordinary want of civilization into supplying an urgent need which makes the market for artificial light as sure as the market for food and clothing. Furthermore, by the same process of evolution, buyers of commodities that are basic necessities, as soon as progress makes them ready, are always prone to force the supplier to give them a more and more lifelike quality.

"For the commodity of light the public is wrong in depending on the gas companies for the reason that for simple people the ideal is that which approximates natural daylight. The public has incontestably taken the taste for a light which is intense and white, and they demand it at all times."

Herz had been in Paris only a few months when he and Dr. C. C. Soulages, whom he had known during his previous sojourn there, formed a business to exploit the incandescent-lamp patents of Richard Werdermann, a German inventor. Next, he founded a well regarded scientific and industrial review, *La Lumière Electrique,* which brought out its first issue on April

15, 1879. (It continued to be published under the same name until January, 1917, when it was merged with *La Revue Electrique* to form *La Revue Générale de L'Electricité*).

Herz's by-line began to appear on learned articles, and his signature on letters to his editor, in which he mingled boasts of his achievements with protests of his modesty. "I do not think that my efforts, crowned with success as they were, have closed the door to all progress on the subject of artificial lighting," he wrote, adding plaintively; "I would be desolated if this were so, because it would deprive me of the pleasure of finding myself again in the vanguard of future progress."

He called himself a man who "has judged people and situations well, has been able to forge ahead up to now by intuition and common sense, and from the beginning has never failed to be proved right." Ernest A. Vizetelly, a London journalist who lived in Paris, "once heard him insinuate that some of Edison's inventions were really his own."

Promptly after establishing a business base in Paris, Herz set out to ingratiate himself with French politicians, taking on willingly the most piddling errands to win their favor. Among his souvenirs was the following note from Agenor Bardoux, Minister of Public Education, dated February 21, 1878: "Sir: I have the honor to inform you that I have entrusted MM. Andre and Angot with a mission to America, to Ogden in the Territory of Utah, to take astronomical and photographic observations of the transit of Mercury across the Sun next May. I should be grateful to you, sir, if you would be so good as to assist in the accomplishment of this very interesting mission by using your influence with the railway companies which run the train service between New York and Ogden. Thanks to your influence, MM. Andre and Angot might obtain free passes going and returning, and the free carriage of their luggage or, at any rate, a considerable reduction on the ordinary rates. This would be an inestimable benefit to these learned gentlemen and would enormously facilitate their difficult task."

What Herz might have told the Minister to suggest such influence with the Union Pacific Railroad, and what he did about the request, were not indicated by pleaders of his cause.

Herz cultivated the acquaintance of Senator Adrien Hebrard, the powerful publisher of *Le Temps*. He met Clemenceau through Hebrard, "which was not a bad sponsorship," Clemenceau commented later. Herz impressed him so well that when Clemenceau, estranged from his wife, went to Marseilles to help fight a cholera epidemic in the 1880's, he left an instruction: "In case of death I want my children raised under the direction of M. Cornelius Herz."

Other important men became Herz's associates. He founded an electrical syndicate with Hebrard, de Reinach, Paul Dalloz, director of the *Moniteur Universel,* Jules Bapst, director of the *Journal des Débats,* and Georges Berger, Superintendent General of Exhibitions. James G. Blaine, President Garfield's Secretary of State, appointed Herz honorary delegate of the United States to the International Congress of Electricians held in connection with the International Electrical Exhibition in Paris late in the summer of 1881. Blaine told him in the letter of appointment that his name had been "strongly presented" by the United States executive commissioner to the exhibition. The next year Herz and his syndicate partners formed a committee to promote the Munich Electrical Exhibition.

Herz became a heavy backer of Marcel Deprez, the physicist, in experiments in the long-distance transmission of electricity, a venture in which the Rothschild banking house also was associated. When the Academy of Sciences honored Deprez in 1885 for his success, he gave fervent thanks "first and foremost" to Herz, "who during two years supported with the greatest energy and with all the means in his power the cause of electrical transmission of force to a great distance, and thanks to whom I was able to carry out the experiments of Munich, the Northern Railway, and Grenoble."

By now Herz had risen far beyond such petty political contracts as cadging railroad passes for junketing savants. He was a savant in his own right. He soared through the grades of the Legion of Honor, and when he reached the peak on March 28, 1886, becoming the first United States citizen to receive the Grand Cross, his friend, General Georges Boulanger, wrote to him emotionally: "No one was more worthy than you to obtain it because of the services which you have rendered and are daily rendering to science and to your adopted country. All true Frenchmen will rejoice, but none of them will be as happy as your devoted friend who cordially shakes both your hands."

When Boulanger, as Minister of War, sent a military mission to the United States six months later to buy machinery for the manufacture of the Lebel rifle, the small-caliber repeater that succeeded the chassepot as the French army's standard weapon, Herz's man, Leon Chabert, an engineer, was on hand to meet the officers in New York and put them in touch with equipment manufacturers.

Herz had a piece of the financing of the rifle's manufacture. He also had money in the Wenger railway air brake. He owned real estate in Paris, in Berlin, in Aix-les-Bains. He had a mansion at 37 avenue Kleber, near the Etoile, and later moved to another at 78 avenue Henri Martin, not far from the Bois. He became an art collector—a classic short cut to status for hustlers of every age and place.* He soared from political errand boy to the central spot in a labyrinthine scheme to detach Italy from the Triple Alliance and make her an ally of France.

To help pave the way in Italy for Herz "to open a fresh field for his activity in the interest of both our countries," General Luigi Menabrea, a noted physicist and mathematician who was Italy's Ambassador to France, beseeched the French Premier and Foreign Minister, Charles de Freycinet, to have the Republic grant "some new distinction" to Herz, "whose high scientific attainments have won him the support of all the votaries of science."

Herz and Francesco Crispi, Premier of Italy, exchanged letters, addressing one another "My dear Crispi" and "My dear

---

*(Herz had a multitudinous collection, but its accumulation did not reflect his customary shrewdness. When Christie's sold it for Mrs. Herz in April, 1899, its 186 oil paintings, 13 watercolors, and 14 drawings brought scarcely 270,000 francs. There were a few good works—Charles Francois Daubigny's "Banks of the Seine," then regarded as one of his best, a river scene by Carot, Fromentin's "The Halt," two Venetian scenes by Ziem, Carolus Duran's "Lady in First Empire Costume," a portrait of the Poissy stationmaster that Messonier had painted on a 3-by-2-inch panel to keep a promise to the railroad man, a Rousseau seascape, two small panels by Troyon, a Detaille monochrome. But for the most part, Herz's art investments failed to work out. For example, he was an enthusiastic supporter of Georges Croegaert, a Belgian who showed at the Paris Salon in the 1880's; he owned 17 of Croegaert's paintings, but all Christie's could get for the lot of them was 3,625 francs.)

Herz." Herz hired Louis Guillot, the Deputy for Isère, as his private secretary. Levi P. Morton, United States Ambassador to France, invited Herz to dinner. Joseph Bertrand, permanent secretary of the Academy of Sciences, wrote to Herz "with hearty thanks for the persistent generosity of the doctor toward distressed men of science." Ferdinand de Lesseps autographed a photograph to him, "*Souvenir au brave Dr. C. Herz.*" The *Journal de Goncourt* mentioned him, a retrospective approximation of a mention in today's gossip columns; it said: "Frantz Jourdain,* who has come to spend the day, expatiates on the intrigues of Clemenceau and of Wilson with Dr. Herz." It was Herz, said Charles de Lesseps, who introduced him to Daniel Wilson's father-in-law, Jules Grevy, President of France, taking him along for a visit at the President's country home at Mont-sous-Vaudrey.

The attempt to define Herz's association with the Panama Canal Company was the fiercest and most ramifying legal conflict the company's bankruptcy produced. Almost from the instant Herz revealed that de Reinach had paid him 2,000,000 francs out of the company's cornucopia, the controversy created a dangerous issue for a procession of French ministries and an expensive embarrassment to the British government. For a brief time one aspect of it was even an item on the agenda of the State Department of the United States.

Herz protested that his association with the Panama Canal Company was entirely tangential. Charles de Lesseps insisted it amounted to a hold-up. Testifying before the examining magistrate who prepared the instructions in the bribery case against him, Charles de Lesseps said that Herz had forced himself on the company while it was trying, for the first time, to get government permission to run the lottery in order to sweeten its big bond issue.

"M. Herz, who had often met my father as a member of the Academy of Sciences, sought him out," he said, "and stressing that he, Herz, had great influence, asked to be put in charge of the financial role of the issue, saying he'd take all the necessary steps to assure the passage of the law through his personal influence."

*(Frantz Jourdain, rambunctious Belgian architect and publisher.)

A letter attesting the agreement and approving the financial outlays of the bond issue was drawn up, he said, and Herz began to demand money as soon as the document was in his hands.

"How much did Cornelius Herz take either from the company or from de Reinach," the magistrate asked de Lesseps, who had been brought from Mazas Prision for the interrogation.

"I don't know what M. Cornelius Herz got from M. de Reinach," he said. "I know the Panama company paid him a sum of 600,000 francs in September and December, 1885, a first sum of 100,000 and a second of 500,000."

He said he had discounted notes for 600,000 francs that Herz held from a contractor named Dauderni, who died before the scandal broke and thus could not be called for corroboration; when Herz began to pressure the company for money, de Lesseps said, he handed back the notes, thus paying off "to get M. Cornelius Herz off our back." He protested repeatedly that Herz had powerful political connections and was therefore "not a person the company could alienate."

He said he returned the Dauderni paper either to Herz or de Reinach; he did not specify which one, or when. He thought it was at the same time that he got back the letter of agreement, put it in a sealed envelope, and deposited it with a *notaire*— that much-esteemed man of trust whose counsel and quasi-legal services are almost indispensable to the conduct of the personal affairs of the French. He said his notary, Maître Mahot de la Querantonnais, did not know the contents of the envelope, which bore an inscription approximately as follows: "If this letter hasn't been retrieved by such and such a date, the paper will be burned."

"This paper was burned by me in Maître Mahot's presence after the deadline indicated in the inscription," de Lesseps said. "I haven't seen Herz since. It was in 1887 that the envelope was burned."

From this 600,000-franc beginning, the legend of Herz's gleanings from the Panama harvest began to expand until it became a 10,000,000-franc blackmail that bled Baron de Reinach of his fortune; Herz's most relentlesss accuser, Albert Imbert, the court-appointed administrator of de Reinach's estate, named that sum as the price for which the doctor had peddled his influence to de Lesseps. He said Herz had insisted that de Reinach endorse the contract as the canal company's financial agent, but then used the endorsement to force the Baron into a lifelong pay-off that ruined him.

Herz's name began to sprinkle the newspapers of Europe and the United States on December 3, 1892, the day the canal company investigation identified him as the recipient of "bearer" checks for 2,000,000 francs. The references were miniscule at first, such as the *New York Herald's:* "Two checks for one million francs each bear the name of Cornelius Herz, the electrician;" but in San Francisco they were clue enough to stir the city editor of the *Evening Bulletin* to enter a momentous instruction on his assignment sheet. On December 10 the assignment produced a page-one story that revealed the genesis of the bankroll Herz had brought to Paris.

W. H. Lyon, a retired brewer with an almost pathological concern for his credit rating, had been one of Herz's wealthy patients in San Francisco, the *Bulletin* reported; "the baker was paid daily for bread delivered, and sunset never came with Mr. Lyon owing any man a cent."

"Shortly after Dr. Herz disappeared, Mr. Lyon was surprised almost to madness by the receipt of a note from a leading bank calling attention to the fact that Mr. Lyon's note for $10,-000 would shortly fall due," the story continued. "In amazement, Mr. Lyon went to the bank and there saw his signature, which he could not dispute, affixed to a note for $10,000. The money was drawn by Dr. Herz. A week later came another note from the bank, and investigation by Mr. Lyon revealed a second note for $10,000, also discounted by Dr. Herz. Other notices followed fast, with the result that Mr. Lyon found that Herz had obtained $80,000 on eight notes of $10,000 each. His supposition was that Herz had had him make these notes while under electrical treatment and in a sort of hypnotic condition. Mr. Lyon went to Paris and besieged the doctor, but never got his money back."

The *Bulletin* rested on its scoop, and twelve days later the *San Francisco Examiner* captured the story; on December 22 the *Examiner* enlightened its readers with a three-column account under the following page-1 headline:

The Panama Affair

A ROBBER OF HIGH DEGREE

DR. CORNELIUS HERZ, THE PANAMA CANAL SHARK

LEFT MANY SAN FRANCISCO VICTIMS

MEDICAL CHARLATAN AND CONFIDENCE MAN
FLEECED RICH AND POOR OUT OF THOUSANDS

STORY OF HIS PACIFIC CAREER

How Lyon, the rich brewer, was duped out of
$100,000 by the slick sharper. Milton S. La-
tham paid $30,000 to experience; Seiler, Ladd,
Keating, and some prominent Hebrews
fleeced; member of the Health Board; robbery
of Dr. Stout; talks with the victims.

These disclosures churned up a week-long sensation in the
newspapers of Herz's old home towns—New York and Chicago
as well as San Francisco. He had turned up on the West Coast,
their stories said, with a young wife, the former Bianca Saroni
of New York, $700 in cash, and a medical library consisting
solely of John Mayne's *Dispensatory and Therapeutical
Remembrancer,* a twenty-six-year-old, 329-page work in which
"prescriptions for all diseases known and mythical were
printed in technical phrases so that they might be copied by an
uninformed medical man and serve to conceal his ignorance of
the principles of *materia medica.*"

Learning that Dr. James Simpson, another young physician, had recently opened an office at Kearney and Sutter
Streets, which he used only in the afternoons, Herz rented it
from him for morning office hours. Moving in, he promptly
hung out a shingle stating that he himself was a pupil of "the
famous Dr. Soulage of Paris, a specialist of diseases of the
brain."

The next year, just when California adopted a law demanding acceptable evidence of a medical education from everyone
prescribing for the sick, Herz announced that his father was
gravely ill in Chicago and rushed there, leaving his wife and an

ailing infant daughter in Dr. Simpson's care. Immediately on his return, four weeks later, he submitted to the California Board of Examiners a diploma dated March 10, 1874, from the Chicago Medical College, whose register he had signed "Cornelius Herz, B.S., M.S., College of the City of New York," although the City College records show only a bachelor's degree for him.

His new credentials were good enough to win him an appointment to the Board of Health of the City and County of San Francisco; Governor Romauldo Pacheco of California appointed him on September 18, 1875.

Herz also won the confidence of Dr. A.B. Stout, a respected practitioner with a fine medical library. They formed a partnership and set up offices in the Adams Building in Kearney Street, in a $250-a-month suite that bristled with Herz's electrical gadgetry and quickly became the gathering place for devotees of modish medicine.

Herz was a teetotaler, smoked only a little, and lived in modest lodgings, but he spent money lavishly on horses and carriages, fine clothes for himself, and small parties at theaters that offered facilities for entertaining backstage.

In 1877 Dr. Herz and his family, consisting of his wife and two small daughters, Irma and Edna, sailed for Europe from New York on the steamship *Etruria,* just three hours after he had cashed a $30,000-draft from Milton S. Latham, president of the London & San Francisco Bank. The draft was drawn on Drexel, Morgan & Co., the New York bankers, to whom Latham, a trifle late in growing suspicious, had telegraphed a stop-payment order. While Latham was his patient, Herz had induced him to invest in the Paris electrical industry.

Other contributors to Herz's economic development did not learn of their misfortune so promptly. One of them was Paul Seiler, an electrician with whom the doctor formed the firm of Seiler & Herz. "I thought I could protect my own interests well enough, even if I did know he was a fraud, so I formed the partnership," Seiler said.

He paid $13,000 for his overconfidence. Notes bearing the firm's signature came pouring in on him after Herz left town.

Seiler insisted that Herz did not know an anode from a

cathode; either Seiler spoke from rage or Herz found a competent ghost writer when he got to Paris.

Other victims the newspapers listed were the San Francisco Almshouse superintendent, M. J. Keating, a Democratic politician whom Herz took for $4,000; George S. Ladd, a brother Mason in Mount Moriah Lodge, who donated $5,000, and Dr. Stout, who learned after Herz's disappearance that he was on his departed associate's paper for a total of $20,000 and went bankrupt trying to make it good.

Two stubborn San Franciscans got their money back, the *Examiner* reported. One was J.W. Winter, a neighbor of Herz and Stout in the Adams Building, who went to Paris and collected $1,500. The other was Stephen D. Field, an engineer who was a nephew of Cyrus Field, financier of the Atlantic cable. He chipped in $1,500 for the exercise of Herz's supposed influence in Paris to win concessions for several of Field's patented telephonic devices, including an electric call box. He traveled to Paris with Herz, and when Herz shaved off his beard as their train neared Chicago, it dawned on Field that the doctor did not want to be recognized in his old college town. In Paris, when it became evident that Herz was attempting to exploit the relationship with Cyrus Field, the inventor determined to get his money and go home. He burst in on Herz one morning with the announcement that he needed $1,000 in a hurry for an important trip to London, and Herz handed over the cash readily.

San Franciscans, who had seen Herz in the full exercise of his continental charm, were far less astonished to learn of the heights to which he had scrambled than were the doctor's City College classmates and teachers. One of them told the *New York World:* "Nobody who knew Herz ever thought he would amount to anything." David Leventritt, a classmate who became a New York State Supreme Court Justice and later chairman of the New York City Bar Association's Character Committee, remembered him as "just an average kind of chap," a "short, stout fellow with nothing striking about him." In the recollection of Professor Adolph Werner, Herz's old teacher of German language and literature, "he didn't do anything to attract attention to him and consequently he escaped especial notice."

Herz was in London when the Panama scandal caught up

with him. It was his custom to spend his winters in England, where his three older children, Irma, Edna, and fourteen-year-old Raoul Caliste, were being educated. The boy was at Eton, where his housemaster was the Rev. Arthur C. Benson, son of the Archbishop of Canterbury; Herz's three younger children were with their mother in Paris.

Summoned to appear before the investigating committee of the Chamber of Deputies on December 13, ten days after he had telegraphed that he was the man who had cashed the two 1,000,000-franc "bearer" checks, Herz sent his excuses and attached a medical certificate stating that he was suffering of diabetes, albumenuria, and "incidental bad health," and could not risk the journey across the Channel. Dr. Thomas Lauder Brunton, discoverer of the use of amyl nitrite in the treatment of angina pectoris, and Drs. David Ferrier and Malcolm Macdonald McHardy, professors of neuropathology and ophthalmology, respectively, at King's College, London had signed the certificate.

The patient was living at a West End hotel, the Burlington, in Cork Street, under siege by a mob of reporters. At the end of the year Dr. McHardy recommended that he spend the winter at the resort town of Bournemouth on the Channel.

Herz rented Boscombe Towers, the Bournemouth home of Sir Henry Drummond Wolff, the British Ambassador to Spain; but when he arrived there he found the water pipes frozen, and so he installed his family at the Tankerville Hotel while repairs were made.

There, on January 17, he received the first official word of the seriousness of his position. It came in a letter from the Grand Chancellor of the Legion of Honor, General Fevrier, telling him he was accused of blackmailing de Reinach and taking Panama money without earning it, and inviting him to appear the next day before a Legion committee appointed to hear his defense. The communication was dated January 14.

Herz replied at once, sending a medical certificate and saying: "I have been invited to give explanations tomorrow and defend myself without knowing against what, since your dossier has not been communicated to me.

"I think I understand that I am accused of having received from the Panama Company (1) two checks of 1,000,000 each; (2) a sum of 600,000 francs.

"On the first point, I have only to confirm my letter to the [Chamber's] commission of inquiry: these two millions were paid to me by M. de Reinach without my knowing their origin, and to pay part of his debt to me that we had definitely settled by a document of July 18, 1889, deposited with the Rothschild bank in Frankfort.

"I am sending you my account with the office of M. Fontana, Paris notary, showing that I have used this money in acquiring buildings and not to corrupt Deputies.

"On the second point, I wish that M. Charles de Lesseps would state precisely the declaration which serves as the sole basis of the accusation; M. de Lesseps certainly did not say that he handed over to me personally any sum.

"The truth is that I turned over to M. de Reinach the drafts signed by Dauderni the contractor and he negotiated them to the amount of 600,000 francs to the company. This was a loan that I made from Reinach, not from the Panama company. If the Panama company accepted these drafts, it was a loan the company made to Reinach on this paper, and if he thought it appropriate to bring my name into this affair, I have no responsibility.

"On the second count of the indictment relative to blackmail of M. de Reinach, I protest energetically against any such imputation.

"Blackmail supposes the extortion, by threats, of sums to which one has no right. My case is entirely different.

"I was the creditor of Reinach. I asked him to settle the account. First he opposed me dishonestly, then he undertook to get rid of his creditor by attempting to have him poisoned. I threatened him with seeking my payment by all legal means. I threatened him with handing him over to the justice of his country. In the end he recognized his debt.

"But to complete my defense I ask authorization that would not be refused to the vilest of malefactors, to make known to me for my defense the dossier that accuses me, and I ask a delay of three weeks to get together my data and draw up my statement."

The same day Herz replied to the Legion, a summons directing him to appear before an examining magistrate was served on him. He replied again with medical certificates stating that he could not travel, and asked appointment of a judicial commission to examine him at Bournemouth, which was permissible under English law, for he was a free man. Instead, the examining magistrate, Judge Tiburce Franqueville, issued a warrant for his arrest the next day, charging him with complicity in the alleged frauds for which the two de Lessepses, their canal company associates, and Eiffel were then on trial.

At midnight on January 19 two Scotland Yard detectives arrested Herz on an extradition warrant. They found him in bed, looking alarmingly ill. Mrs. Herz summoned her husband's local physician, Dr. William Frazer, who told them Herz could be moved only at the risk of his life, and certified that he was suffering of an "affection of the heart, great prostration, and functional derangement."

The detectives telephoned to London for instructions and were ordered to let Herz remain in bed but to keep him in custody. Franqueville then issued a second warrant, but it was not executed. Herz was merely notified of it since he already was under arrest. This one charged him with extorting money by menaces: "He made Baron Jacques de Reinach sign on May 9, 1888, a bond for 10,000,000 francs payable one day after the Panama company had received the proceeds of the first payments made on the lottery bonds which the company was then seeking parliamentary authority to issue. The issue was not taken up in full. Nevertheless, after various attempts at blackmailing, of which some evidence appears in the letter from Reinach to Chabert, (annexed,) Cornelius Herz on 10 July, 1888, sent to Marius Fontane, managing director of the Panama company, the telegram a copy whereof is annexed, in which he threatened Fontane to ruin Reinach and his friends unless he was paid the 10,000,000."

On January 28 the French government published in its *Journal Officiel* a decree signed by President Carnot, expelling Grand Officer Cornelius Herz from the Legion of Honor for "committing an offense against honor." The decree also pointed out that the offenses of which Herz was accused were outlawed by the three-year statute of limitations and "cannot be made the subject of criminal proceedings before the courts of law."

The same day, on the basis of more documents that Imbert, the administrator of de Reinach's estate, dug out of the Baron's files, Franqueville issued a third warrant, which charged that Herz, although actually in debt to de Reinach, falsely claimed up to the end of 1890 to be his creditor, and with this false claim extorted considerable sums of money from him. France demanded extradition under its treaty of August 14, 1876, with Britain.

The British extradition act provided that once arrest on an extradition warrant had taken place, the prisoner had to be arraigned before a police magistrate in the Bow Street court in London. It demanded that the nation seeking extradition produce evidence that, under English law, would justify the accused person's commitment for trial if the offense alleged had been committed in England; in this event the magistrate would hold the accused for trial, but otherwise had to order his discharge. The act did not permit release on bail in the event of adjournment, and provided no special procedure for dealing with a prisoner too sick to be arraigned.

Therefore, unless Herz could get up to London and win his release in the Bow Street court, he had to remain a prisoner. The provisions of the act shackled him to his sickbed for more than three years.

The Tankerville Hotel was a cheerfully furnished villa on the shore road; its terraced lawn, planted with pine trees and surrounded by hedges of evergreen, descended to a pleasant bay. It had accommodations for thirty guests, and Herz rented the entire establishment.

A constant procession of physicians, lawyers, reporters, family friends, and business associates moved through the hotel, including several politicians among the numerous visitors from France. Despite eyewitness reports of Herz's ghastly appearance, the story spread that he was malingering, for the "public was prepared on the contrary to believe that Cornelius was able to succeed in any trick or deceit he chose to play on his adversaries, even to convincing them that he was at death's door when he was in perfect health."

A half dozen famous British doctors, including Dr. Russell Reynolds, Queen Victoria's physician, who went to Bournemouth at the Home Secretary's request, and Sir Andrew Clark, president of the Royal College of Physicians, examined Herz frequently and certified the gravity of his illness. Dr. Rey-

201

nolds said Herz was so sick he could not be moved from his bedroom to a bigger room on the same floor of the hotel.

But these professional judgments by leaders of the British medical establishment "failed to prevent the most persistent and gross misrepresentations appearing in the public press, both French and English," Dr. McHardy commented to the Home Secretary.

The French government, at the British Foreign Office's invitation to come and see for itself, sent Dr. Charcot, who died only a few months later, and Dr. Brouardel.

They arrived at the Tankerville Hotel at 11 p.m. on January 21, armed with British Home Office authority to conduct the examination, whether or not Herz's own physician or a medical representative of the British government was present. After one look at the patient they hastened to apologize and withdrew, postponing the examination until the next day, when Herz's doctors were also at hand.

In their report Charcot and Brouardel said: "Cornelius Herz declares himself to be forty-seven years of age. He looks at least sixty-five. His face is pale, colorless, the eyes bright. The muscles of the limbs are flabby. It is evident that during these last months the patient has grown physically thinner. The weakness is extreme."

Their report, widely published, "hardly noticeably checked the continuance of false charges in the French press," the *British Medical Journal* said, adding that "indeed one of the late Dr. Charcot's last public acts was definitely to refute *Figaro*'s allegation that Drs. Brouardel and Charcot had been hoaxed at Bournemouth by a substituted patient provided by the English physicians in place of Dr. Herz, and winked at by the English authorities."

Dr. Brouardel told how Herz, himself, supplied another proof of his identity. "Turning to Dr. Charcot, he said, 'You do not recognize me, Dr. Charcot,'" Brouardel related. "The latter replied that he had never seen him before. 'You are mistaken, sir,' returned the patient. 'I was an intern under you in 1867, when you replaced Dr. Marotte at the Pitié Hospital. I can see you now sketching a blood clot from the femoral vein, which was the shape of a serpent's head.' Dr. Charcot remembered these details when Cornelius Herz reminded him of them."

On November 4 the French government sent Brouardel back to Bournemouth, this time with Dr. Georges Dieulafoy, to examine Herz again. Their examination produced a report to the government at Paris that it was now safe to move the patient to Bow Street for a hearing on the extradition writ.

Their prognosis, as far as it went, agreed with that of the British doctors, one of whom, Brunton, carried the forecast several steps further. After examining Herz in September, he had reported: "His circulation is now so far restored that I do not think he is likely to die of collapse, and that he might run the risk of being brought up to London. I think there is an undoubted risk in this movement, but he seems to be getting steadily worse, and unless he can get free of his anxieties I do not think there is any chance of recovery, and I do not think he can last for more than a year. It would therefore be worth his while to run the risk of death on the way up, but what I fear is that if he is remanded to prison the excitement will bring on a fit of angina pectoris which will kill him. I should therefore fear that such a remand would simply amount to a sentence of death. The most recent news is that the tendency to despair has so further interfered with Dr. Herz's very insufficient sleep that unless relief can be brought to him by a speedy settlement of his case, he will probably lose his reason if not his life."

On June 13 the *Cour de Cassation,* the highest French court, had reversed the fraud conviction of Ferdinand and Charles de Lesseps, Fontane, Cottu, and Eiffel on the ground that prosecution for the acts of which they were found guilty was outlawed by the statute of limitations. These were acts in which Herz was accused of being their accomplice. Almost exactly a year later the examining magistrate at Paris threw out the complicity charges against Herz; but he still faced the charge of blackmail.

Letters and telegrams to de Reinach and others, copies of correspondence found in the Baron's duplicate letter book, notes attributed to Herz, and documents subpoenaed from banks and dug up in searches of his home and offices formed the mass of material on which the prosecution built the blackmail case.

The extradition papers included an agreement addressed to Herz under date of May 9, 1888, extracted from de Reinach's duplicate letter book: "It is agreed that in accordance with our verbal agreement dating from the first application of the Panama company to obtain a lottery loan, you shall receive 10,000,000 francs the day after the company itself gets from the public the first cash payment on the lottery bonds which it is now seeking parliamentary sanction to issue. It is also agreed that I shall also retain out of this sum all moneys that you owe to me, also all moneys that you owe to the house of Kohn, Reinach & Co., capital, and interest. Out of balance then to come to you it is also agreed that there shall be taken the sum necessary to pay all your debts in Paris through M. Chabert, whom you have appointed for that purpose. These presents are to be returned to me as soon as payment is made, their return to be my discharge."

The application for extradition also included the following telegram sent from Frankfort to the Panama company secretary, Marius Fontane, at 9 rue Charras, Paris, the headquarters of the Suez Canal Company: "Your friend is trying to cheat. He must pay or blow up, and if he does, his friends will blow up with him. I will break up everything sooner than be robbed of a cent. Notify, for there is just time. Cornelius Herz."

The date of the telegram was July 10, 1888, eight days before the two 1,000,000-franc checks to "Bearer" were sent to Herz in Frankfort.

From de Reinach's files the prosecution also produced a copy of a letter to Herz's associate Leon Chabert, dated November 28, 1888, in which the Baron threatened to give the Attorney General of France documentary evidence that Herz had extorted millions from him if Herz attempted further blackmail.

The prosecution added, as another indication of blackmail, an extract from a telegram in which Herz told his private secretary, the former Deputy, Guillot: "As for Reinach, you may depend upon it that he will act promptly from tomorrow; that is settled; you understand why we can reckon on him. Tell him so for me."

To plead his case in France, Herz retained Edouard Clunet, an expert in international law. Item by item, Maître Clunet waged a muscular counterattack in arguments and citations that filled a 250-page book entitled *Mémoire À Consulter,* an English translation of which by W. F. Craies, a London barrister, was published under the title, *Statement of the Case for Dr. Cornelius Herz.*

Clunet denounced the prosecution as a political maneuver, for which the British law would not sanction extradition. He said the political opposition in France used the Panama scandal to smear the government and the form of government that prevailed, and that the government panicked and made Herz the scapegoat.

The opposition's tactics, he said, "consisted in attributing to an absent man the most hateful parts in the scandals, in accumulating against him the most terrible accusations, and in associating with this creature of their imagination, painted in the blackest colors, the government in the first place and also the whole republican party."

Even if the prosecution were not politically motivated, Clunet insisted, 1) the crimes with which Herz was charged were not extraditable offenses under the British act; 2) but even if they had been, they were outlawed by the statute of limitations; 3) the prosectuion initiated in the correctional courts was illegal because Herz was a Grand Officer of the Legion of Honor and jurisdiction to proceed against Grand Officers was vested in the Court of Appeal; 4) and even if none of those contentions were valid, Herz was not guilty of any of the charges.

In the most serious charges to pour forth from the Panama scandal—the wholesale corruption of public officials—Herz was never implicated as a principal or as an accomplice of any of the accused, Maître Clunet pointed out; of all those accused, only Charles Baïhaut, the former Public Works Minister, was convicted of taking a bribe, and only Charles de Lesseps of giving it to him.

"Two great cases before the courts, a judicial investigation, a parliamentary inquiry lasting over 63 sittings and assisted by the depositions of 158 witnesses, nine domiciliary searches or seizures, have failed to establish the unwarranted charges of 'buyer of consciences,' of 'master cheat,' of 'traitor to his country' launched from the tribune, apparently at an absent man but in reality at the ministry and the republican party by a deputy in whom, it may be said, after the decision of the Court of Assize in the Norton case, critical capacity and care for fairness run not so high as political passion," Clunet said.

The 600,000 francs that Charles de Lesseps said Herz squeezed out of him was not an extorted payment, Clunet protested, but the proceeds of a transaction between Herz and de Reinach, an advance against security for the same amount "in the form of bills signed by a solvent contractor, Dauderni, and guaranteed by a solvent banker, de Reinach."

"But where the inaccuracy of M. Charles de Lesseps becomes flagrant is here," the advocate declared. "If the 600,000 francs in question had been a gift to Dr. Herz in one form or another, the accounts of the company would show a trace of it; it would appear on the list of sums distributed; M. Flory, the expert accountant, would have pointed it out. We know that he published at the end of his report 'an account of the recipients' in 15 columns and 129 quarto pages, which minutely enumerates all the names of the agents, brokers, banks, newspaper correspondents, &c. who received any sum whatever from the Panama company. It is a catalogue of more than 2,000 names. That of Dr. Herz is not among them. The 600,000 francs are not mentioned."

Herz blackmailed neither the Panama company nor de Reinach, Clunet said; the Baron owed him some money, and he simply sought to collect it. "Even if he did it on violent terms, even if he used threats of imputations or disclosures of a defamatory character," the advocate argued, "an angry creditor—genus *irritabile creditorum*—would not have committed an offense even if he had tried to frighten his debtor."

There were no such threats in the telegram from Frankfort to Fontane, he said. Moreover, the telegram was not sent from French soil, and the prosecution could never find the original to prove even that Herz had been the sender. To support his contention that Herz had an honest claim against de Reinach, Clunet, in the ink of strenuous advocacy, prepared a long, detailed inventory of the intertwined business interests of the two men, their personal relationships, villainies on the part of de Reinach, and responses by Herz that appeared almost exalted in their magnanimity.

According to his account, they had begun to do business together the year after Herz arrived from California, and their association encompassed the whole conglomeration of the doctor's ventures. Yet the records of their dealings with one another were so haphazard and deficient that at one point the banker had to ask Chabert how much he had paid, through Chabert, to Herz.

Clunet said de Reinach's first written acknowledgment of his debt to Herz was in a letter dated June 16, 1886. At that moment the French government was debating the Panama company's application for permission to float a lottery bond issue, with de Reinach the head of the issuing syndicate.

The banker wrote:

> My dear Herz:
> You know my arrangement with the Panama company as to the formation of the syndicate to carry out the proposed lottery loan of the company. I now confirm our previous arrangements on this subject, which are that I should pay you 7/10 of the sums which I receive on this business as and when I receive them myself..
>
> J. de Reinach

Two days later he wrote again:

> My dear Herz:
> I confirm to you my letter of the 16th inst., and have to tell you that the sum I am to receive from the Panama company has been raised to 10,000,000. You know that M. de Lesseps has reserved the right to dispense of some 100,000 francs of the said sum.
>
> Yours devotedly,
> J. de Reinach.

When the government asked for further data on which to base its decision, the company withdrew its application, and the issue was not floated. Two years later, desperate for money, the company again applied for permission to float a lottery loan, and while the application was being debated, de Reinach sent Herz a new promise to settle. This contract was dated May 11, 1888:

> To Dr. Herz: In accordance with verbal agreement dating from the first application of the Panama company

to obtain a lottery loan, you will be entitled to receive 10,000,000 francs on the day after the Panama company itself gets from the public the first cash payment on the lottery bonds which it is now seeking Parliamentary sanction to issue. It is agreed that out of this sum you shall repay me all that you owe me and also what you owe to the house of Kohn, Reinach & Co., capital and interest. The return of these presents shall serve as my discharge.

Yours etc.
J. de Reinach

This time the government, to its subsequent regret, approved the application, and the lottery bond issue was brought to market on June 26. But the public took up scarcely 40 per cent of it, and on July 1 Herz was still clamoring for money from de Reinach.

"Now Dr. Herz had a document in his hands, (the acknowledgement of 11 May 1888) with which, as he had threatened, he could attack the banking account of M. de Reinach," Clunet said. "If Dr. Herz died, how much simpler things would be for the debtor."

And so, the lawyer charged, de Reinach plotted to have Herz killed.

Louis Andrieux, the discursive star witness at the parliamentary investigation of the Panama affair, took full credit for ferreting out the plot. He told the investigating Deputies that Herz had released him from his professional obligation as one of the doctor's Paris lawyers so that he might tell this tale of de Reinach's dark intention: "Herz, in Paris, had received a letter from Brazil, signed by somebody named Amiel. This Amiel explained that he was hired to poison M. Cornelius Herz and he had received a substantial down payment for putting an end to M. Cornelius Herz's days, but that once he had the money he preferred to flee to Brazil with the hope of speculating with it and building a business with this money, preferring to escape the responsibilities of the actual act to which he at first had lent himself.

"Amiel added that he had met with a person whose name he could not give because he had never known it, but these interviews took place around the Madeleine at various meeting places that had been given to him.

"Cornelius Herz was doing this, he was getting information on the identity of Amiel; he asked me to work on it, and I found out that it was a former agent of the *Sûreté Générale* of the Prefecture of Police who had been fired from everywhere. This was certainly the man who could have lent himself to such a game. The information did not have a great value, as no one knew any more. One could suppose that this man was only hoping to get a free trip home. He said, 'If I were in Paris it would be easier to find who hired me and to denounce to M. Cornelius Herz the person who wanted to end his days.'

"I insisted that before sending him any sum whatsoever, Amiel send to his correspondent the letters written to him, as he said, giving the mysterious meeting places in which to plan the deed. Amiel decided to send an envelope, and the verification of the address brings us to recognize the writing of the Baron de Reinach, who, without further precaution, put his own hand to addressing the letter he had sent to this person.

"When this communication was made, no further doubts existed, as M. Cornelius Herz had maintained before that two persons could be interested in his disappearance, and at the time, he alternately accused Baron de Reinach and General Boulanger. This second hypothesis seemed to me the most possible, and it was to this that I attached the most. The discovery of this scrap that I mentioned settled the question. It was indeed Baron de Reinach."

When Herz confronted de Reinach with his bits of evidence, Andrieux testified, the Baron denied passionately any evil intent, exclaiming to his aggrieved associate: "What, you took that seriously! I only wanted to get you off my neck, make you leave the country and go farther away."

It was out of the context of this plot to kill Herz, Maître Clunet said, that the prosecution extracted a document and used it in an attempt to incriminate Herz in blackmail. Clunet insisted that de Reinach, anticipating the possibility of disclosure of his murder plot, began to fabricate a defense for himself by inserting in his duplicate letter book the following communication, ostensibly sent to Chabert on November 28, 1888:

"My dear Chabert:

"I received letter of yesterday. Not only do I refuse to pay Dr. Herz any more, but if he does not keep quiet, I shall claim from him by legal proceedings repayment of all the sums which he has received since the Panama business, for neither in law nor in fact is anything due to Dr. Herz. He did nothing and is not entitled to any remuneration. The failure of the issue, the Panama bonds, prevented the company from repaying me the money I spent, and if in making payment to Dr. Herz I yielded to blackmailing threats, which if carried out might have compromised the Panama issue, and to the pressure put on by his friends, that does not constitute any valid engagement. I repeat that if Dr. Herz, a Grand Officer of the Legion of Honor and, as he says, future Ambassador of the United States to Paris, and as he prides himself, a man intent on leaving an honorable name to his children, I say that if he stirs a step I will at once lay a complaint before the Attorney General and will produce all the receipts and checks on the Bank of France starting with the first check for 600,000 francs which Dr. Herz took from the Panama company, documents which clearly show how many millions he has wrongfully appropriated. I will also hand to the public prosecutor all letters and telegrams which I have from Dr. Herz which will make clear what means of intimidation he used to attain his object. They will thus know in France, in Germany, in Italy, in Switzerland, in the United States the methods by which Dr. Herz makes his money. I have never profited a cent by all these sums. My hands are clean. Let Dr. Herz and all those who have profited by this ill-gotten money rest assured that I shall refuse all communication, verbal or written, and I refuse all interviews with anyone whatsoever. I regret to have to make this communication to you, but I mean to be done with it once and for all and I will not be exposed to any more blackmailing or exactions. The law protects me.

Yours,
J. de Reinach.

To the prosecution this letter was evidence, provided post-humously by the blackmailer's own victim, that Herz was a blackmailer. To counsel for the defense, it was just a fake.

"Indeed, if M. de Reinach was injured, why did he not lay his complaint?" Maître Clunet demanded. "The formalities are simple. A letter is enough, not prepaid, addressed to the Attorney General of the Republic."

De Reinach, he said, had prepared the copy of the letter for his book of duplicates only to "make a pretext for his conduct and make up a brief for himself," should he be shown up as the instigator of Herz's murder. But when the plot was foiled and his complicity revealed, Clunet said, the intended victim, "touched by his repentance and his tears, pardoned him."

But Herz's forgiveness carried a price tag, which he disclosed in a telegram to de Reinach from Basel on December 16 that was one of the stiffest declamations in their long and acrimonious dialogue: "Your distinctly odious conduct becomes more and more astonishing. Not only do you break contracts and promises of the most formal character, but you go on to forget my kindness, and the benefits I have conferred on your people. The recollection of them jars you. You have dared to threaten me with a great disaster, and with a light heart you challenge me to battle. I am sorry for your blindness. How dare you say that you owe me no gratitude, how dare you lie so shamelessly. In forty-eight hours you will have irrefutable proofs of your falsehood. Very often you have displayed in my presence great contempt for the government and law of your country, and spoken of all the Ministers and high magistrates as if they were your humble servants. Well, then, try now to prove you are right. You lied again when you talked this way, for you will not find, either in the government or among the judges of France, anyone who can have anything to do with your dishonest methods or who will share to the slightest extent the fearful consequences and the just penalties which your conduct more and more swiftly bring upon you. Pay me what you owe me, beg my pardon for your base conduct, and perhaps I will once more consent to forgive everything."

Their mutual friend, Chabert, returning from a meeting with Herz, brought de Reinach a personal reminder of the kinds of disclosures his old partner might make, and pleaded with him to avoid an explosion by settling up.

"I have seen some of your letters; I assure you they are very imprudent and very compromising," he telegraphed to de Reinach. "You write of commissions on the land which you hold at Bordeaux and which were to be sold to the War Department, of commissions to be given him in the Chemin de Fer Economiques and South of France Railway, and you are a director of these companies."

Chabert warned de Reinach that "a cataclysm is coming" and that Herz, demanding stubbornly "the two million which you promised him." was so determined on an all-out fight that he "has classified all the letters which you have written to him and is going to get them printed."

The telegram brought de Reinach to see Chabert the next day; their intimate conversation produced enormously varied impressions on the two men. Chabert, reporting to Herz at Weisbaden by letter on December 27, mentioned a new Panama scheme involving American participation and said he had told de Reinach that Herz was "well in with Blaine," who was soon to become Secretary of State of the United States again in the Cabinet of President Benjamin Harrison. This bit of name dropping was effective, Chabert told Herz; it "interested him much," and de Reinach was in a mood to settle up as soon as he could get out of a financial squeeze. He said the banker had been "driven off his head by the Panama fiasco and is under stress of claims for 1,500,000 francs" that he had guaranteed the canal company, "but he is taking fresh breath now that these negotiations are in good progress."

Herz was asked to intervene in these negotiations, which contemplated American private-sector financial assistance in the canal project, Clunet said, because of his "powerful connections in the United States as an American citizen and an official delegate of the American government at the Electrical Exhibition of 1881." But he made no comment on a long, tough letter de Reinach wrote to Chabert the day after their meeting, setting forth his own version of their discussion:

December 20, 1888

My dear Chabert:
To avoid all ambiguity regarding our conversation yes-

terday, I am going to state it precisely to you. Either Dr. Herz acts as he should act, or he certainly will be acting as an honest man should not act. In the first case he has only to make an assignment to the Panama company and its administrators in payment of the balance of that which he said was due him, and to me in guarantee, or else he could do the reverse and make an assignment to me that I myself assign in my turn to the Panama company. This procedure would be a bit longer, but if he follows that procedure of an honest man, it is necessary that they be issued before December 31 so that they might go to the company while it was not in bankruptcy. If the doctor chooses this course I think he will be able—thanks to his friendship with the President (Bl...?)—to be useful to a new Franco-American scheme for forming a new company that will have the job of completing and exploiting the canal. He will be able to reap very great benefits—benefits that then will be legitimately acquired because he will have worked for the affair. I must also tell you that at this time I am not in any scheme.

If Dr. Herz chooses the other course, which he has shown me in his numerous dispatches, he is very mistaken if he thinks he frightens me. It is not the one who offers money who is guilty, but rather the functionary or member of the government who accepts it.*

No, my engagements with respect to Dr. Herz are the engagements he asked me for, and I don't know how he used the sums he received from me. He indeed asked and obtained from me, for the railroad of the Littoral, 100,000 francs. (I have his receipt on the check he cashed.) He also told me that he gave them to Monsieur X, Deputy, but you remember that I questioned Monsieur X on this subject and he denied in the most explicit manner taking a *radi* of this sum. Therefore Dr. Herz is mistaken if he thinks that he scares me with

*see Notes

this publication. It is on him that everything will bounce back, because I have carefully preserved his letters and receipts and I will publish them in my turn. I have shown you some samples of the letters that he remembers and that will portray him sufficiently. It will also be seen that he drew by my hands on the public fortune in France the following sums, and I overlook the small sums because Dr. Herz likes to work only on a large scale:

Malacca canal	87,500	francs
Rothschild business	1,500,000	
First Panama business	600,000	
Second Panama business	8,000,000	
Military beds (second time)	2,250,000	
Littoral	100,000	
Total	12,537,500	francs

and I am omitting what I have said.

The public will also know that I have saved him six times from bankruptcy (not so from failure), it will know the Drexel Harjes business and the Leonide Leblanc* business etc. I will conceal nothing at all to make better known the state of things. Finally, Dr. Herz is not aware that the decorations of the Legion of Honor conferred on foreigners do not render the latter Legionnaires by any means, and they come under the jurisdiction of ordinary courts. It is peace or war, whatever he wants. I am completely ready. Best to you.

J. de Reinach

Not long after this exchange of fulminations, Herz and de Reinach were back in harness, a reconciliation typical of a monumentally ambivalent relationship that Andrieux had remarked on to the Deputies, saying, "it fluctuated strongly, according to the times."

The vehicle for this new association was the scheme to detach Italy from the Triple Alliance. It was from a long, coded telegram from Herz, dealing solely with this project, Maître

*see Notes

Clunet charged, that the prosecution lifted the following passage and used it as a foundation of a blackmail indictment: "As for Reinach, you may depend upon it that he will act promptly from tomorrow; that is settled; you understand why we can reckon on him. Tell him so for me."

"Jealous of Herz having conceived the plan we have just described, and of the glory which would redound on its author, de Reinach seeks by underhand methods to defeat it in order to be able to resume its realization on his own account" was the explanation Clunet offered.

To support it, he put into his brief the entire exchange between Herz and Guillot, Herz's private secretary. It was an exchange that dripped with diplomatic expertise and the familiar mention of some of the best known public men in France and Italy: de Freycinet, the French Minister of War at the moment; Jacques Spuller, the Minister of Foreign Affairs; Rouvier, the Finance Minister; Pierre Deluns-Montaud, Minister of Public Works the year before; Albert Billot, former Director of Litigations in the Foreign Office; Clemenceau, leader of the radical party; the Italian Ambassador, General Menabrea; the Premier of Italy, Crispi:

Herz at Rome, to Guillot, 31 boulevard des Italiens, Paris, February 16,1890:

Pray decipher this with care and read it to all whom it may concern. It is clear that if the Ambassador is not named in concert with me, effect cannot be given to what has been tacitly agreed. If on the contrary effect is given, logic indicates the utility of naming at once a person who, although he is *bien entendu* a *persona grata* to the Italian government, is also a personage in concert with whom one could go quickly into the question of ways and means. Assuming the actual state of affairs, that is to say the impracticability of obtaining the acceptance of any one of the names already put forward, I take the liberty of submitting to the competent power the name of Deluns-Montaud, a personage who is, I can affirm, at this precise moment better qualified than any other to carry out the negotiations actively and to obtain in a short time a conclusion of a new political treaty between Italy and France. Once obtained, this result which we are all seeking will be glorious for France, for our Minister of Foreign Affairs, for Italy, I venture to say ultimately for Germany and for humanity at large, and also in a small way for your humble servant.

Cornelius Herz

Ask Clemenceau to bestow himself with vigor and speed. If necessary work other influence so as to hasten as much as possible the solution we require. A few days from now I shall arrange matters. As for Reinach, he is positively idiotic just now. You may depend upon it that he will act promptly from tomorrow. That is settled. You understand why we can reckon on him. Tell him so for me.

Herz

Go and see friend Rouvier again. Tell him that I am very grateful for the high and vigorous attitude he has taken in the matter which interests us all and beg him to accept a thousand thanks.

Herz

Guillot to Herz, Laurati Hotel, Rome, February 17: Interview Spuller and Deluns-Montaud excellent results. All went well. Spuller will ask Menabrea *père* on Wednesday if Deluns-Montaud is acceptable. Great eloquence of Deluns-Montaud has produced the unexpected result. Spuller must give reply to Deluns-Montaud Thursday. It also results from this interview for Deluns-Montaud that Reinach has played you false with Spuller. As for me, I have proof that Reinach is playing you false with Crispi. I think the moment has absolutely come for you to see Crispi again and bring him completely on your side. On Wednesday evening Menabrea *fils* will tell you if Spuller has kept promise.
Guillot to Herz, February 18: Have seen Freycinet this

216

morning have explained position of affairs to him, he will work for us. As for Reinach, I believe it is better not to let him know his infamous conduct. Then after tomorrow, when Spuller shall have spoken of Deluns-Montaud to Menabrea *père* you will at once have Reinach summoned to Rome as agreed with Rouvier so you will have Reinach in your hands and will make him harmless. I have just left Menabrea *fils*, all is quite arranged for tomorrow.

Whatever treatment they administered to de Reinach, it appeared to be effective. In a letter to Herz, under the name of his father-in-law, A.S.Saroni, at the Hotel Bellevue, Brussels, on March 3, Guillot, signing himself "Raoul," reported the following: "Reinach wished (1) to communicate to me the contents of a note about Billot which he is going to have inserted in tomorrow's issue of *La Paix*. This note says that this appointment is not yet made and that Billot's character is not such as to suit the post of Ambassador to Rome; (2) Reinach says that he has seen Rouvier, that he has spoken to him very forcibly, and that Rouvier has given his word of honor to get Spuller to change his determination."

Despite all these serpentine maneuvers, nothing happened. Billot, not Deluns-Montaud, went to Rome, and fifteen years later, when he wrote his book, *La France et l'Italie*, Italy was still a member of the Triple Alliance.

The sputtering relationship between Herz and de Reinach persisted until the Baron died. When the scandal sheets started their attacks on him in the fall of 1892, he wrote to Herz twice for help: "My name is again in the paper; please do the necessary to avoid," and "Please do the necessary that the *Intransigeant* does not reproduce the note of the *Cocarde*." Three times on November 19, 1892, the Baron sent Herz a frantic message regarding the visit with Rouvier and Clemenceau. The next morning de Reinach was found dead in his bed. Exactly two months later, Herz was entombed in the Tankerville Hotel.

As a result of his dealings with de Reinach, Herz faced a civil suit as well as criminal prosecution. The Panama Canal Company's trustee in bankruptcy, Achille Monchicourt, demanded that de Reinach's estate pay back more than 9,000,000 francs that he had received from the company. The court-appointed administrator of the estate, Albert Imbert, settled with him for 3,000,000 francs and sought in turn to retrieve de Reinach's payments to Herz.

Herz having proclaimed that the 2,000,000-franc payment de Reinach made to him went for the purchase of Paris real estate, not to corrupt politicians, Imbert attached the property. He also brought suit in the First Chamber of the Civil Court of the Seine to establish that its purchase, in Mme. Herz's name, was only a straw-man transaction and that the property was really Herz's and thus was subject to creditors' claims. Monchicourt intervened on the Panama company's behalf to support Imbert's application and also to demand return of the 600,000 francs Charles de Lesseps said he had given Herz in 1885. On February 15, 1894, the court ruled in their favor.

The property consisted of Herz's mansion at 78 avenue Henri Martin and buildings at 4 boulevard Flandrin and in the rue de la Faisanderie. Imbert and Monchicourt fixed their total value at 1,500,000 francs, and Imbert then negotiated a deal with Herz to settle the de Reinach estate's claim for that amount. Acting with a power of attorney from her husband, Mme. Herz signed the compromise in Paris on March 10, 1894, and on May 2 the court ratified it.*

Though Herz had to pay a heavy price for the compromise, his family and friends, and the press as well, felt that it had bought the desperately sick prisoner of Bournemouth peace of mind by removing the threat of criminal prosecution and extradition proceedings that had burdened him so long. A *Figaro* story said that the deal with Imbert not only settled the extradition question, but that as further relief from the penalties imposed on him, Herz would seek revocation of his expulsion from the Legion of Honor. The *New York Tribune*'s Paris correspondent announced that Herz would "henceforth be free to return to Paris and to take up his business affairs, his social, and probably, too, his political relations, just as if nothing had happened."

"Indeed, if anything, he comes back to us more powerful, more influential, and more feared than ever," the *Tribune* re-

*see Notes

porter wrote. "Although known to possess most damaging secrets concerning many of the most prominent statesmen, officials, and politicians of the day, he has betrayed no one, he has maintained silence under the greatest provocations, and he has managed to live through and to emerge head erect from such a storm of obloquy as seldom falls the lot of any one man. Every conceivable crime from murder to treason has been laid at his door by the press and by boulevard gossip."

On June 11 the examining magistrate, Franqueville, threw out the complicity charge against Herz. But to the consternation of the sick man and his entourage, the magistrate recommended that Herz stand trial for blackmail.

The trial convened on July 27 in the Correctional Court of the Seine, with Maître Clunet presenting medical certificates of Herz's incapacity not only from Drs. Brunton, McHardy, and Frazer, but from distinguished new authority, Sir Richard Quain, physician extraordinary to Queen Victoria.

The court rejected their depositions. When the prosecution charged that Herz was faking his illness, the court pronounced him in contempt and heard witnesses. Imbert testified that he had found numerous instances of blackmail by Herz, and accountants presented their testimony that Herz had extorted a total of 11,190,000 francs from Baron de Reinach, 4,675,000 of it being Panama company funds. The prosecution demanded the maximum penalty, and on August 3 the court imposed it, five years in prison and a 3,000-franc fine.

Maître Clunet appealed at once to the Court of Appeal, on the ground that it had sole jurisdiction for a trial of Herz because he was a Grand Officer of the Legion of Honor when the acts for which he was tried were alleged to have taken place. He cited Article 10 of the French law of April 20,1810, on the organization of the judicial department and the administration of justice: "When Grand Officers of the Legion of Honor, generals (in command of a division or a department), Archbishops, Bishops, presidents of consistories, members of the *Cour de Cassation*, of the Court of Accounts, of the Imperial Courts, and prefects are accused of misdemeanors (*délits de police correctionelle*), the Imperial courts (of Appeal) shall take cognizance of them in the manner prescribed by Article 479 of the Criminal Procedure Code." Article 479 provided that when any of these eminences committed such an offense, except in discharge of his duties, the Attorney General in the royal court of appeal would haul him before that court for decision on the matter.

The Court of Appeal did not rule on Clunet's arguments for almost ten months; then, on May 15, 1895, it rejected them. Herz's last resort was the *Cour de Cassation*, France's highest court of appeal. But on August 2 this court sustained the ruling of the Court of Appeal. The high court based its findings on the premise that immunity from prosecution in inferior courts did not derive from Herz's possession of the Grand Cross, because it had been bestowed on him as a foreigner. This was exactly what de Reinach had warned him against in his bitter communication through Chabert almost seven years earlier.

But to win an extradition writ and gain Herz's custody, France had, in effect, to prove his guilt again; she had to convince a Bow Street magistrate that the case she had would have warranted Herz's trial before a jury in Britain had the alleged crime been committed there.

While British law, as it stood, saved Herz from an immediate transfer to a French jail, it also denied him an opportunity to face the charge and win his freedom from his Bournemouth imprisonment, since he was too ill to travel to Bow Street and Bow Street was sole jurisdiction in extradition cases.

Although a few persons in France were willing to admit even a nodding acquaintance with Herz, in England he was blessed with the support of a small band of insistent champions. Their immediate goal was to get him his day in court. His physicians turned polemicist and prodded the Home Office with memorials. The *Times* of London opened its columns to them. The *Law Journal* protested "an arrest under circumstances verging on inhumanity." The law firm of Herz's solicitor, Sir George Lewis, a great expert on criminal law and friend of the Prince of Wales, demanded of the Home Secretary: "Is this poor man, conscious of his innocence, to be allowed to linger at Bournemouth until death releases him from the warrants under which he is in custody, and who, we respectfully ask, would be responsible for his death, considering that he is in custody under an extradition warrant issued by an English magistrate?"

Members of Parliament from Aberdeen to Kent, representing all political parties, made speeches in behalf of an amendment to the extradition act and put questions repeatedly to a succession of Liberal and Conservative Ministers. The Liberal Party's Home Secretary, Herbert Asquith, assured Arthur Sackville Trevor Griffith-Boscawen, Conservative member for Tunbridge, that "the English government in this matter is doing nothing but what its treaty obligations with France require," and that he would be delighted to finish "what is to us an extremely expensive and very disagreeable duty."

At last a change in the law made its way past all the parliamentary whistle stops, and on February 19, 1896, France and Britain ratified the consequent modifications of their extradition treaty. The amended law permitted a magistrate to hold a bedside hearing in Bournemouth and then dispose of the case in a Bow Street trial that Herz did not have to attend.

On the morning of April 27,1896, a dozen policemen surrounded the hotel in which Herz had been lying ill for forty months, and the court marched in: Sir John Bridge, Chief Magistrate of the Metropolitan Police Courts, Sir John's chief clerk, two Home Office physicians, three members of Herz's medical team, his solicitor, Sir George Lewis, the barrister, Craies, two lawyers for the French government, the representatives of the Treasury, and Inspector Bartels of Scotland Yard, whose only function was to identify the man in the bed.

The Chief Magistrate admitted Herz to bail of £2,000,thus leaving him free to get out of the hotel if only he could, and adjourned the proceedings until May 4 in Bow Street. There he handed down his decision that "no jury could possibly be expected to convict," that the letters cited as menaces to de Reinach said only: "Pay me that thou owest" and that the prosecution must therefore be discharged.

"No jury would say that in this case this was a menace, and further no jury would say that there was not money due," Sir John said. "A man has a right to use a certain amount of threats, I will not say how much, to get the money due him. Then there is another question to be considered in this case, which is, of course, a very large one. The difficulty of getting a jury to convict in a case of this kind is the long time since the occurrences and the death of Baron de Reinach, admitting that on both sides there were enormous transactions between them

221

and there are no books that show these transactions. How is it possible with complicated accounts and no books to come to any conclusion as to what the accounts between the parties really were. Therefore I cannot say that this gentleman should be committed for extradition.

"I cannot help saying that it is a matter of importance to consider what would have been the result if I had come to a different conclusion. The law as it now stands would be that I should have had to commit Dr. Herz to a prison where it would have been impossible to send him, or else to order him to be confined to his own house or room until such time as he could be sent to prison or could be extradited. But we have it on the evidence of medical men that such a time will never come, and it would be quite useless, only occasioning great grief to his relations and causing Dr. Herz himself to sink rapidly instead of slowly to his grave.

"One cannot have visited Bournemouth and seen Dr. Herz without feeling that the case is one of the saddest one has ever seen or without a feeling of pity for the wife and children who have been so carefully tending him. At the same time this has not influenced me in the decision I have arrived at. I am satisfied that I could have come to no other decision."

A new French parliamentary investigation into the Panama affair, convened the next year, found Sir John's decision not only "contrary to the good will" that the British government had shown at the start, but one that left Herz free to "try his hand again at some new extortions against our country."

The new inquiry resulted from Emile Arton's arrest at long last in London on November 17, 1895. Although he was wanted in Paris as the pay-off man in the Panama company's alleged purchase of parliamentary favor, the British court refused to extradite him except on other charges standing against him: fraud, forgery, and embezzlement in the bankruptcy of the Dynamite Company, of which he was an executive. But after he was convicted and sent to prison on those charges, he waived the protection of the extradition writ and volunteered to stand trial for bribing legislators, thus uncorking a deluge of incrimination that swept the Chamber of Deputies into yet another investigation.

Arton's effusions led to the arrest and trial of two Deputies, a Senator, and five former Deputies, despite his insistence that the notebook in which he said he listed his Panama handouts to legislators was not a record of bribes but only of gifts to hard-up friends in return for their friendly support of the lottery measure.

After a week of testimony the prosecution dropped the case against four of the defendants, and the jury acquitted the rest, the verdict rousing the courtroom audience to a shout of, " *Vive la République!*"

"It is clear that Arton* put in his notebook imaginary payments and that the only man to whom he offered money was himself!" the *Times* of London's Paris correspondent observed.

The investigating Deputies, moving at a more laborious pace than the trial court, invested months in running down leads that promised any degree of involvement, interrogating hundreds of witnesses, perusing mounds of documents, and eventually marshaling their findings in a 1,312-page report.

The big fraction of the report they devoted just to the doings of Cornelius Herz emphasized the mystery of his participation in the Panama affair, but did not clear it up.

On July 5, 1897, the committee chairman, Ernest Valle, put the key question to Imbert, administrator of de Reinach's estate, who was Herz's principal accuser: "We have found a note from Baron de Reinach titled 'Herz Blackmail,' in which the sum indicated was 10,000,000. Why did M. de Reinach give 10,-000,000 to Cornelius Herz?"

The Panama company, Imbert said, contracted to pay Herz for his help in winning government approval of its first application for authority to issue lottery bonds, and de Reinach endorsed the contract as the company's financial agent. But the government did not grant its approval.

"It is then that in 1888, I believe—I give you here, gentlemen, my impression—someone named Arton offered his cooperation," Imbert said. "He was coming back from Panama with de Lesseps and told him: 'I can take care of this business.' And the mission previously assigned to Herz was assigned to him.

*After serving his sentence for the Dynamite Company crimes, Arton went back into business and became a director of a Paris bank in the rue des Petits-Champs. He committed suicide on July 18, 1905, by taking cyanide in his office at 13 rue Lafitte.

Herz then returned from the North Cape threatening and saying: 'You cannot give to someone else what you have given to me.' He was told that his contract was valid only for 1886. He said, 'Not so, it is always effective, and I intend for you to settle.' "

The tie that bound de Reinach and Herz was a letter Herz demanded from the Baron to replace his contract with de Lesseps, Imbert testified. It was the letter in which de Reinach acknowledged that the 10,000,000 would be due Herz the day after the Panama company collected the first installment payment on the 1888 lottery issue.

"One speaks of a secret between Herz and Reinach," he said. "There was no secret. Herz had Reinach by the throat with his contract of 10,000,000."

Imbert insisted, however, that the letter implied the intention to make the payment proportionate to the success of the issue, and since only 40 per cent of the bonds were sold, Herz was due only 40 per cent. But Herz, he said, always replied: "That does not concern me. If you do not pay, I will tell everything."

"There was always the menace," Imbert said.

To the parliamentary investigators this was an inadequate explanation. There must have been something more that Herz had on de Reinach, they said, but as to what it may have been their report did not give a clue.

"We have shown," the report said, "the Baron de Reinach, despite all his vain efforts of resistance, always ended up acceding to the demands of his associate or accomplice, and letting the latter squeeze him for bigger sums than he himself had received for these purposes from the Panama company and snatch away small French savings, so impudently and criminally despoiled.

"It is our conviction that the ineluctable domination of Reinach by Herz could not stem solely from any explanation of ordinary business contracts and financial settlements; that in addition there had to be added a real or supposed influence that was attributed to Herz on certain politicians and figures in government, but that there must have been, above all, some important secret involving Panama and even other matters concerning Baron de Reinach and that Cornelius Herz was in a position to reveal and was constantly threatening to."

In Britain, Imbert's testimony was an aggravation to the freed but still bed-ridden Herz. He replied to it by inviting the investigating committee to Bournemouth to hear his own version and receive documents and correspondence that he offered to supply in full.

The committee approached him warily. Its first step was to send two of its members to Bournemouth to verify his signature on the invitation. Returning to Paris, one of them, Jean Plichon, Deputy for the Nord, told *Le Soir* that when he and his colleague stated their mission, Herz exclaimed: "Doesn't everyone in Paris from the President of the Republic down know my signature!" As soon as the English newspapers picked up the item in *Le Soir*, Herz telegraphed Plichon: "The majority of the statements therein are lies."

Immediately on assuring itself that the invitation to Bournemouth was not a fake, the committee scheduled a hearing to be held there at 3 p.m. on Thursday, July 22, and Valle, the chairman, notified Herz by telegram on July 17. The investigators decided to rendezvous the morning of the hearing at the Waterloo Station in London. Valle was going ahead to Cardiff on private business and would join them at Bournemouth.

But on July 19 Herz wrote to Valle that the committee should have consulted him before setting a date. He said he needed time to receive and examine the files, for which he had asked in the various civil and criminal actions brought against him, and proposed a postponement until 3 p.m. on August 12.

Unfortunately for the committee, Valle left for Cardiff before Herz's letter arrived on the morning of July 20, and no one opened it until his colleagues had started on their own journey, bound for a night out in London before coming to grips with their adversary at Bournemouth the next afternoon. The first they heard of his objections was from the Paris newspapers, which had picked up his letter from the *Times* of London.

Their junket was aborted at the very moment "when the twenty-five Deputies were about to step aboard the Channel steamer, each with the government allowance of three louis (twelve dollars) in the pocket of his tweed tourist suit."

The Paris press had saved the committee from a needless

and expensive journey to England. For the rescue it collected in a toll of heavyhanded irony.

The *New York Tribune* reported that "French Deputies have seldom before afforded such ground for ridicule," and in the convulsion Herz had become "the man of the day."

"His photographs are displayed in the shop windows of the boulevards," the *Tribune* said, "and in the flood of Parisian caricature Dr. Herz appears almost as a 'hero' in comparison with the French Deputies, the French parliamentary commissioners, and the French magistrates, who are all handled without gloves."

Herz protested he had no hand in their embarrassment. "If I'd wanted to make fools of them, all I'd have had to do was to let them come on to Bournemouth and then tell them what I wrote to them," he said. "Instead, I think I did the right thing. I gave them ample notice. If some of them had already left, it's because they wanted a trip to London. You don't have to leave on Tuesday to be in England Thursday."

The *Figaro*, remarking that some unkindly spirits regretted Herz's prompt notification because it deprived them of the spectacle of "this band of birdbrains" dragging themselves home wearily from a fruitless trip across the Channel, sniggered even at the clothes the junketing Deputies wore: "Ever since they almost went to Bournemouth, our investigators now present themselves at the Palais Bourbon in traveling clothes, and they seem to have particular views on what's elegant for tourists. They show vests of an audacious cut, sweaters of great fantasy, and ties that would frighten a bull, hats that would make Aristotle dream and compel him to add something new to his chapter. It is sometimes a clown's hat and sometimes a rag, wrinkled and hanging, or else a big black hat such as the Auvergnats wear. Certain dandies wear a white felt hat which they put over one ear, and one constantly looks for a feather. The loveliest of all is that of M. Valle, very high and very large. It is the color of amadou. It takes the most varied forms and the most surprising. It is a protean hat. At one moment one would have taken it to be the felt hat of Louis XIII, now a Puritan's hat, such as that which Cromwell's roundheads carried. Sometimes M. Valle pushes it back and bends it. He then thrusts one hand behind his back, one in his sweater, and one imagines Napoleon."

The mid-summer flood of parliamentary mortification that Herz had managed to uncork gave him nothing more than one last wry laugh in his long and losing fight with the French government.

Two months earlier he had made a demand for heavy damages, writing to the President of France, Fclix Faure: "I claim from the French government an indemnity of $5,000,000 for the false imprisonment upon false charges upon which I was illegally detained at the instance of the French government, which arbitrarily discarded or mutilated the laws of France in order to attain their ends in regard to me."

Receiving no reply, Herz retained Edward Lauterbach, a New York lawyer, to appeal to the President of the United States to intervene in behalf of the claim. Lauterbach, a City College classmate of his client, was three times chairman of the New York County Republican Committee and had been New York delegate-at-large to the Republican National Convention that nominated President William McKinley the year before. Six days after he filed Herz's appeal, the State Department notified him that it saw "no grounds whatever for diplomatic intervention on behalf of Dr. Herz."

Lauterbach continued to press the claim combatively, putting before the State Department a voluminous brief containing Maître Clunet's entire statement in the extradition case, official documents certifying every vital statistic of Herz's life, and the bitter affidavits of three women who had attended Herz devotedly for years—his wife, his secretary, Isabel Scott Turner, and his nurse, Mary Alice Winifrede Delahaunt.

The women charged that the French had doublecrossed him, that representatives of the French government had lured him into compromising the suit of the de Reinach estate by dangling in front of him like a carrot a promise to withdraw the criminal charges.

"With each new step in the prosecution he grew steadily more ill," his wife said, until even Maître Clunet, who had stubbornly opposed the compromise, at last advised it, telling her: "They have got him like a rat in a hole, and any sacrifice of money is preferable to sacrificing his life."

His secretary said that almost up to the minute the Correctional Court of Paris had pronounced sentence, Herz's household and his friends believed confidently that he would be freed as a result of his deal with Imbert. When he was summoned to the trial, she said, "we were immediately informed by the government through their friends and agents that this was the way the government had chosen to finish the matter, and they guaranteed that it would be satisfactory for us." Instead, she recited, the court refused to let Clunet present his case, disregarded the medical certificate, found Herz guilty by default, and imposed the maximum penalty on him.

On December 12, 1899, the State Department reaffirmed its refusal to intervene, despite an oral presentation by Lauterbach which, Secretary John Hay informed him, had "much impressed" the department.

Herz, who had moved into the Bournemouth Hotel at the beginning of 1893, left it only twice: on January 22, 1898, when he was taken for a brief drive around the town; and on July 7, 1898, when he was removed to Willesden Cemetery in northwest London, where he was buried in a grave marked by an unobtrusive granite monument bearing the inscription:

> Sacred to the memory of Dr. Cornelius Herz
> Who died at Tankerville
> Bournemouth
> July 6th, 1898, aged 52.

His death inspired a mixed refrain on both sides of the Atlantic.

"Charlatan though he was, he was not without feelings of gratitude, more especially for the numerous Englishmen who interested themselves in his case," London's *Pall Mall Gazette* said in a well adulterated tribute.

The *San Francisco Examiner*, which had rolled up the shade on Herz's California career, was more delicately ambivalent. It said: "Dr. Herz's brilliant attainments brought him into contact with many prominent people in this city, and everyone he met had cause to remember him. He found it an easy matter to raise funds by his various schemes, and always forgot to return the money he raised."

The New York newspapers awarded Herz a substantial play, *nil nisi bonum*, despite competition for space with the Spanish-American War and the loss of 580 persons in the collision off Nova Scotia of the French liner *Bourgogne* and the British sailing ship *Cromartyshire*.

Almost lost among these big stories was an item from Washington reporting an announcement by Senator John Tyler Morgan of Alabama that he would call up immediately a bill proposing that the United States build a canal across the Central American isthmus, this one by way of Nicaragua.

12

At the age of thirty-two Georges-Emile Lemarquis had a law practice that was perhaps the most multitudinous in the annals of advocacy.

Lemarquis had been only an obscure functionary of the Civil Court of the Department of the Seine until July 4, 1893. On that day the court elevated him to a position of intimidating power over a large section of the French business community and set off a chain of reactions with a monumental consequence—completion of the Panama Canal.

The court-appointed Lemarquis attorney for the unfortunates who held the billion francs of bonds that Ferdinand de Lesseps's Universal Panama Canal Company issued in the eight years before it went bankrupt in 1889. Thus he had more than 200,000 clients.

In the four and a half years since the de Lesseps company's bankruptcy, its liquidation had only inched along, the receivers beset by serious illness, the government more intent on prosecution and self-defense, the opposition on vendettas, than on financial recovery.

Joseph-Mathieu Brunet, a former Minister of Public Education, who was the first receiver, became so ill after a year that he asked the court to name a coreceiver. Its appointee, Achille Monchicourt, became the sole receiver when Brunet died on March 8, 1890. Three years later illness compelled Monchicourt, in his turn, to ask for a coreceiver.

The collapse of de Lesseps's company had raised a massive public doubt about the feasibility of the entire canal project. To evaluate it expertly, Brunet set up an examining committee of eleven French and foreign engineers, headed by Inspector General Guillemain, director of the National School of Bridges and Highways. It made an intensive study, including an on-the-spot examination by five of its members. Two months after Brunet's death, the committee reported that in its opinion the plant on the isthmus was in good condition and probably sufficient to finish the job, and that a canal with locks was feasible and could be built in eight years at a cost of 900,000,000 francs, of which 562,000,000 francs would be for construction and the rest for administration and financing.

Monchicourt thereupon bought an extension of the expiring Colombian concession, which had demanded completion of the canal within ten years of the organization of the de Lesseps company. Lucien Napoleon Bonaparte Wyse, who had obtained the concession at Bogota in 1879, went back there for the receiver, and on the day after Christmas in 1890 signed an agreement in which Colombia stipulated that if a new canal company were formed and work resumed by February 28, 1893, the government would allow another ten years for completion. For its cooperation the Colombian government charged 10,-000,000 francs in gold and 5,000,000 francs in paid-up shares of the successor company. Bonaparte Wyse demanded a 1,000,000-franc fee, but the receivers said he had not performed his mission exactly as ordered and that the job was worth only 400,000 francs, an estimate the court sustained.

No successor company was in sight on the stipulated deadline, but five weeks later the Colombian government, for an additional 2,000,000 francs gold, gave the receivership another extension, until October 3, 1894, to form one.

On July 1, 1893, the Chamber of Deputies took a giant step to streamline the liquidation and rejuvenate the canal project; it passed a special act providing for the appointment of a *mandataire*, or attorney, to represent all the bondholders, and gave him full powers to bring actions and make settlements in their behalf. Three weeks after the court named Lemarquis to this office, it appointed Jean-Pierre Gautron to serve as coreceiver with the ailing Monchicourt, who died the next winter.

The chief problem the new team faced was unmistakable.

"Construction could not be carried on except by a new company, but one primary difficulty was in the way; to form a new company, money was necessary," Lemarquis explained. "But it is certain that in the condition in which we found the liquidation of the company, and the operation itself, it was useless to try to get new funds from the public. The risk was too big."

He and his associate thereupon devised a simple, pragmatic solution, and applied it unrelentingly. "We decided to levy on the undue profits the syndicators had realized and the wealth of the company's responsible administrators," Lemarquis related.

In the summer of 1894, with the approach of the postponed deadline for organizing a new company to build the canal, they incorporated the *Compagnie Nouvelle du Canal de Panama*, with a capitalization of 65,000,000 francs, of which investors would subscribe 60,000,000 at the rate of 100 francs a share, and the rest would represent the paid up shares due Colombia as part payment for the first extension.

Lemarquis and Gautron had no expectation that they could finish the canal for this sum, but hoped it would be ample to advance the undertaking to a point at which they could present a detailed completion plan and cost projection.

Their first action was to bring a test case against Hugo Oberndoerffer, a roly-poly mercenary who not only had reaped an outsized profit on the canal company's bond issues but also obtained an enormous fee, ostensibly for suggesting the lottery device as a way to sell a sticky issue.

"I engaged the syndicates in the person of M. Hugo Oberndoerffer because it looked to me as if a suit against him would be the easiest to win," Lemarquis said.

The court attributed an ill-gotten gain of 3,653,201.50 francs to Oberndoerffer and ordered him to pay it back with interest. Lemarquis let him settle the judgment by subscribing to 3,-800,000 francs of the new company's stock.

Prodded by this judgment, sixty-three other members of the so-called underwriting syndicates toppled like a row of dominoes; they bought 3,285,700 francs of the new company's shares. These contributors, members of groups organized when Baron Jacques de Reinach was the old company's financial agent, had enjoyed an arrangement under which they advanced 2.50 francs for each bond issued, for which they were rewarded on a sliding scale that assured them of their money back if the issue was only one-eighth successful, and a 400 per cent profit on a complete sellout. The court ruled that the chance they took was so minimal it was no risk at all.

Lemarquis, in addition, squeezed 1,337,000 francs in outright restitution out of twenty-four members of the earlier syndicates. The de Lesseps company had given them options on bonds at a discount from the public offering price, but permitted them not to exercise the option until they had sold the bonds at a markup. This risk-free commitment, too, merited no reward, in the court's opinion.

Lemarquis got 10,000,000 francs in subscriptions to the new company's shares from three great French banks—*Crédit Lyonnais, Société Générale,* and *Société Générale de Crédit Industriel et Commercial*—on the ground that they had collected considerable sums from the de Lesseps company in syndicates and otherwise without sufficient justification. The first two institutions chipped in 4,000,000 francs each, and the third, 2,000,000 francs. From the bankrupt company's administrators, or their heirs, came 7,885,000 francs in stock subscriptions.

Then the liquidating team decided to attack contractors, still solvent and within reach of French law, who had shared in the old company's benefactions. "The best case we had to bring against the contractors was the one against Eiffel," Lemarquis said.

They threatened to bring an 18,000,000-franc breach of contract suit, and settled for Eiffel's subscription to 10,000,000 francs of the new shares. Three other contractors agreed to subscribe for 5,150,000 francs, and in addition the four, in settlement of claims of their own totaling 13,463,644 francs for services to the bankrupt company, agreed to accept 232.37 francs in cash and the balance in lottery bonds computed at a third of their face value.

Couvreux & Hersent, the friendly contractors, who had not disclaimed misleading statements the de Lesseps company attributed to them in promoting its stock in 1880, accepted Lemarquis's assessment of a 300,000-franc subscription to the stock of the new company, then voluntarily doubled it.

All these subscriptions left the liquidators approximately 20,000,000 francs short of their announced goal of 60,000,000 francs, and on September 22, 1894, they offered the remaining shares to the public. The public subscribed for less than 3,-500,000 francs of the stock.

Gautron thereupon made up the deficit by buying the unsold shares with funds available to the liquidation. These included the proceeds of the transactions with Dr. and Mme. Herz, the de Reinach estate, the estate of former Agriculture Minister Francois-Paul Barbe, who was a major beneficiary of de Lesseps company largesse, and of the judgment against Charles Baïhaut, the former Public Works Minister.

✓   On October 20, 1894, just eleven days before time to organize a new canal company ran out, the *Compagnie Nouvelle du Canal de Panama* achieved corporate existence. Meeting at the French Horticultural Society's auditorium at 84 rue Grenelle, it elected a board composed of well known bankers, industrialists, and jurists, including representatives of the three banks that had subscribed for the shares, and took over the bankrupt company's concessions from Colombia, its construction work and matériel on the Isthmus of Panama, and all its plans, studies, and documents.

Gautron also put in trust for its benefit the shares of the Panama Railroad, for which the de Lesseps company had paid almost $20,000,000 and which had closed 1893 with assets of approximately $15,175,000 and liabilities of $13,500,000, for a surplus of $1,800,000; title to the shares was not to pass to the new company until it had completed the canal or paid 20,000,-000 francs, (about $4,000,000) to the liquidator.

In exchange for the properties and concessions Gautron handed over, the new company, by bylaw, earmarked 60 per cent of its earnings for the liquidator, who also had bought more than a quarter of its stock. Thus, for the benefit of Lemarquis's corral of shareholders, who had subscribed more than two thirds of its funds, only a withered fraction of its revenues would remain.

✓   Even with 60,000,000 francs cash in bank, the first requirement of the New Panama Canal Company was to establish credibility. Its charter provided for the appointment of a special five-member engineering committee to report on the work being done and the conclusions to be drawn from it, the report to be rendered when the company had spent half its capital; at that time a special meeting of the shareholders would decide whether or not to complete the canal and, if it decided to go ahead, by what ways and means.

To endow its ultimate decisions with maximum invulnerability, the company also established an international board of fourteen eminent engineers which would represent "the widest possible experience, the severest judgment, and the most independent conclusions." They would conduct their own investigation.

Its chairman was a retired Inspector General of the French Department of Bridges and Highways, and its members included the chief engineer of the Croton Aqueduct in New York, a General of the United States Army Corps of Engineers, the chief engineer of England's Manchester Canal, a former technical director of works of the Kiel Canal, a former director of the technical academy at Darmstadt, noted Russian and Colombian engineers, as well as a half dozen much respected French technicians. To consider all financial and statistical questions, the company set up an adjunct board headed by Paul Leroy-Beaulieu, a famous economist who had been an outspoken and persistent critic of the de Lesseps enterprise.

Between February, 1896, and September, 1898, the international technical board held ninety-seven regular meetings and numerous informal ones, and sent several of its members to the isthmus for a firsthand examination. At the same time the new company resumed operations on the isthmus, which Brunet had been compelled to suspend in May, 1889. Its working force grew to 2,000 men, and it complied with the terms of its concession by excavations along lines that appeared certain to be useful whatever plan was adopted. In November, 1898, the international board rendered its report, declaring its unanimous confidence in the "entire feasibility and practicability of completing the canal."

In December, with half its capital spent and the statutory committee reporting, the New Panama Canal Company adopted a plan for a canal with eight locks, its general location the same as that selected by the old company, and its cost, exclusive of financing charges, estimated at 509,250,000 francs.

But by now the Panama canal appeared to be in jeopardy of powerful competition; the United States government was giving every indication of becoming the builder of a canal of its own along the Nicaragua route. The likelihood that this threat would become a competitive fact had grown persistently since 1885, when Aniceto G. Menocal, an engineering authority on transisthmian canal routes, conducted a new survey for the United States Secretary of the Navy. He had again recommended the Nicaragua route, as he had done at the Paris canal congress of 1879 that voted for the Panama route.

In 1887, acting for the Nicaragua Canal Association of New York, Menocal obtained a concession from the Nicaraguan government. It permitted two and a half years for preliminary work, and ten years thereafter for completion of a canal, with Nicaragua to receive a minimum of $4,000,000 on a guarantee of 6 per cent of all securities issued to finance the project.

The old Panama Canal Company was still in business, though doddering; but when Ferdinand de Lesseps learned of Menocal's proposed Nicaragua canal, he reacted with characteristic cheer. It would be useful only for irrigation purposes, he told the *London Standard,* because the locks its promoters contemplated would make transit so slow that a voyage around the Horn would be preferable.

The financial structure of the Nicaragua project rested largely on a foundation of hopeful promises exchanged by two corporations that evolved from the Nicaragua Canal Association: one a construction company, the other a company to exercise the concession.

The former, the Nicaragua Canal Construction Company, was chartered under Colorado law on June 10, 1887, with a $12,000,000 capitalization. The other, the Maritime Canal Company of Nicaragua, operated under a Vermont charter until February, 1889, when Congress passed and President Grover Cleveland signed a bill granting it a federal charter.

Under a contract between the two corporations, title to the work as it progressed was vested in Maritime, which paid for it with shares of its capital stock and with obligations for first mortgage bonds it was to issue.

On November 30, 1887, the construction company sent out a survey party headed by Menocal, who had become its chief engineer. His second in command was Robert Edwin Peary, a young Navy lieutenant, for whom the voyage was tropical preparation for a career in Arctic exploration.

The Panama Affair

On October 22, 1889, almost two and a half years to the day from Nicaragua's ratification of the concession, construction began with a ceremonial turning of the first spadeful of earth. The route chosen was from Greytown on the Caribbean to Brito on the Pacific, a port-to-port distance of 169.448 miles, of which only 26.783 miles would be man-made canal. The rest of the passage would be by way of the San Juan River, Lake Nicaragua, and the basins in the valleys of the Descado, San Francisco and Tola rivers. Construction cost was estimated at $65,000,000.

Soon 1,600 men were at work on the canal. They built wharves, warehouses, and landing facilities, officers' quarters, hospitals, workshops, and a thousand feet of breakwater at Greytown. They assembled a powerful dredging plant, excavated almost two miles of canal to a depth of 17 feet and a width of 100 to 230 feet, laid 11 miles of railroad along the route, and strung 60 miles of telegraph wire.

The construction company spent almost $4,500,000 in cash, and in payment for plant issued $2,900,000 in securities. Investments by world-famous financiers burnished its prospects; early in 1892 its president, former United States Senator Warner Miller of New York, announced with satisfaction that Andrew Carnegie, John W. Mackay, H.O. Armour, Cornelius N. Bliss, and H.M. Flagler had become large shareholders. But in the panic of 1893 the company was thrown into receivership.

It had assets but could not realize on them. In its treasury were more than $14,875,000 of Maritime stock and almost $5,-600,000 in Maritime's obligations for first mortgage bonds not yet issued. But Maritime, with a $100,000,000 capitalization and permission by charter to double it, reported to the Secretary of the Interior in November, 1893, that since its organization it had sold only $1,014,500 of its shares.

Associates in the Maritime Canal Company and new investors strove assiduously to revive the construction company, bringing forth a barrage of reorganization plans. A commission appointed by President McKinley re-examined the project and estimated that the canal could be built for $133,000,000. Another commission filed a further report in favor of the Nicaragua route. Senator John Tyler Morgan of Alabama gave the undertaking powerful support, saying: "Should the canal cost the people of this country $300,000,000 it would be money well laid out, and even upon the basis of such an expenditure the investment would bring us a handsome profit in the shape of reduction of tolls and the fostering of our commerce on the high seas." He proposed an amendment to the act of incorporation that would cancel Maritime's previously issued shares, direct the Federal government to invest heavily in a new issue, and empower the President of the United States to appoint most of the company's directors.

None of these efforts to rehabilitate the project succeeded. As time for completion of the canal under the terms of the concession began to run out, a new syndicate sprang up around William R. Grace, former Mayor of New York, and Edward R. Cragin, who had recently helped General Horace Porter raise funds from the public to build Grant's Tomb.

The new syndicate's lawyer told the Commerce Committe of the House of Representatives that its members included John J. Astor, Levi P. Morton, Robert Goelet, and other tycoons of similar renown, and that one of its professional associates was Lyman E. Cooley, chief engineer of the Chicago drainage canal.

Recognizing there was little likelihood that Maritime could meet the deadline for completion of the canal, President Jose Santos Zelaya of Nicaragua granted a "promise of contract" under which the Grace syndicate would receive a concession to build a canal the day after the old one expired. To bind the contract, the Grace group engaged to pay the Nicaraguan government $100,000 on ratification and an additional $400,000 four months later. It made the down payment, then abandoned the project.

While these transactions were in progress and the New Panama Canal Company, in Paris, was anxiously approaching its own time of decision, the opening of a waterway across the isthmus of Central America had become of momentous concern to the people of the United States. The war with Spain, and the voyage of the battleship *Oregon,* second largest in the United States Navy, dramatized the urgent need for a maritime short cut between the east and west coasts. Rushing to take part in the battle against the remnants of the Spanish fleet at Santiago harbor, Captain Charles Edgar Clark needed approximately six weeks to bring the *Oregon* around the Horn from San Francisco to Cuban waters.

The rumble of the rising American interest was audible in Paris, and the report to the New Panama Canal Company from its distinguished panel of independent consultants had been in the hands of the company scarcely two days when it notified President McKinley of the findings.

Hailing its Panama route as "indisputably the maritime highway which can be opened to navigation in the shortest time and at the least possible expense," the French company also sent its director general, Maurice Hutin, and Lemarquis, the de Lesseps bondholders' *mandataire*, to inform the American Congress and the public of its plans to complete its own canal.

The company's secretary, Edouard Lampre, explaining its strategy to the United States Senate Committee on Interoceanic Canals, said: "We have plenty of cash in France to build it, but the rivalry with the Nicaragua route, and the possibility of the Congress of the United States passing a resolution for the construction of the Nicaragua canal has frightened the people there, so we thought it best to seek some kind of a combination here to build the canal, then with the assistance of the United States, and now to let the canal go to the United States if they will have it."

Hutin and Lemarquis put up at the Hotel Waldorf in New York, reinforcing an already formidable American representation in the person of William Nelson Cromwell, a lawyer of imposing mental endowments who, as the *New York World* described him, could "smile as sweetly as a society belle and at the same time deal a blow at a business foe that ties him in a hopeless tangle of financial knots."

"He is an artist at pulling a badly involved company out of a hole," the *World* said, and, continuing its eulogy, "has more ways of getting around a seemingly hopeless proposition than seem possible to his adversaries. He is one of the readiest talkers in town. No life insurance agent could beat him. He talks fast, and when he wishes to, never to the point."

Cromwell headed the law firm of Sullivan & Cromwell, which had become general counsel for the Panama Railroad Company in 1894, and counsel for the New Panama Canal Company in the United States two years later.

On February 28, 1899, the lawyers and Hutin offered the United States an opportunity to invest in the company's

Panama canal project. Although the company had never proposed and did not seek "any appropriation of financial aid from the United States in the completion of its canal," they wrote to President McKinley, it recognized "a national sentiment in favor of acquiring some pecuniary interest in any canal connecting the Atlantic and Pacific oceans."

As a result, the company would extend to the United States government every assistance in examining the Panama canal works, and if the government then adopted the Panama route, they told the President, the company would be willing to reincorporate under the laws of one of the states of the Union, and would transfer its concessions and property to this new corporation. It would then give the United States such representation on its board of directors and such opportunity to acquire an interest in its securities "as may be permitted by its concessions, which of course, must be scrupulously observed."

Three days later President McKinley approved an act of Congress empowering him to make a thorough investigation to determine "the most feasible and practicable route" for a canal across the Central American isthmus, and the cost of building it and putting it under the exclusive "control, management, and ownership of the United States."

Acting under this authority, the President appointed an Isthmian Canal Commission comprised of some of the foremost military, naval, and civilian engineers in the United States, who began at once a long and painstaking study of every aspect of an Atlantic-Pacific canal. In the summer of 1899 they went to Paris, where the French company gave them complete access to its data and convened for their benefit a meeting with its international technical board, even bringing some of its members from distant countries.

Early in 1900 the Isthmian Canal Commission went to the isthmus, and on April 10 Admiral John G. Walker, its chairman, put three specific questions to Hutin, who had become president of the French company:

> "1. Is the New Panama Canal Company willing to sell to the United States all of the rights, privileges, and franchises, together with all the works, railways (including the Panama Railway), telegraph or telephone

lines, buildings, lands, plant, material, drawings, and documents of every description which it owns or controls in connection with the construction of a canal across the Isthmus of Panama?

"2. Is the company able—that is, has it the legal power —to give a clear title to such rights, franchises, property, etc., of every description, free of all encumbrance or claim of any nature from any person whatsoever, and particularly from the stockholders or creditors of the old Panama Canal Company?

"3. For what sum, in cash, will the company transfer to the United States all of the rights, privileges, franchises, property, etc., of every description which it owns or controls in connection with the construction of a canal across the Isthmus of Panama?"

Walker pointed out to Hutin that the commission had no authority to accept or reject terms. He said it was gathering information for the President of the United States and was operating under a law that contemplated "only the complete 'control, management and ownership' of the canal by the United States, and not a partial or joint control with private corporations or individuals."

Hutin did not answer the Admiral for ten weeks, but on April 26 he took the precaution of buying a six-year extension of the Colombian concession for 5,000,000 francs gold, although it still had four and a half years to run. This payment, to the government of Colombian President Manuel Antonio Sanclemente, was a calculated risk, made in the face of a warning from revolutionists that if they came to power, they would reject the extension, which they contended only the national congress had authority to grant.

But without the concession the Paris company had nothing to sell, and, unless it could persuade the Colombian government to amend an inhibiting provision of the franchise, no likely customer to whom to sell it. This provision not only forbade the company to cede or mortgage its rights to any nation or foreign government, under penalty of forfeiture, but, in the case of the Panama Railroad's concession, imposed forfeiture for the mere act of trying to cede or transfer its privilege to a foreign government. Thus it became impossible for Hutin to answer Walker responsively. This was only one of Hutin's troubles in attempting to dicker with the United States. For the first time in more than a half century of intermittent agitation for a transisthmian canal, legislation authorizing the government to build one had advanced in the United States Congress to the point at which affirmative action appeared probable to political forecasters.

The measure, introduced by Representative William P. Hepburn, an Iowa Republican, authorized the President to acquire rights of way for the Nicaragua route from the Nicaraguan and Costa Rican governments, appropriated any sum necessary to get them, and empowered the President then to direct the Secretary of War to build the canal.

Sullivan & Cromwell reacted with a statement exhorting Congress to take no action "without waiting for the report of the Isthmian Canal Commission after having appropriated $1,000,000 to secure information upon which to base its action, and after having invited information of the New Panama Canal Company's project, the information of its surveys and plans as well as its valuable records, statistics, and data, the result of the accumulation of years of labor and investigation." The lawyers at the same time denied the "rumor that the company is or has been offering its works, plant, or machinery for sale" and took the occasion to assert: "The company has at no time had or maintained any lobby in Washington, and any statement to the contrary is untrue. It relies upon the merits of its project and the advance condition of its work, and is confident of the completion of the canal."

Disregarding these admonitions, the House, on May 2, passed the Hepburn bill by a vote of 225-35.

When Hutin eventually answered Walker's April 10 letter on July 26, it was only to say that the company's administrative board was preparing a reply to the questions and to ask how soon the Admiral wanted it. Walker said he would like to have it as soon as practicable, but no later than October 1.

The canal company, handcuffed by a concession that did not leave it free to sell to its likeliest customer, sustained a holding action. It did not reply until November 26, and then Hutin told Walker that in view of the commission's lack of authority to negotiate, "nothing decisive at this time could result from a categorical answer to certain of your inquiries."

But the spring of 1901 brought a sign that Colombia would release the company. On April 29 the Colombian Minister to Washington, Carlos Martinez Silva, wrote to Hutin: "In order to facilitate preparation of the complete report of the Isthmian Canal Commission, I would beg you to inform me, at least in a general way, what would be the conditions under which your company would be disposed to cede its franchise to the government of the United States, of course with the necessary authorization of the Colombian government."

To this inquiry, Hutin needed only two days to reply that if Colombia consented, his company would sell its concession and all its property to the United States government. He said the price would be determined, so far as possible, "by amicable valuations and agreement" and that "if a considerable difference of opinion should arise, recourse would be had, as is just and equitable, to arbitration in the usual form." He also revealed that in fixing a price the company would be looking for additional compensation in the form of annual payments or a lump sum "for the eventual profits which its concession would have enabled it to make."

This exchange, Admiral Walker told Hutin, who was then in Washington, encouraged him to hope that "you will take up the subject once more and give me such additional information as you feel at liberty to do, particularly in reply to the first and third questions."

Hutin, in his answer, reiterated what he had told the Colombian Ambassador—that the canal company would arrive at a price through negotiation and arbitration. Walker commented that "as a basis for these negotiations there should be some expression of the views of the company as to the value of its property." On June 28 Hutin, back in Paris, cabled to Walker: "Will send you in about a fortnight detailed valuation of company property." On July 25 he cabled to the Admiral: "We intend sending you by next mail detailed valuation company's property, but preparation has required much more time than contemplated."

Although the next mail brought no such data to the commission, Walker and Hutin arranged to meet in Washington again in the fall; but on September 5, Leon Czolgosz shot and fatally wounded President McKinley at the Pan American Exposition at Buffalo, New York. Nine days later, the day the President died, Hutin cabled punctiliously to Walker: "Under present sad circumstances, do you still think I should meet you in Washington about October 1?"

"If you intend naming price for property and concessions, there should be no delay," the Admiral answered.

Before Hutin sailed on October 9, he sent Walker some figures, in a document entitled: "A Study Concerning the Estimated Value of the French Company's Contribution to the Canal Undertaking in Case of a Transfer of Our Concession to the United States Government."

"You will kindly note," Hutin requested in a covering letter, "that we have viewed these values in their intrinsic consistence, in what they really are in themselves, without any reference to their relation with the comparative expenses of either canal; in short, for the proportion of usefulness they actually present in the Panama Canal undertaking, supposed to be completed and regarded solely in itself. They represent what might be called the real and absolute value of our contribution."

He hastened to add that the sums set forth were subject to negotiation, which might alter them to "a more or less important degree."

Walker told Hutin, who arrived in Washington a day after his letter did: "The paper you now submit does not yet give a definite answer to the question, but it contains the elements from which a final sum can be obtained." He offered to continue informal discussions if Hutin thought the commission could be helpful in preparing the company's "final proposition."

On October 22 the Admiral prodded the reluctant vendor again, reminding him that Congress would convene on December 2 and that the President should have the commission's report substantially earlier.

On November 5, with Hutin still having named no firm price, Walker performed his own addition of the numerous figures set forth in the company's wordily titled study, and told him: "These figures I understand to aggregate 565,500,000 francs, or $109,141,000."

"The total, in francs, is correct, and I presume also the rate of exchange you have adopted," Hutin hastened to reply. "But whether each of these amounts is singly considered or their total, it is essential to preserve their true character. They represent, as has already been explained on different occasions verbally and in writing, valuations that the company believes just, because it has established them with the greatest care and regard for material exactness. But the company admits that they may be criticized and that it would make reasonable concessions if they were justifiable."

The isthmian canal commissioners thereupon considered their long, laborious pursuit of a firm price ended, and on November 16, 1901, sent their report to Theodore Roosevelt, new President of the United States. "After considering all the facts developed by the investigations made by the commission, and the actual situation as it now stands," they told the President, "this commission is of the opinion that 'the most practicable and feasible route' for an isthmian canal, to be 'under the control, management and ownership of the United States,' is that known as the Nicaragua route."

It was a matter of price, they said. Exclusive of the yet undetermined costs of concessions from the Central American governments whose territories the various routes would cross, the commission projected a construction cost of $189,864,062 for the Nicaragua Canal, and the cost of completing the Panama Canal at $144,233,358 plus the $109,141,500 purchase price Walker's additions had produced.

The commissioners thought that what the Paris company had to sell was worth only $40,000,000, which they arrived at by valuing the useful portion of the completed excavations at $27,-474,033, the maps, drawings, and records at $2,000,000, and the 68,500 Panama Railroad shares at their $100 par value, and adding 10 per cent of this $36,324,033 total to cover possible omissions. The $6,850,000 figure they put on the railroad shares was barely 30 per cent of the price de Lesseps had paid for them in 1882, but was twenty-six times the railroad company's net income for 1901.

"There are certain physical advantages, such as a shorter canal line, a more complete knowledge of the country through which it passes, and lower costs of maintenance and operations in favor of the Panama route," the commissioners advised the President. "But the price fixed by the Panama Canal Company for a sale of its property and franchises is so unreasonable that its acceptance cannot be recommended by this commission."

The new company's failure to make the sale appeared to enrage the Panama investors even more than the de Lesseps company's bankruptcy had done. "The opinion in financial circles is that by playing a game of finesse, and refraining from making a reasonable firm offer in dollars and cents to sell the canal outright, those who conducted the negotiations destroyed the company's last and only hope of salvation," the *New York Tribune* explained from Paris.

Hutin resigned, and Marius Bo succeeded him as president. Police were called to quell a riot at a shareholders' meeting on December 21, after which the directors managed to submit a resolution that blamed the rejection on a "misunderstanding which must be dissipated."

"We believe that there is here only a misconception," they said in a report to the meeting, "for the company has never intended to fix a price but only to offer a basis for discussion. The communications previously received permitted it, besides, to count upon the commission's lending itself to that discussion. But the commission has considered that its authorization did not extend to negotiating, and it has made its report, stating therein as the price demanded by the company the total of it valuations."

The company asked permission to renew negotiations on the basis of the commission's own $40,000,000 figure. "The few speakers who secured a hearing urged adoption of the board's proposals as being the shareholders' only salvation," the *Tribune* reported. "One speaker said it was plainly impossible for the company to finish the canal, as it could not raise money in France or in the rest of Europe."

The meeting then authorized the company to try again, and just before the new year Lampre sailed on the steamship *Aquitaine* to represent the company at the bargaining table. Suddenly, while its emissary was still en route, the company transformed its strategy, accepting advice from a new and noisy quarter, and after two years of coy evasion named a firm price.

The Panama Affair

Throughout much of the year 1901, Philippe Bunau-Varilla had barnstormed the United States, extolling the merits of the Panama canal. In a frenetic tour of lecturing, hectoring, and pamphleteering, he had importuned the members of the Canal Commission, audiences of influential businessmen up and down the country, the powerful Ohio Republican Senator, Marcus Alonzo Hanna, other members of the United States Senate, even President McKinley.

A small, trim man with a spiked mustache and a bristling sense of his own rectitude, Bunau-Varilla had a broad variety of reasons—economic, emotional, patriotic, professional—to be a champion of the Panama project. As a twenty-five-year-old engineer, he had gone out to the isthmus for the de Lesseps company, become its temporary chief engineer by surviving yellow fever and several seniors who succumbed to it; then, with two other engineers and his brother, Maurice, later publisher of *Le Matin*, had formed the contracting firm of Artique, Sonderegger, Bunau-Varilla et Cie., to work on the Culebra cut. After the bankruptcy of the de Lesseps enterprise, he had continued to battle doggedly for the realization of its objective, even going to St. Petersburg to try to induce Russia's Finance Minister to participate in a new venture. Finally, he had a substantial personal interest in the success of the Panama project; Artigue, Sonderegger, Bunau-Varilla et Cie., was one of the contracting firms Lemarquis had herded into membership in the risky New Panama Canal Company's family of stockholders. The Bunau-Varilla firm subscribed to 2,200,000 francs of the new shares, and settled its own claim of 1,912,000 francs against the old company for 86.70 francs cash and the balance in lottery bonds.

In the spring of 1901 he spent more than 135,000 francs to publish three lengthy appeals in the French press for money to complete the canal, promising to subscribe 2,000,000 francs on his own if an attempt were made to raise 500,000,000 francs of new money. His campaign brought in other pledges of only 200,000 francs.

Immediately after the riotous meeting of the stockholders, he denounced the company's strategy to Bo, the new president, and Henri Germain, head of *Crédit Lyonnais,* one of the banks that Lemarquis had dragooned into becoming big shareholders in the company.

"What is needed is not to negotiate, it is to fix a firm price," Bunau-Varilla lectured them. "Yesterday you might still have done it; today it is too late. Yesterday you might have negotiated and got sixty, perhaps seventy million dollars. Today the battle is lost. You can make an offensive attack again only if you accept the figure of $40,000,000, at which the commission has placed that part of the company's property which she can use in her project. This estimate is wretchedly low, but as you have let the opportunity slip by, you must grab at any solution still possible. You still have fourteen days before you. If on January 7, at the opening of Congress, the price is not settled, you will have accepted an unparalleled responsibility."

At 11 a.m. on January 4 the directors met at the company's offices at 7 rue Louis-le-Grand, almost next door to Lemarquis's residence, and gobbled up Bunau-Varilla's counsel. They rushed a cable to Jules Boeuvfé, an official of the French Embassy at Washington, requesting that he "inform Admiral Walker immediately and without awaiting Lampre's arrival that the company declares itself ready to transfer to the government of the United States on the payment of $40,000,000 its properties and concessions estimated at that amount by the Isthmian Canal Commission in its last report page 103 in conformity with the terms and conditions of said report."

Making sure that it could not possibly be misunderstood, the company assiduously delineated its intent in two more cables sent to Walker in the week that followed. The first, on January 9, said: "The New Panama Canal Company declares that it is ready to accept for the totality, without exception, of its property and rights on the isthmus the amount of $40,000,-000, the above offer to remain in force up to March 4, 1903." On January 11 Bo informed the Admiral: "Offer of sale of all our property applies also to all maps and archives in Paris."

In consequence of these offers, the Isthmian Canal Commission on January 18 filed a supplementary report that stated: "The unreasonable sum asked for the property and rights of the New Panama Canal Company when the commission reached its former conclusion overbalanced the advantages of that route, but now that the estimates of the two routes have been nearly equalized, the commission can form its judgment by weighing the advantages of each and determining which is the more practicable and feasible.

"There is, however, one important matter which cannot enter into its determination, but which may in the end control the action of the United States. Reference is made to the disposition of the governments whose territory is necessary for the construction and operation of an isthmian canal. It must be assumed by the commission that Colombia will exercise the same fairness and liberality if the Panama route is determined upon that would have been expected of Nicaragua and Costa Rica should the Nicaragua route be preferred.

"After considering the changed conditions that now exist and all the facts and circumstances upon which its present judgment must be based, the commission is of the opinion that 'the most practicable and feasible route' for an isthmian canal to be 'under the control, management and ownership of the United States' is that known as the Panama route."

On June 19, 1902, the long and bitter fight against the Hepburn bill, which had authorized construction of a Nicaragua canal, came to an end when the Senate adopted an amendment introduced by Senator John Coit Spooner, a Wisconsin Republican, that transformed the House bill into an entirely new measure.

It authorized the President to build a canal on the Panama route if the United States could get a good title to the French company's properties, and the proper concessions from Colombia, and, if not, to go ahead with the Nicaragua project. It empowered the President to spend $40,000,000 for the French company's property and franchises, gave him a preliminary appropriation of $10,000,000 for either route, and authorized an individual appropriation of $135,000,000 for the Panama project and $180,000,000 in the event the Nicaragua route was selected. A conference committee accepted the Spooner amendment without change, and both houses of Congress promptly adopted the conference report.

Late on Saturday night, June 28, 1902, President Roosevelt signed the Isthmian Canal Bill with an ordinary steel pen, which became a historic possession of Mark Hanna, its redoubtable proponent.

With the signing of the act, all parties to the transaction

began a brisk cleanup of the legal and diplomatic details that still littered the path to a closing.

Arbitrators settled a dispute between the New Panama Canal Company and the liquidator of its bankrupt predecessor over the division of the forthcoming payment from the United States: 206,000,000 francs at the prevailing rate of exchange. They ruled that before dividing the proceeds according to the stipulated formula of 60 percent to the old company and 40 per cent to its successor, the liquidator would receive 20,000,000 francs for handing over the Panama Railroad shares, and the new company would get back the 5,000,000 francs it had paid Colombia for extending the concession in 1900.

The office of the United States Attorney General, Philander C. Knox, conducted a search of title, and on October 25 Knox reported to President Roosevelt: "I am of the opinion that the United States would receive a good, valid, and unencumbered title."

Secretary Hay promptly began to negotiate with Dr. Tomas Herran, Colombian *chargé d' affaires* at Washington, for Colombia's approval of the transfer of its concession, and on January 22, 1903, they signed the Hay-Herran Convention. Under its terms, Colombia authorized the French company to sell its isthmian property and concessions to the United States, to which it ceded a 30-mile-wide strip of land between the Atlantic and the Pacific; Colombia would retain sovereignty over the territory and the United States would have administrative control for police and sanitation purposes; in return, the United States would pay Columbia $10,000,000 on exchange of ratifications, and, starting nine years thereafter, $250,000 dollars a year in gold.

The United States government then made it first formal acceptance of the French company's offer to sell. On February 17, the Attorney General informed its management: "By direction of the President of the United States, I have the honor to say that the offer of the New Panama Canal Company, as contained in your telegrams of January 9 and 11, 1902, through Admiral Walker, to sell the property and rights on the Isthmus of Panama and in Paris, to which offer M. Gautron, liquidator of the *Universelle Interocéanique* Panama Canal Company assented, with the approval of the Civil Tribunal of the Seine, is hereby accepted, subject to the modifications of articles 21 and 22 of the concessionary contract by the ratification of both countries, and the going into effect of the pending treaty concerning the Panama canal between the United States and Colombia, now signed and awaiting ratification."

The United States ratified the treaty on March 17. Colombia never did. On July 9 a spokesman for the Colombian government told the American Minister at Bogota that he did not think the Colombian Senate would ratify the Hay-Herran Convention without two amendments, one stipulating a $10,000,000 payment from the French company for permission to sell the concession, the other increasing the initial United States payment to $15,000,000.

During the summer Senator Jose Domingo Obaldia was appointed Governor of Panama, and on September 11 the American Minister advised Secretary Hay from Bogota: "Senator Obaldia's separatist tendencies are well known, and he is reported to have said that should a canal treaty not pass, the Department of Panama would declare its independence and would be right in doing so. That these are his opinions there is no doubt."

Revolution was a chronic political condition on the isthmus, where the United States, under its Treaty of 1846 with the Republic of New Granada, from which Colombia evolved, guaranteed that the "free transit from one to the other sea may not be embarrassed in any future time while this treaty exists." In the fifty-seven years since the signing of the treaty, fifty-three "revolutions, rebellions, insurrections, civil wars, and other outbreaks" had taken place there, President Roosevelt recalled in a subsequent editorial in *The Outlook*, reviewing his course in the Panama affair.

"Twice there had been attempted secessions of Panama," he wrote, "and on six different occasions the Marines and sailors from United States warships were forced to land on the isthmus in order to protect property and to see that transit across the isthmus was kept clear, a duty we were by treaty required to perform."

His intelligence reports in the summer of 1903 forecast another revolution immediately after adjournment of the Colombian Congress in October. "Acting in view of all these facts, I sent various naval vessels to the Isthmus," President Roosevelt wrote. "The orders to the American naval officers were to maintain free and uninterrupted transit across the isthmus, and, with that purpose, to prevent the landing of armed forces with hostile intent at any point within 50 miles of Panama. These orders were precisely such as had been issued again and again in preceding years—1900, 1901, and 1902, for instance. They were carried out. Their necessity was clearly shown by the fact that a body of Colombian troops landed at Colon and threatened a reign of terror, announcing their intention of killing all the American citizens in Colon. The prompt action of Captain Hubbard of the gunboat *Nashville* prevented this threat from being put into effect; he rescued the imperiled Americans, and finally persuaded the Colombian troops to reembark and peacefully return to Colombia."

The state of Panama declared its independence of Colombia on November 4, and two days later the revolutionary junta governing the new Republic named as its first Minister to Washington the kinetic Frenchman, Bunau-Varilla, who claimed major credit for inciting, quarterbacking, and helping to finance the revolt.

The new Minister's mission was to negotiate a canal agreement with Secretary Hay, and on November 18 they signed the Hay-Bunau-Varilla Treaty, giving Panama the same remuneration the Hay-Herran Convention would have brought to Colombia.

Panama ratified the treaty on December 2, the United States on February 23, and two months later the shareholders of the New Panama Canal Company, with only three dissents, approved the sale to the United States and authorized their directors to liquidate their company.

The company wanted its $40,000,000 handed over in Paris and was willing to pay the expenses of the transaction. To accomplish it, buyer and seller appointed the banking house of J. P. Morgan & Co. as their special disbursing agent, and Morgan went to Paris to handle the delivery in person.

His firm shipped $18,000,000 in gold to France, bought exchange on Paris for the balance in several European markets, and paid the money into the Bank of France, which the canal company had designated depositary.

Bo, the company's president, and Albert Rischmann, one of his directors, executed the conveyance for the canal company; Assistant Attorneys General W. A. Day and Charles W. Russell signed it for the United States on May 2, and Morgan left Paris the next day for Aix-les-Bains. His firm's services cost the canal company approximately $35,000.

The United States repaid the $40,000,000 to Morgan's on May 9, delivering the largest treasury warrant it had ever issued, the largest previous warrant having been for the $7,200,000 paid to Russia for Alaska in 1868. Out of the payment to the Bank of France, Gautron received 128,600,000 francs for distribution to 226,296 bondholders, a payout of about 10 cents on the dollar of their investment in the de Lesseps enterprise.

The balance of the American payment went to 6,796 shareholders of the New Panama Canal Company, at least 70 per cent of whom were shareholders from its organization. They received approximately 130 francs per share. Thus the new company's original shareholders, both the willing and unwilling, who held their stock thoughout the company's anxious career, got their money back with interest that amounted to approximately 3 per cent per annum. Who constituted the other 30 per cent of the stockholders, who speculated in the stock, what their profits were, was never disclosed.

"Doubtless in Paris, and perhaps to a lesser extent in New York, there were speculators who bought and sold in the stock market with a view to the varying conditions apparent from time to time in the course of the negotiations, and with a view to the probable outcome of the negotiations," Roosevelt said in *The Outlook*. "This was precisely what speculators did in England in connection with the outcome of the battle of Waterloo, and in our own country in connection with Abraham Lincoln's issuance of the Emancipation Proclamation and other Acts during the Civil War."

The United States did not get the stock books either of the de Lesseps company or its successor. Senator Philander Knox, Roosevelt's former Attorney General, advised him subsequently; "We did not buy the corporations or their stocks; we bought only their property."

The United States did buy the new company's archives, but in the opinion of a law officer of the War Department's Bureau of Insular Affairs, who examined the documents of title that passed to the United States, neither stockholder lists, stock ledgers, nor transfer books were "of such nature as necessarily or even properly to be considered a part of its archives."

Nor would Cromwell, the company's New York lawyer, identify the stockholders. The most he would reveal, in protracted and insistent questioning by the Senate Committee on Interoceanic Canals, was that he was not one of them.

"I have not received or obtained benefit, directly or indirectly, in the remotest manner that human ingenuity could describe, to the extent of a single farthing from any syndicate, combination, organization, or party soever in connection with the sale of the Panama Canal," was his cosmic denial. "I was never interested in the securities of the New Panama Canal Company, nor in the securities of the old Panama Canal Company, I have never owned a dollar in either company or had a pecuniary interest in the remotest character in either, and consequently I never had a single dollar benefit therefrom."

But as far as others were concerned, his testimony was a classic of encloisterment; the whole subject of his work with the New Panama Canal Company, he said, was "covered by the seal of professional confidence."

"How long would that professional lockjaw last?" asked Senator Morgan, an undiscouraged interrogator.

"From 1896, and it is still in vogue," Cromwell replied.

The sale to the United States brought a mournful cry from Charles de Lesseps, back in France from his longtime exile in London. "Why must so many efforts have been made and so much French money have been spent and wasted at a dead loss; why has not the Panama Canal remained a French enterprise?" he asked emotionally when a reporter for *Le Gaulois*, the royalist newspaper, came to interview him.

But with a vestige of the cheeriness that was his father's invariable reaction to disaster, he squeezed a drop of practical solace out of the turn of events. "At any rate," he said, "everything will not be lost; French investors will be able to recover some trifle of what they lost in the disaster by which the work was unjustly overtaken."

The physical delivery of the canal works took place on the morning of May 5, 1904, at the headquarters building of the

New Panama Canal Company on the Cathedral Plaza in Panama City. Renaudin, the company's representative on the isthmus, summoned the principal employees and read a cable from the home office directing him to hand over to the United States government. Then Lieutenant Mark Brooke, U.S.A., read a signal from the Secretary of War of the United States, William Howard Taft, directing him to accept the property.

They signed a document, written in English, French, and Spanish, that attested the delivery, and Brooke raised the flag of the United States over the headquarters of the Panama Canal.

Bibliography

ADAM, George, *The Tiger: Georges Clemenceau,* N.Y., Harcourt, Brace, 1930. Called Adam in Sources

d'ALLEMAGNE, Henry R., *Prosper Enfantin et les Grandes Entreprises,* Paris, Librairie Grund, 1935

AUCHMUTY, James Johnston, *Sir Thomas Wyse, the Life and Career of an Educator and Diplomat,* London, P.S. King & Son, Ltd., 1939. Called Auchmuty in Sources

BARKER, Edward Harrison, *France of the French,* N.Y., Charles Scribner's Sons, 1909. Called Barker in Sources

BARRES, Maurice, *Leurs Figures,* Paris, Juven, 1911

BEATTY, Charles, *De Lesseps of Suez, the Man and His Times,* N.Y., Harper & Bros., 1956

BERTAUT, Jules, *Paris, 1870-1935,* N. Y., D. Appleton, Century, Inc., 1936. Called Bertaut in Sources

BISHOP, Joseph Bucklin, *The Panama Gateway,* N.Y., Charles Scribner's Sons, 1915. Called Bishop in Sources

BONAPARTE WYSE, Lucien Napoleon, *Le Canal de Panama, l'Isthme Americain,* Paris, Hachette, 1886

BOOTH, A.J., *Saint-Simon and Saint-Simonism,* London, Longmans, Green, Reader & Dyer, 1871. Called Booth in Sources

BOURSON, Alexander, *Clemenceau,* Paris, Rene Julliard, 1949. Called Bourson in Sources

BOURSON, Alexander, *Le Scandal du Panama,* Paris, 1931

BRUUN, Geoffrey, *Clemenceau,* Cambridge, Harvard University Press, 1943

BUNAU-VARILLA, Philippe, *Panama, the Creation, Destruction and Resurrection,* London, Constable & Co., 1913. Called Bunau-Varilla in Sources

CERMOISE, Henri, *Deux Ans au Panama,* Paris, C. Marpon & E. Flammarion, 1886. Called Cermoise in Sources

CLEMENCEAU, Georges, *Le Silence de M. Clemenceau,* Paris, Albin Michel, 1929

CLUNET, Edouard, *Statement of the Case for Dr. Cornelius Herz,* (translated from his *Mémoire à Consulter* by W. F. Craies, of the Inner Temple, Barrister-at-Law) privately printed, 1893, by Harrison & Sons, St. Martin's Lane, London W.C. Called Clunet in Sources.

COLQUHOUN, Archibald Ross, *The Key to the Pacific, the Nicaragua Canal,* London, Archibald Constable & Co., 1895. Called Colquhoun in Sources

COUBERTIN, Baron Pierre de, *The Evolution of France under the Third Republic,* N.Y., Thomas Y. Crowell & Co., 1897. Called Coubertin in Sources

CURTIS, M. R., *Three Against the Third Republic,* Princeton, Princeton University Press, 1959

DANSETTE, Adrien, *Les Affaires de Panama,* Paris, Perrin, 1934

DANSETTE, Adrien, *Le Boulangisme,* Paris; A. Fayard, 1946. Called Dansette in Sources

DICTIONNAIRE DES PARLEMENTAIRES, 1789-1889, A. Robert, E. Bourloton, G. Cougny, Paris, Bourloton, 1891. Called *Parlementaires, 1789-1889* in Sources

DICTIONNAIRE DES PARLEMENTAIRES FRANCAISES, 1889-1940, compiled under the direction of Jean Jolly, archivist of the National Assembly, being issued by Presses Universitaires de France. Called *Parlementaires, 1889-1940* in Sources

EDWARDS, Albert, *Panama, the Canal, the Country, and the People,* N.Y., Macmillan, 1912

ERLANGER, Philippe, *Clemenceau,* Paris, Editions Bernard Grasset, 1968

LES FEMMES CELEBRES, Paris, Mazenod, 1960

FITZGERALD, Percy Hetherington, *The Great Canal of Suez,* London, Tinsley Bros., 1876. Called Fitzgerald in Sources

FRANCE, *CHAMBRE DES DEPUTES, ANNALES DE LA,* various dates. Called *Annales* in Sources

FRANCE, *CHAMBRE DES DEPUTES, 5 Legislature, Session de 1893, Rapport Général Fait au Nom de la Commission d'Enquête Chargée de Faire la Lumière sur les Allégations Portées à la Tribune à l'Occasion des Affaires de Panama.* Three volumes: (1) overall report by Deputy Ernest Vallé and reports by investigators of individual phases. Called Inquiry, 1893, Vallé in Sources; (2) testimony of witnesses before the Investigating Committee. Called Inquiry, 1893, Depositions in Sources, followed by date of testimony; (3) report by Auguste Flory, auditor, to examining magistrate, with annexes thereto. Called Inquiry, 1893, Flory in Sources, and report of Armand Rousseau to Minister of Public Works. Called Inquiry, 1893, Rousseau in Sources

FRANCE, CHAMBRE DES DEPUTES, 6 Legislature, Session de 1898, Rapport Général Fait au Nom de la Commission d'Enquête sur les Affaires de Panama. Called Inquiry, 1898, in Sources

GALTIER-BOISSIERE, Jean, *Histoire de la IIIème République,* Paris, Crapouillot, 1935. Called Galtier-Boissière in Sources

GONCOURT, Edmond, *Journal de Goncourt,* Paris, Fasquelle et Flammarion, 1956. Called Goncourt in Sources

GORGAS, William Crawford, *Sanitation in Panama,* N.Y., Appleton, 1915. Called Gorgas in Sources

GREAT BRITAIN, FOREIGN OFFICE. Authentic and Official Correspondence Concerning the Case of Dr. Cornelius Herz, an Invalid Untried Prisoner since January 19, 1893, Arrested and held under an English police magistrate's warrant obtained illegally as alleged. Called Great Britain, Foreign Office in Sources

GRENVILLE-MURRAY, E.C., *Round About France,* London, Macmillan, 1878. Called Murray in Sources

GRENVILLE-MURRAY, E.C., *The Men of the Third Republic,* Philadelphia; Porter & Coates, 1873

HANOTAUX, Gabriel, *Contemporary France,* London, Constable, 1909

HILLARET, Jacques (pseudonym of Col. Auguste Andre Coussillan), *Dictionnaire Historique des Rues de Paris,* Paris, Les Editions de Minuit, 1963

HURLBERT, William H., *France and the Republic,* London, Longmans, Green, 1890. Called Hurlbert in Sources

HYNDMAN, H.M., *Clemenceau, the Man and His Time,* N.Y., Frederick A. Stokes Co., 1919

KELLEY, Frederick M., *The Practicability and Importance of a Ship Canal to Connect the Atlantic and Pacific Oceans,* N.Y., G.F. Nesbit & Co., 1875

LAWTON, Frederick, *The Third French Republic,* Philadelphia, Lippincott, 1909. Called Lawton in Sources

LATIMER, Elizabeth Wormeley, *France in the Nineteenth Century,* Chicago, A. C. McClurg & Co., 1896. Called Latimer in Sources

DE LESSEPS, Ferdinand, *Recollections of Forty Years,* N.Y., D. Appleton & Co., 1888. Called *Recollections* in Sources

DE LIVOIS, Rene, *Histoire de la Presse Française,* Paris, Les temps de la Presse

259

LONERGAN, W.F. *Forty Years of Paris,* N.Y., Brentano's, 1907. Called Lonergan in Sources

MACH, Gerstle, *The Land Divided,* N.Y., Alfred A. Knopf, 1944

MEYER, Arthur, *Ce que mes yeux ont vu,* Paris, Librairie Plon, 1912

MINER, Dwight C., *The Fight for the Panama Route,* N.Y., Columbia University Press, 1940

MORAND, Paul, *1900 A.D.,* London, William Farquhar Payson, Ltd., 1931

NELSON, Dr. Wolferd, *Five Years in Panama,* N.Y., Belford & Co., 1889. Called Nelson in Sources

PARRIS, John, *The Lion of Caprera,* N.Y., David McKay Co., 1962. Called Parris in Sources

QUESNAY DE BEAUREPAIRE, Jules, *Le Panama et la République,* Paris, F. Juven, 1899. Called Quesnay in Sources

ROBINSON, Tracy, *Fifty Years in Panama,* 1907, 2nd edition, N.Y., The Trow Press. Called Robinson in Sources

RODRIGUES, J.C., *The Panama Canal,* N.Y., Charles Scribner's Sons, 1885. Called Rodrigues in Sources

ROOSEVELT, Theodore, *The Works of Theodore Roosevelt: Presidential Addresses, State Papers, and European Addresses,* N.Y., P.F. Collier & Sons, 1910

SIEGFRIED, Andrew, *Suez and Panama,* N.Y., Harcourt, Brace, 1940. Called Siegfried in Sources

SMITH, G. Barnett, *The Life and Enterprises of Ferdinand de Lesseps,* London; W.H. Allen, Ltd., 1895. Called Smith in Sources

SMITH. J. Lawrence, *Interocean Canal,* privately printed, 1880

SUAREZ, Georges, *La Vie Orgueilleuse de M. Clemenceau,* Paris, les Editions de France, 1930

THOMAS, Lately, *Sam Ward, King of the Lobby,* Boston, Houghton, Mifflin Co., 1965

U.S., DEPARTMENT OF STATE, Domestic Letters, Vol. 138, June-Aug., 1881

U.S., DEPARTMENT OF STATE, Annex, Miscellaneous Letters, Dec. 15, 1898. Consists of documents filed in Herz petition for U.S. intervention in his demand for indemnification by France. Called Herz, Documents, State in Sources

U.S., PANAMA CANAL TITLE, Opinion of the Attorney General upon the title proposed to be given by the New Panama Canal Company to the United States. Transmitted to President Theodore Roosevelt by Attorney General Philander C. Knox, Oct. 25, 1902. Washington, Government Printing Office, 1903. Called Knox in Sources

U.S., REPORT OF THE ISTHMIAN CANAL COMMISSION, 1899-1901; Rear Admiral John G. Walker, president. Delivered to State Department Nov. 30, 1901; transmitted to Congress by President Theodore Roosevelt, Dec. 4, 1901. Washington, Government Printing Office, 1904. Called ICC in Sources

U.S., DEPARTMENT OF NAVY, Bureau of Navigation, *The Maritime Canal of Suez,* by J.E. Nourse, Washington, Government Printing Office, 1884

U.S., CONGRESS, 46th Congress, 2nd Session, Executive Document No. 112, President Hayes's message to the Senate

U.S., CONGRESS, 46th, 3rd, Miscellaneous Document No. 16, De Lesseps's testimony before House Select Committee on Interoceanic Ship Canal

U.S., HOUSE OF REPRESENTATIVES, 49th, 1st, Misc. Doc. No. 395, Lieutenant W. W. Kimball's report on Panama Canal

U.S., HOUSE OF REPRESENTATIVES, 50th, 1st, Misc. Doc. No. 599, Lieutenant C.C. Rogers's report on Panama Canal

U.S., SENATE, 56th, 1st, Misc. Doc. No. 188, New Panama Canal Company developments

U.S., SENATE, 57th, 1st, Misc. Document No. 123, supplementary report of Isthmian Canal Commission

U.S., SENATE, 57th, 1st, Misc. Report No. 783, Interoceanic Canal, Minority View

U.S., SENATE, 59th, 2nd Misc. Document No. 401, testimony before Committee on Interoceanic Canals

U.S., CONGRESS, 60th, 2nd, Misc. Document No. 589, letter by War Department Insular Affairs Bureau law officer

VASSILI, Count Paul *France from Behind the Veil,* N.Y. and London, Funk & Wagnalls Co., 1914

VIZETELLY, Ernest A., *Court Life of the Second French Empire,* (Court of the Tuileries), N.Y., Charles Scribner's Sons, 1907. Called Tuileries in Sources; *Republican France, 1870-1912,* Boston, Small, Maynard & Co., 1912. Called Vizetelly in Sources; *Paris and Her People,* N.Y., Frederick A. Stokes, 1919. Called Paris in Sources

PERIODICALS AND BROCHURES

AMERICAN ACADEMY OF ARTS AND SCIENCES, proceedings, Vol. XXXI, "Viscount Ferdinand de Lesseps," by Henry Mitchell

AMERICAN ARCHITECT & BUILDING NEWS, March 10 and Aug. 18, 1883, articles on Panama Canal, quoting *Le Génie Civil*

AMERICAN GEOGRAPHICAL SOCIETY, report rendered Dec. 9, 1879, by Dr. W.E. Johnston as delegate to International Canal Congress, Paris 1879. Called Johnston in Sources

AMERICAN HERITAGE, Aug., 1963, "The Man Who Invented Panama," by Eric Sevareid

THE ART JOURNAL, Nov., 1889, article on Secretan sale

BOSTON SOCIETY OF CIVIL ENGINEERS, paper by Charles D. Jameson, 5-19-86

BULLETIN DU CANAL INTEROCEANIQUE, external house organ of Panama Canal Company. Called *Bulletin* in Sources

CONGRES INTERNATIONAL D'ETUDES DU CANAL INTER-OCEANIQUE, Paris, March 15-29, 1879, *Comptes Rendus.* Called *Comptes Rendus* in Sources

COSMOPOLITAN, June, 1894, "The Panama Scandal," by Maurice Barres. Called Barres in Sources

ENGINEERING, London, 2-17-82 and 4-7-82

FORTNIGHTLY REVIEW, London, 1-1-97, "Dr. Cornelius Herz and the French Republic," By Sir Edward J. Reed; 3-1-1903, memoir by J.S. Alger; Oct. 1904, "Statesmen of the Third Republic," by Baron Pierre de Coubertin

FORUM, March, 1893, "Story of a Colossal Bubble," by E. Lambert

THE GREEN BAG, Boston, Vol. 7, 496 *et seq.,* "Imprisonment of Dr. Cornelius Herz"

THE LEISURE HOUR, Aug., 1880, "Across Panama," by J.A. Owen

LIPPINCOTT'S MAGAZINE, June, 1885, "Letters from the Isthmus," by John Heard, Jr.

LA LUMIERE ELECTRIQUE, 12-1-79 and 9-9-82

THE MENTOR (Crowell Publishing Co.), Oct., 1928, "The Love Story of Georges Clemenceau," by Alice F. Brown

THE NATION, 10-2-90 and 10-9-90, articles on General Boulanger; 3-2-93, comment on Khedive's sale of Suez shares; 1-28-1902, "Case of Bunau-Varilla"

NATURE, 8-20-85, "Piercing the Isthmus of Panama, abstract from *La Nature*

NEW YORK CHAMBER OF COMMERCE, report by John Bigelow, April, 1886. Called Bigelow in Sources

NORTH AMERICAN REVIEW, Aug. 1879, article on Panama Canal by A.G. Menocal; July, 1880, article on canal prospects by Ferdinand de Lesseps; Sept. 1903, "Why the Panama Canal was Originally Chosen," by Crisanto Medina

NORTH DAKOTA HISTORY, Jan.-Apr., 1946, "The Career of Marquis de Mores in North Dakota," by Golphen

OUTLOOK, 12-10-98, "The Panama Canal Scheme," by E.V. Smalley; 4-2-04, "Makers of the Canal"; 10-7-11, "How the United States Acquired the Right to Dig the Panama Canal," by Theodore Roosevelt

REVIEW OF POLITICS, Vol. 12, No. 3, July, 1950, "The First National Socialist," by Robert F. Byrnes, analysis of career of Marquis de Mores

REVIEW OF REVIEWS (English), Oct., 1890 and Nov. 1891, articles on General Boulanger; Jan., 1893, "Panama Scandal"

REVUE GENERALE D'ELECTRIQUE: Commemorative brochure published with the compliments of, Paris, Nov. 13, 1935, at *Société Française des Electriciens* celebration of 50th anniversary of Marcel Deprez's long-distance transmission of electricity.

SATURDAY REVIEW OF POLITICS, LITERATURE, SCIENCE AND ART, London, 11-19-92 and 11-26-92, Panama Canal scandal; 7-6-89, Secretan art sale

SCIENTIFIC AMERICAN, 1-19-90, "Panama Canal Bubble"

SCOTTISH REVIEW, April, 1889, "Panama Canal Scandal"

SCRIBNER'S MAGAZINE, Oct., 1933, "The Great Frenchman," by Roger Burlingame

THE SPECTATOR, 10-3-91, Boulanger obituary; 11-26-92, "The Panama Scandal"; 12-17-92, "Development of the Panama Scandals", 12-24-92, "French Republicans at Bay"; 3-4-93, "M. Ferry's Election"; 6-24-93, comment on Clemenceau and Norton case; 4-3-98, "Revival of the Panama Canal Scandals." Called *Spectator* in Sources

TEMPLE BAR, May, 1884, "Courts of the Presidents"

WESTMINSTER REVIEW, Vol. 118, 393, "The Courts and the Ministries"

Sources and Notes

In the listing of sources, the following abbreviations are used:

New York Times	*NYT*
New York Tribune	*TRIB*
New York Herald	*HERALD*
New York World	*WORLD*
Times of London	*TIMES*
Pall Mall Gazette	*PMG*

Chapter I

2   Heavy industry wage scale: *Etude Statistique sur les Salaires des Travailleurs et le Revenu de la France;* miners' housing costs: Hurlbert, 295; Eiffel Tower strike: *TIMES,* 12-21-88 5:3

2   *"Petites gens de bas de laine"*: *NYT,* 12-25-92 17:1-3; de Lesseps on Suez shares: *TRIB,* 5-21-82 2:3-4; dividends: *North American Review,* July, 1880; Khedive's stock sale: *Nation,* 3-2-82

3   De Lesseps's construction forecast: *North American Review,* July, 1880; "As for the salubrity . . .": *ibid.*

3   Comparative prices of canal shares, "The Panama stock has never . . .": *TRIB,* 5-21-82 2:3-4

4   Isthmian canal searches: *Rodrigues*

4   Lopes Gomera, "It is quite true . . .": *Nelson;* ". . . that phenomenal bigot . . .": U.S. Senate speech by *Chauncey M. Depew,* 1-14-04

4   Europeans' searches for canal route: *Rodrigues*

5   Napoleon III, "When you have severed . . .": *TUILERIES,* 371

5   Goethe to Eckermann, "I should wonder if the United States . . .": *Colquhoun,* 163-64, quoting from *"Conversations of Goethe with Eckermann and Soret,"* Oxenford translation, ed. 1883, 222-23.

6   Explorations by Latin American governments: *Rodrigues*

6   Kelley's interest: *U.S. House of Representatives, 46th Congress, 3rd Session, Miscellaneous Document No. 16;* history of the Raspadura: *Every Week Magazine,* 4-24-1938

6-7   Vanderbilt's venture, U.S. Government explorations, and Nicaragua route recommendation: *Rodrigues*

7-8   Suez-Panama visions, *TIMES,* 8-28-79 9:5; Saint-Simon biographical: *Booth,* 105 *et seq.*

8   Enfantin and the Suez Canal: *ibid.,* 219-33

8   Voyage of the Clorinda, Garibaldi— " . . . the man who defends . . .": *Parris,* 20-22, quoting Alexandre Dumas's *Mémoires de Garibaldi,* Brussels, 1860

8   De Lesseps's departure from diplomatic service: *NYT,* 12-8-93 1:3; also *Fitzgerald,* Vol. I, 4., quoting de Lesseps's lecture to *Société des Gens des Lettres,* 1870

9   Ancient canal routes of Egypt: *NYT Saturday Review of Books and Art,* 1-16-97, quoting Anatole France

9   "It was a work of peace . . .": *ibid.*

10   "The father of this young man . . .": *Fitzgerald,* Vol. I, 16-17

10   How de Lesseps became enchanted with the idea of a Suez canal: *ibid.,* 5-6

10-11   "When he came to see me . . .": *ibid.,* 7

11   "His situation, the welcome . . .": *ibid.,* 18

11   Enfantin's efforts: *Booth,* 219-33

11   Benoit Fould's mission for de Lesseps: *Recollections,* Vol. I, 193; Achille Fould's mission for Napoleon III: *Tuileries,* 60

11-12   News of Abbas's murder reaches La Chesnaye, de Lesseps handles Said diplomatically: *NYT Saturday Review of Books and Art,* 1-16-97, quoting Anatole France; Said—"I am satisfied and I accept . . .": *Fitzgerald*

12   "The camp begins to be astir . . .": *Recollections,* Vol. I, 167-69

Maron J. Simon

23   "... one of those chimeras ...": *Mitchell,* quoting Stephenson

23   De Lesseps flies tricolor from London hotel room, barnstorms United Kingdom: *PMG,* 12-9-94, 1

23   Details of United Kingdom tour: *Recollections,* Vol. II, 312

23-24   Data on Mme. de Lesseps: *Republican France,* 349 *et seq.* ".... overdressed, overfed and underexercised": *TRIB,* 7-29-83

24   Father's loss on sale of *rentes: NYT,* 12-29-96 3:4

24   Ferdinand de Lesseps fared equally badly in government service: *Bigelow,* quoting de Lesseps's Topographical Society speech

24-5   Empress Eugenie at Suez opening: *NYT Saturday Review of Books and Art,* 1-16-97, quoting Anatole France; de Lesseps tried to help her when Second Empire fell: *TIMES,* 12-20-96 3:6 and 12-29-96 3:4

25   "M. de Lesseps, I am one of your stockholders", "... scarcely a small tradesman ...": *Recollections,* Vol. I, 150

25   "Everybody had imagined that the Panama enterprise ...": *TRIB,* 7-7-95

25   Buys Türr-Wyse concession: *Inquiry, 1893, Flory,* 21-2

26   "Patronage Whip": *Spectator,* 11-26-92

26   Herz, assistant surgeon major: *Clunet,* 252

26   Canal company formed: *Inquiry, 1893, Flory,* 11

26-7   "In these provincial tours ...": *Johnston*

27   Breakfast at Lyon: *TIMES,* 7-11-79

27   Appleton's job, testimony before U.S. House of Representatives Special Committee to Investigate Panama Canal Co., etc.: *TRIB,* 2-15-93 12:2

27   First stock issue fails, circular attributes blame: *Inquiry, 1893, Flory,* 11-12, also *TRIB,* 2-25-80 1:6 to 2:1-2

28   Construction job to be "by contract or for a royalty, as I prefer ...": *Recollections,* Vol. II, 201, quoting circular

28   "... I shall solve that myself ...": *ibid.*

28   Birth of *Bulletin du Canal Interocéanique: Inquiry, 1893, Flory,* 12

28   "Mr. de Lesseps has a newspaper ...": *TRIB,* 2-21-80 4:5

28   "The visit of M. de Lesseps to the isthmus ...": *ibid.,* 1-22-80 1:4

29   "He would ride over the rough country . . .": *Robinson,* 146

29   " . . . her form was voluptuous . . .": *ibid.,* 143

29   Toast to the press: *TRIB,* 1-22-80 1:4

29-30   Philosophy of optimism: *ibid.*

30   "Lesseps himself told me . . .": *TRIB,* 1-13-89 13:1-2

30   Wyse-Reclus estimates and revisions: *Inquiry, 1893, Flory,* 7, 9, 13

30-31   De Lesseps's prospectus: *TRIB,* 2-25-80 1:6 to 2:1-2

31-32   Levasseur's forecasts and explanation: *Inquiry, 1893, Flory*

32   "Remember in the course of your lifetime . . .": *Scottish Review,* April, 1889, quoting Mohammed Ali

32   "If the committee had decided to build a locked canal . . .": *TRIB,* 2-27-80, quoting de Lesseps

32   "For what he *has* done . . .": *ibid.,* 2-29-80 7:3, quoting Whitelaw Reid

32-33   De Lesseps's testimony before House Select Committee on Interoceanic Ship Canal: *U.S. 46th Congress, 3rd Session, Miscellaneous Document No. 16*

33-34   President Hayes's message to the Senate: *U.S., 46th Congress, 2nd Session, Executive Document No. 112*

34   Outrey's note: *U.S. 57th, 1st, Senate Report 783, "Interoceanic Canal, Minority View",* 3-19-1902, 33-34

Chapter 3

35   Clamor for canal shares: *Rodrigues,* also *TIMES,* 3-2-81 5:3

35-36   "My forecasts are completely realized . . .": *Inquiry, 1893, Flory,* 17-18, quoting de Lesseps in *Bulletin,* 11-15-80

36   Abel Couvreux's Brussels speech, " . . . certain that these prices are still in excess . . .": *ICC,* 202

36   "American Committee formed, Navy Secretary enlisted to head it": *U.S. House of Representatives, 52nd, 2nd, Report No. 2615,* 3

36-37   "Today I received a letter . . .": *NYT,* 2-15-88 5:2, quoting President Grant

37   *Publicité* costs of first issue: *Inquiry, 1893, Flory,* 21; de Girardin on board: *ibid.,* 26

Chapter 4

46-47   Blanchet's troubles with the route and the site of the company town: *American Architect & Building News,* 3-10-83, 110, and 8-18-83, 74, both quoting *Le Génie Civil*

47   Digging starts: *Engineering,* 2-17-82

47-48   Couvreux & Hersent contract: *ICC, Historical Notes,* 197-213, also *Inquiry, 1893, Flory,* Annex 3, 261-63

48   Meade's report: *TRIB,* 3-9-82 1:2

48   "It is necessary at any price . . .": *Inquiry, 1893, Flory,* 205

48-49   De Lesseps's letter to Holguin: *Bulletin,* 7-1-81

49   Stockholders approve railroad-purchase bond issue and other borrowing: *Inquiry, 1893, Flory,* 38-39, also Annex 12, 405-409

49   Report on health of working force: *TIMES,* 6-30-82 5:2

50   Details of Sept., 1882, bond issue: *Inquiry, 1893, Flory,* 39; underwriters too timid, had no risk: *Inquiry, 1898,* Tome III, 54

50   "With $30 million already invested . . .": *TRIB,* 9-28-82 4:3

50-51   Contractors ask out, contract terminated amicably: *Inquiry, 1893, Flory,* 44

51   Dingler named to boss new setup: *TIMES,* 2-3-83 5:2

51   Canal route, Dingler's new estimates: *ICC,* "Historical Notes", 197-213

51-52   De Lesseps goes to London on Suez business: *TRIB,* 7-29-83 3:1

52   "Our works director, M. Dingler . . .": *Inquiry, 1893, Flory,* 45-47

52-53   Details of October issue: *ibid.*

52   "M. de Lesseps is being twitted . . .", "An enterprise like the Panama canal . . .": *TIMES,* 9-28-83 3:1

53   Jamaican laborers' wages: *ibid.,* 6-4-84 4:3

53   Deaths in Dingler's family: *Siegfried,* 253

53   Richier quits: *NYT,* 7-15-84 8:4 and 12-25-92 17:1-3

53   *American Architect & Building News*'s pessimistic comment: edition of 5-17-84

54   Details of the sticky issue: *Inquiry, 1893, Flory,* 54-55

54-55-56-57   De Lesseps's remarks at July 29 stockholders' meeting: *TIMES,* 7-28-85 5:3

Chapter 5

Maron J. Simon

Chapter 6

less, from the memories of the Jacobins of 1793. In the same way the *Right* is the camp of the monarchists, followers of the Bourbons, the Orleans, or the Bonaparte house, and the *Extreme Right* combines those who remain attached to the institutions of the old form of government, and who would like to see the privileges of the nobility and the clergy restored in the form in which they existed before the taking of the Bastille. The *Center* comprises the reasonable, the moderate in views; on the one hand those who, without being wholly republican, will accept the Republic frankly, if they see that such is the wish of the country (this is the *Left Center*); on the other hand, those who would go as far in the path of liberal and democratic concessions, but who will find it difficult to renounce the monarchial form of government.")

87	Boulanger and Duc d'Aumale: *Vizetelly,* 297-98, also *ADAM,* 84
88	" . . . one could detect in him . . .": *Coubertin,* 215
88	"This reproach could already . . .": *ibid.,* 216
88	*"Partira pas!": Adam,* 84
88-89	" . . . more effective power than was ever . . .": *TEMPLE BAR,* May, 1884
89	Decorations price list: *Galtier-Boissiere,* 73
89	Wilson conviction, appeal court's reversal and reasoning: *Vizetelly,* 312; "Rather late": *TIMES,* 3-28-88 5:2
89	*"Ah, quel malheur . . .": Parris,* 312
90	Ferry epithets: *Vizetelly,* 307
90	" . . . better to retain Grevy . . .": *ibid.,* 305
90	" . . . hatred of the Germans blinded . . .": *Review of Reviews* (England), Oct. 1890; League of Patriots organized: *TIMES,* 3-12-89 5:1
90	" . . . remain the faithful and devoted . . .": *ibid.,* 12-1-87 5:1
91	" . . . the plan was simple . . .", "If I were overridden . . .": Clemenceau's Salernes speech, 8-8-93
91	Boulanger called to meet royalists: *Latimer,* 433
91	"Anything else, my dear general . . .": *ibid.,* 435
91	Grevy's billiards companion: *Vizetelly,* 229
91	Deroulede shouted down: *TIMES,* 12-2-87 5:1-2
92	Grevy out, Carnot in: *ibid.,* 12-3-87 7:1-2

92   Boulanger's hybrid party, compulsory retirement: *Vizetelly*, 318; "Main Drain", *Adam*, 89

92   Boulanger all things to all men: *Vizetelly*, 318

92-93   Boulangists "in", " . . . the general reaped a harvest": *Coubertin*, 225

93   " . . . with what money no one knew . . .": *ibid.*, 224

93   Photo in African hut: *Latimer*, 437

93   "With gaze impenetrable . . .": *Coubertin*, 225

93   Sword of marengo: *Paris*, 170; 55,000-franc monthly allowance: *Vizetelly*, 323; Duchesse d'Uzes's slush-fund; *ibid.*, 323-24; Cliquot fortune: *ibid.*, 317; Louise Michel exiled to Caledonia; *ibid.*, 69; not long out of jail: *ibid.*, 376

93   Footnote: English *Review of Reviews*, Oct. 1890

93   " . . . now one of the pillars . . .": *Lonergan*, 159

94   " . . . a cabinet of Natural History . . .": *Coubertin*, 117

94   " . . . it was his known integrity . . .": English *Review of Reviews*, Oct. 1890

94   Elder Carnot's funeral: *TIMES*, 3-21-88 5:2

94   "Boulanger will bring us cheap bread": *Latimer*, 437

95   " . . . the deftness of a toreador . . .": *PMG*, 6-23-93 3; Floquet struck from a shrub: *Lonergan*, 87; nature of wound: *TIMES*, 10-1-91, 3

95   Boulanger to Tangiers with newly divorced Mme. Bonnemains: *Vizetelly*, 328-29

95   " . . . however extreme his views . . .": *TIMES*, 1-7-89 5: 1-2

95   Paris election costs 15 per cent of slush fund: *Vizetelly*, 330

95-96   Message of sympathy to de Lesseps: *TIMES*, 12-17-88 5:2

96   Bergnac peasant's letter: *TRIB*, 1-13-89 13:1

96   Boulanger buys Panama bonds: *TIMES*, 1-7-89 5:5; Premier only says he is sorry: *ibid.*, 1-12-89 5:1

96   De Lesseps for Boulanger: *NYT*, 1-28-89 1:2-3, also *TRIB*, 2-4-89, editorial

96   "M. Floquet is in power . . .": *TIMES*, 1-12-89 5:1

96-97   Election night excitement, Boulanger organization's efficiency: *NYT*, 1-28-89 1:2-3

97   "Tried and dignified republican . . .": *Coubertin*, xix

97   Election night details: *NYT*, 1-28-89 1:2-3

97   "I did not desire . . .": *NYT,* 1-29-89, quoting *London Daily Telegraph*

97-98   "I had no conception . . .": *Lonergan,* 85

98   League of Patriots dissolved: *TIMES,* 3-12-89 5:1; close tail on Boulanger: *Vizetelly,* 334

98   Boulanger flight crosses up Chincholle: *Lonergan,* 89

98   Dillon fetches him home: *Vizetelly,* 334-35

98   Exhibition's lottery loan: *TIMES,* 4-16-89 5:2

98-99   Boulanger attacks parliamentarians, indicted, flees to Brussels, ousted from Belgium, convicted, local elections end political career: *Vizetelly,* 335-39

99   "Marguerite à bientôt": *Spectator,* 10-3-91, 1

99   "Here lies General Boulanger . . .": *Galtier-Boissiere,* 73, quoting Clemenceau; "It seems as if . . .": W. T. Stead, English *Review of Reviews,* Oct. 1890

99   "It is true that despite . . .": *Annales,* 12-20-92

Chapter 7

100   "Civil and foreign war is . . .", "Your program is mine . . .": *World,* 11-22-92 1:6

100   "His mouth and all the . . .", "I detected at once . . .": *Barres*

101   Engineering committee to Panama, Bonaparte Wyse gets new concession: *ICC,* 57; "French thriftiness responds . . .": *TIMES,* 9-11-91 3:1; 100,000 sign petition: *ibid.,* 1-6-92 5:4

101   Panama question to Minister of Justice: *ibid.,* 6-23-90 5:6

101   Prinet appointed: *ibid.,* 6-12-91 5:5; his first step: *ibid.,* 6-15-91 5:6

102   De Lesseps dresses for inquiry: *Smith,* 310

102   "What a terrible nightmare . . .": *ibid.*

102   Searches and seizures: *TIMES,* 9-9-91 3:3 and 9-10-91 3:2

102   Deputies demand action: *ibid.,* 1-6-92 5:4

102   *Micros* data: *Inquiry, 1893, Depositions,* 12-2-92, 182-190

102   "This man who has lied . . .": *La Dernière Bataille,* 325; " . . . an anti-phrase . . .": *ibid.,* 338

102-103 Martin names alleged corrupters: *Inquiry, 1893 Vallé,* 5; identification of Blanc: *ibid.,* 11

testimony, *Inquiry, 1893, Depositions,* 12-22-92, 573-74, also *Bourson,* 121 *et seq., Clemenceau,* by Philippe Erlanger, 267

116   Constans slapped Laur, later dropped from government: *Lonergan,* 152, 154-55, also *Vizetelly,* 348

117   Platform of *La Justice:* Clemenceau's Salernes speech, 8-8-93

118   Circulation only 15,000: *Vizetelly,* 266; Could not make ends meet: *Bourson,* 129

118   *La Justice* notice of Herz stock repurchase: *Inquiry, 1893, Depositions,* 12-14-92, 489

118-119   Attack on Herz begins: *Journal officiel,* 12-16-92, 1825, also *Clunet;* de Cassagnac could "never find words": *Greenville-Murray,* 71

119   Riot in the Chamber, bribery charges ordered: *Smith,* 353-54

120   Details on arrests and search for Cottu: *TRIB,* 1-1-93 15:5; Cottu biographical data: *WORLD,* 12-17-92

120   "Worthy of Mazas," description of prison: *TRIB,* 2-5-93 16:5

120   Ferdinand de Lesseps unaware: *Smith,* 355

120   Comfort in jail, menu: *TRIB,* 1-17-93 1:3

121   Suspend parliamentary immunity for ten: *Smith,* 358

121   Deves the conciliator: *Vizetelly,* 249

121   "With his sanguine complexion . . .": *Barres*

122   Deputies act impetuously: *Spectator,* 12-24-92

122   Senate acts next day: *Smith,* 358 *et seq.*

122   Café Procope: *The Men of the 3rd Republic,* also *Parris,* 172-73

122   "Everywhere where it is sought to take me . . .": *Smith,* 360

122-123   Rouvier's appearance: *WORLD,* 12-21-92, lead story; "What I have done . . .": *Spectator,* 12-24-92

123   "Oh you hypocrites . . .": *HERALD,* 12-22-92 7-4

123   Dugue de la Fauconnerie: *Barres*

123   Proust and Bourgeois: *ibid.*

123   Proust resigns Chicago post: *NYT,* 12-8-92 5:3 Note: The liberation of the "Angelus" to public bidding from its exalted niche in the mansion of its jealous owner was the direct result of a scandal that shook the French financial community at the height of the Boulanger agitation.

The collapse of an attempted worldwide corner on copper by the owner of the painting, E. Secretan, president of the Metals Company, touched off a run on the *Comptoir d'Escompte,* which had overextended itself in banking him. The head of the bank, Isaac-Pierre-Marie-Eugene Denfert-Rochereau, committed suicide, and Secretan was sentenced to six months in jail, the court also ordering the sale of his art collection.

The Secretan collection had come to be as well known in Paris as the Wallace Collection was in London—but much more difficult to see. It was housed in Secretan's palatial home in the rue de Moncey, the former residence of Count Pillet–Will, regent of the Bank of France, on the rising ground toward Montmartre, next door to Guy de Maupassant's former home. Secretan owned 168 oils, water colors, and drawings, and several sculptures, the best known of them Falguiere's "Diana."

Among the works of the old masters were one of Canaletto's Venetian scenes, Rembrandt's "Portrait of his Sister," and "Man with Armor," Rubens's "Abagail Meeting David," Sir Joshua Reynolds's "Widow and Child," Van Dyck's "Portrait of Lady Cavendish," Pieter de Hooghe's "Dutch Interior," Fragonard's "The Happy Family," Boucher's "Sleep of Venus," Jacob Ruysdael's "Water Gate," the portrait of Peter van der Broeke of Antwerp and the two small oval portraits of Scriverius and his wife by Franz Hals, Velasquez's "Portrait of Philip IV," and a Hobbema landscape and his "Water Mill."

The Secretan collection, however, was then most famous for its array of modern art, including Bonington's "On the Beach," Fromentin's "Falcon Hunt," Delacroix's "Giaour," Troyon's "Homeward" and "Garde Chasse," Rousseau's "Hut of the Charcoal Burners," Corot's "Le Matin" and his last finished work, "The Biblis," Courbet's "Roe Cover," Decamps's "Jesus Among His Brothers," Gericault's "Lancer," several works by Millet, and twenty-four oils by Meissonier, four of them unfinished. But the "Angelus," which Secretan displayed in solitary eminence, not hanging on a wall but standing on an easel surrounded by plush hangings, was the copper tycoon's prize, and for weeks its disposal had been the focus of the huge excitement generated by the auction.

It was not clear who had owned the famous painting before him. Millet's son said his father, who had completed the work in 1859, had sold it for 1,800 francs to Ernest Feydeau, the playwright, who sold it in turn for a 1,200-franc profit to the father-in-law of Alfred Stevens, the Belgian painter, and that Stevens's brother, Arthur, sold it for 5,000 francs to Jules van Praet, the Belgian diplomat and historian. Alfred Sensier, Millet's biographer, said it went directly from the painter to his friend, Arthur Stevens, and then to Van Praet.

Samuel P. Avery, Sr., of New York, who rushed to Paris, for the Secretan sale, offered a much livelier account of the early ownership of the "Angelus." He said that Longfellow's brother-in-law, Thomas G. Appleton, of Boston, had visited Millet at Barbizon while the painter was finishing the painting of the two peasants at evening prayer and had offered him 4,000 francs for it on completion. Millet accepted, Avery said; but when he had finished the painting, Appleton was off on a yachting cruise, and Millet, needing money, sold it to Van Praet for the same price.

Van Praet, according to art-world gossip, became irritated by the invariable reaction to the painting—"Why, you can hear the bells!"—and swapped it for a "shepherdess and flock" bon-bon. John W. Wilson, one of the great collectors of the time, later acquired the "Angelus" for 38,000 francs. At the famous Wilson sale in 1881, Secretan and the Egyptian collector, Defoer Bey, battled for it until they had pushed the bid up to 160,000 francs, at which point they decided shrewdly to draw lots for it. Secretan won.

Presently Secretan grew tired of it and sold it to the art dealer, Georges Petit, who intended to sell it to Defoer Bey. Fortunately for Secretan, his dismissal of the painting killed his Egyptian rival's interest in it, too, since Secretan's own regard for it was soon revived when he received through the mails a letter addressed only: "Monsieur the Owner of the Angelus." Enormously impressed by this testimony to the fame attached to the ownership of the painting, he bought it back, paying a 100,000-franc profit to Petit, and thenceforth refused to part with it, even for 500,000 francs, until the court forced him to.

The sale, with bidders on hand from many countries, took place on July 1, 2, and 4, 1889, and produced receipts totaling 6,346,925 francs. An American contingent barely made it; a slow crossing on the steamship *Etruria* made them so late they had to hire a special train to get to Paris in time.

Opening day was blistering hot, and more than 500 bidders and spectators were packed into the auction room of the Charles Sedelmeyer gallery at 4 bis rue de La Rochefoucauld.

The sale began "amidst a buzz of excitement impossible

to describe, very subdued and quiet but deep and strong," and it was announced at the start that each successful bidder would have to pay an additional fee of 5 per cent of the price of the work purchased.

Agnew's bought the Bonington for 29,100 francs. Proust bought Courbet's "Roe Cover" for the Louvre for 76,000 francs. An agent for the Duc d'Aumale, King Louis Philippe's son, paid 190,000 for Meissonier's "Cuirassiers of 1805." The seventy-seven-year-old Meissonier's marriage only that morning to Mlle. Besancon, the devoted housekeeper of the years of his first wife's confining illness, had lifted even higher the excitement of the sale.

At last, at 4:30 p.m., two and a half hours after the auction opened, the auctioneer put up the "Angelus." "Nothing more dramatic than its sale ever took place in an auction room," *The Art Journal* reported.

The bidding opened at 100,000 francs. An agent for James Sutton of the American Art Association bid 220,000 francs. M. Knoedler & Co., acting for the Corcoran Gallery, went quickly to 250,000. At 400,000 Proust disclosed that the French government was interested. Avery bid 490,000.

"Five hundred thousand," Proust replied.

"And one thousand," the American Art Association came back.

"And two thousand," Proust called out; and the auctioneer raised his hammer and knocked down the "Angelus" to France.

"How the men tossed their hats up to the ceiling and ladies sobbed with pleasure," London's *Saturday Review of Politics, Literature, Science and Art* recounted, "how the calm Yankee stepped in 'with his cold music,' and explained that he had made a higher bid, how M. Proust nearly fainted and was fanned by enthusiastic ladies, how the duel began again, until M. Proust had reached the figure of 553,000 francs, how a silence ensued, in which *tout Paris* heard the beating of its own heart, how the hammer fell at last, and the 'Angelus' was the property of France in perpetuity, all this is now a part of history, and far from being the least amusing of its pages."

One month later Sutton bought the "Angelus" from the auctioneers for 580,650 francs, the knockdown price plus the stipulated 5 per cent fee. Twenty-seven art lovers had raised 250,000 to buy the painting for the Louvre, counting on the government for the rest, but the budget committee of the Chamber had failed to report out the appropriations bill before adjournment, so Millet's famous work was transported to New York. Eventually the rich merchant,

Alfred Chauchard, one of the owners of the department store, Grands Magasins du Louvre, paid 856,000 francs to bring it back to France.

De Maupassant next door: *Hillairet,* Vol. 2, 134; Provenance of "The Angelus": *Art Journal,* Nov., 1889; Avery's story of "The Angelus": *NYT,* 7-3-89 2:3; Van Praet, Wilson, Defoer Bey: *Art Journal,* Nov., 1889; Secretan sells to Georges Petit: *TRIB,* 4-15-89 7:1; Details of art sale: *Art Journal,* Nov., 1889; "How the men tossed their hats . . .": *Saturday Review of Politics, Literature, Science and Art,* 7-6-89; Budget committee does not report bill out: *TIMES,* 8-3-89; Chauchard purchase: *Parris,* 158 family, awarded the choice of weapons to Clemenceau, who chose pistols. Millevoye's seconds then interposed further conditions, insisting that if the first two shots produced no results, the combatants would switch to swords and continue until one was disabled. Clemenceau's seconds rejected this remarkable demand. (*TIMES,* 12-26-92 5:2)

131   "... threatened to become the French Kipling": *Vizetelly,* 189

131   Other details of Deroulede biography: *NYT,* 1-30-1914, also *WORLD,* 12-22-92 2:3, Curtis's *Three Against the 3rd Republic,"* 24, quoting Jerome and Jean Thauraud's *The Life of Deroulede*

131   *Le Drapeau* praised Herz: *Clunet,* 263; with Deroulede's concurrence: Clemenceau's Salernes speech, 8-8-93

131   Duel with Laguerre: *Dansette,* 348

131   "Don Quixote in an Inverness cape": *ibid.,* 150

132   "He has never managed to acquire . . .": *NYT,* 1-7-1900 15:3

132   "... valiant soldier and distinguished poet...": *Coubertin,* 220

132   "Men are most often moved . . .": *ibid.,* 259

132   " . . . arrogance often amounting to insolence . . .": *Barres*; " . . . no liking for the Wrecker of Cabinets . . .": *PMG,* 6-23-93 1

132-133   "... there was a respect for M. Clemenceau...": *Spectator,* 6-24-93

133-134   " . . . but even his most bitter enemies . . .": *NYT,* 5-14-79 4:6-7

134   "It began very calmly . . .": *ibid.*

134   "... he did not exactly lead a party...": *Spectator,* 6-24-93

134   " . . . darts flung by a dextrous . . .", " . . . an intensity and a vivacity . . .": *Lonergan,* 74-75

134   " . . . frequently too bitter . . .": *Spectator,* 6-24-93

135   " . . . one of them detestable . . .": *TIMES,* 11-2-92 5:4, quoting Joseph Reinach

135   " . . . even when he appeared the most open . . .": *Barker,* 34

135   "I am accused of having arranged . . .": Clemenceau's Salernes speech, 8-8-93

Chapter 9

146	Note: Pasteur's seventieth birthday was December 27, 1892.
146	Taste for high life to blame: *Saturday Review of Politics, Literature, Science, and Art;* 11-26-92; Deputies' pay and perquisites: Othon Guerlac in *Century Magazine,* Jan., 1904
146	"No door can be opened . . .": *NYT,* 12-25-92 1:2-4
147	"With regard to the waste of money . . .": *PMG,* 1-13-93 3, quoting Emile Zola
147	Trial opens, de Lesseps's judgment by default allowed: *NYT,* 1-11-93 2:2
147	Charles de Lesseps's testimony, salving the press: *TIMES,* 1-11-93 5:3-4
147	"A number of persons offered assistance . . .", " . . . In remunerating financiers and . . .": *TRIB,* 1-13-93 1:2
148	Baïhaut extortion charge: *TRIB,* 1-11-93 5:3-4
148	"American Committee" mention: *ibid.*
148	"The members of syndicates run a risk . . .": *TIMES,* 1-11-93 5:3-4
148-149	All found guilty: *Inquiry, 1898,* Tome I, 26-27
149	Fines and jail terms: *ibid.,* 28
149	Pity from the newspapers: *TRIB,* 2-10-93 1:1-2
149	Attempt to change name of rue Panama: *TIMES,* 1-26-93 5:4; Eiffel company considers name change: *ibid.,* 2-15-93 5:3; Rouen renames quai de Lesseps: *ibid.,* 2-13-93 5:2
149	"Though still living, you already belong . . .": *Bunau-Varilla,* 106
149	De Lesseps at La Chesnaye, *Smith,* 403
150	Thevenet, Roche and Arene cleared: *ibid.,* 389
150	Wife collapses at Baïhaut arrest: *NYT,* 1-10-93 1:1; Clement's kindly gesture: *TIMES,* 1-10-93 5:2
150	Five more defendants cleared: *Smith,* 393
151	" . . . evil genius of the politicians . . .": *TRIB,* 3-10-93
151	"Of all the persons connected . . .": *TRIB,* 1-18-93 1:2
151	Legion of Honor drops Herz: *TIMES,* 1-30-93 5:5, also *Clunet,* 283-285
151	British will not allow questioning of imprisoned fugitive: *TIMES,* 2-14-93 5:4
151	Disorder at bribery trial: *NYT,* 3-19-93 1:3-5

151-152   Radical leaders reply: *ibid.,* 3-9-93 5:1 and 3-11-93 8:1

152   Charles de Lesseps at bribery trial: *Smith,* 411; contrast with appearance in earlier case: *NYT,* 1-14-93 3:1

152   "No, I have time enough . . .": *TIMES,* 3-9-93 5:1-2

152   Testimony at first trial, "Everybody knows what his influence was . . .": *TIMES,* 1-11-93 5:3-4 and 1-12-93 5:1

152-153   "Herz came to my father . . .": *TRIB,* 3-9-93 1:1-2

153   "When de Lesseps was discounting bills . . .": *ibid.,* 3-11-93 1:1

153   " . . . you must extricate me . . .", "I replied that I had not seen M. Herz . . .", " . . . had no knowledge how de Reinach . . .": *TIMES,* 3-9-93 5:1-2

153   Note: Mont-sous-Vaudrey was President Grevy's country home on the little Cuisance River in the Jura.

153-154   Proust, Gobron, Dugue, Beral, Sans-Leroy deny wrongdoing: *NYT,* 3-10-93 8:1

154   Baïhaut collapses and confesses: *TRIB,* 3-10-93 1:1-2

154   Only three found guilty: *Smith,* 435-36

154   Property separation for Mme. Baïhaut: *TIMES,* 3-22-93 5:2

154   United States Congress investigates American Committee: *TRIB,* 1-29-93 2:3

154-155-156-157   Findings of U. S. Congressional committee: *U. S. House of Representatives, 52nd Congress, 2nd Session, Report No. 2615,* 2-6

156   Jesse Seligman's testimony: *TRIB,* 2-16-93 3:1

157-158   Deputies' findings: *Inquiry, 1893, Valle,* 235-40

158   Convictions in earlier trial reversed: *Cour de Cassation Ruling, Inquiry, 1898,* Tome I 28-30; three released: *TRIB,* 6-16-93 11:4

158   Charles de Lesseps served time in hospital, released: *TRIB,* 9-13-93 1:2; government accepts compromise: *Siegfried,* 279

158   Blondin's incipient paralysis: *TRIB,* 3-27-93 1:2; release: *ibid.,* 10-9-93 7:3

158-159   Terror of Etampes: *ibid.,* 5-20-94 16:3; Baïhaut kept from dying daughter: *TIMES,* 1-4-94 5:3; pardoned, returned to "Riviera for prisoners": *ibid.,* 12-12-96 7:5

159   Ferdinand de Lesseps's condition: *ibid.,* 12-8-94 6:1-5, *TRIB,* 11-6-93 16:1; *Goncourt,* entry for 1-6-97

159   "In the tragic hour for his name . . .": *NYT Saturday Review of Books and Art,* 1-6-97

Maron J. Simon

Chapter 10

169   "We are very glad to be your seconds . . .": *TIMES*, 6-21-93
           5:1

169   Footnote: *PMG*, 8-9-93, 6

169-170   Ducret's statement: "We have abstracted . . .": *TIMES*,
           6-22-93 5:2-3, quoting *La Cocarde*

170   Millevoye's hints: *ibid.*

170   "I will accept any form . . .": *ibid.*

170   "For some months these sorry remnants . . .": *TIMES*, 6-
           4-93

171   "M. Clemenceau—who is, as we say . . .": *Spectator*, 6-24-
           93

171   Reasons for hostility to Clemenceau: *Barres*

172-173-174-175-176-177   Session of the Chamber: *Annales*, afternoon
           session, 6-22-93, also *TIMES*, 6-23-93 5:2-3

174   Note: Sir Thomas Lister was British Assistant Under
           Secretary of State for Foreign Affairs.
           Henry Austin Lee was private secretary to the Marquess
           of Dufferin and Ava, British Ambassador to the French
           Republic.
           William Henry Waddington, the French archaeologist and
           statesman, of British ancestry, was Premier of France in
           1879 and Ambassador to the Court of St. James from 1888
           to 1893.
           Alexandre Ribot was a former Premier and Foreign Min-
           ister.
           The Marquis de Reverseaux was French Consul General
           at Cairo.

175   "This inheritor of the Anglophobe tradition . . .", " . . . they
           will next suggest . . .": *TIMES* lead editorial, 6-23-93 9:5

175   "Very stupidly M. Millevoye . . .": *Coubertin*, 264

177   Clemenceau "radiant and justly so . . .": *TIMES*, 6-23-93
           5:2-3; Millevoye hissed: *ibid.*, 6-24-93 7:1 disregarded in-
           structions: *Barres*

177   "Had he been the only one . . .": *ibid.*

177   Forgery traced to Norton: *PMG.* 6-28-93, 6

177   Ducret says de Mores and de Dion checked data: *TIMES*,
           6-24-93

177   Norton's story: *ibid.*, 6-26-93 5:2-3, also *PMG*

177-178   Norton-Ducret trial: *NYT*, 8-6-93 2:6, also *TIMES*, 8-7-93
           3:1-3, *PMG*, 8-7-93

185   Herz's college career: Cohn Library archives, *College of the City of New York*

185-186   Assistant surgeon in French army:*Clunet,* 252

186   Education in Europe: *ibid.,* also Reed's article in *Fortnightly Review*

186   Residence in Chicago: *NYT,* 12-23-92, 5

186   Mount Sinai Hospital incident; from files of the institution. Also related without mention of Herz's name in *Mount Sinai Hospital of New York, 1852-1952,* Random House

187   Herz in San Francisco, becomes "electrical doctor," describes anti-insomnia instrument: *San Francisco Evening Bulletin,* 12-10-92 1:5

187   Physical description of Herz; passport issued 10-23-88, signed by Robert M. McLean, U. S. Minister to France: *Herz, Documents, State*

187   "He told of marvelous cures abroad and talked of kings . . .": *San Francisco Evening Bulletin,* 12-10-92 1:5

188   "In electricity as in all other things . . .": *La Lumière Electrique,* 12-1-79

188   His deal with Soulages: *ibid.*

189   "I do not think my efforts . . .", " . . . has judged people and situations well . . .": *ibid.*

189   " . . . once heard him insinuate that some of Edison's inventions . . .": *Vizetelly,* 358

189   "Sir: I have the honor to inform you . . .", Bardoux's letter to Herz: *Clunet,* 259

189-190   Clemenceau meets Herz, names him mentor of his children: *Le Silence de M. Clemenceau,* 211-12

190   Electrical Syndicate with Dalloz, Bapst, etc.: *Clunet,* 253

190   Appointment by Blaine: U. S. State Department, Domestic Letters, Vol. 138, June-Aug., 1881, 451, letter dated 8-2-81

190   Munich exposition promotion syndicate: *La Lumière Electrique,* 9-9-82

190   Praise from Marcel Deprez: Deprez speech of 10-26-85 reprinted in commemorative brochure published by French Society of Electricians at 50th anniversary celebration in Paris, 11-13-1935

Panama affair, this was the only mention of any association Herz may have had with Drexel, Harjes, the Paris associate of Drexel, Morgan & Co., and the only reference to Leonide Leblanc, the spectacular actress who was the mistress of a succession of prominent men. During the de Lesseps fraud trial *The New York Times* observed in a page-1 dope story: "Apparently the trial will be allowed to end without a mention of the name of Leonide Leblanc, the beautiful ex-friend of the Duc d'Aumale. Her house in Paris was the center of the whole Panama intrigue, and at her dinners these incriminated Ministers, Deputies and editors met the cashiers of the rotten enterprise. She herself feathered her nest luxuriously out of the haul, and was so braided up with every detail that it must have taken large ingenuity to prevent an allusion to her before the Court of Appeal. She is safer before the parliamentary inquiry because it is said that more than half its members were guests under her roof those lavish, hospitable days." (*NYT,* 1-15-93 1:3-4-5)

214   De Reinach-Herz friendship, " . . . it fluctuated strongly . . .": *Inquiry, 1893, Depositions,* 12-22-92, 559, Andrieux's testimony

215   The passage out of context—"As for de Reinach, you may depend . . .": *Clunet,* 214-15

215   "Jealous of Herz having conceived the plan . . .": *ibid.,* 217

215-216-217 Herz-Guillot exchange on diplomatic affair: *ibid.,* 216, 216a, 216b, 217

217   "My name is in the paper again . . ."; "Please do the necessary . . .": *ibid.,* 231; de Reinach's messages to Herz, Nov. 19, 1892: *ibid.* 232

218-219 Imbert-Monchicourt actions to recover from de Reinach estate and Herz: *Inquiry, 1898,* Tome I, 321-29, also *TRIB,* 1-22-93 1:2, 1-28-93 1:1, 1-12-94 1:2, 2-16-94 5:2, *NYT,* 2-16-94 5:2, *TIMES,* 5-4-94 5:1, quoting *Figaro*

218   Mme. Herz signs the compromise: her affidavit of 11-16-97, *Herz, Documents, State*

218   *Figaro* story about revocation of Legion ouster: *TIMES,* 5-4-94 5:1

218-219 Herz " . . . henceforth be free to return . . ."; "Indeed, if anything, he comes back to us more powerful . . .": *TRIB,* 5-20-94 16:3. One of Baron de Reinach's children, Mme. Joseph Reinach, did not participate in this transaction. She was the wife of her first cousin, the Opportunist

Deputy who was a famous journalist and editor of Gambetta's *La République Française.* Estranged from his freewheeling father-in-law, he had returned 40,000 francs of his wife's dowry because he regarded it as coming from Panama money, and he and Mme. Reinach had renounced participation in her father's estate. (*TIMES:* 12-19-92, 5, 1-16-93 5:2, 2-11-93 5:3, also *Knox,* 130, speaks of settlement relating to estate of M. de Reinach, M. Lucien de Reinach, Mlle. Juliette de Reinach)

219	Examining magistrate throws out complicity charge against Herz, but recommends blackmail trial: *Inquiry, 1898,* Tome I, 324-26
219	Court rejects Clunet's certificates from eminent British physicians: Miss Turner's affidavit, *Herz, Documents, State*
219	Herz trial, conviction, sentence: *Inquiry, 1898,* Tome I, 326; also *TRIB,* 7-28-94 5:3 and 8-4-94 7:4, *TIMES,* 7-28-94 5:3, and 8-4-94 5:2
219-220	Clunet appeals, highest court rejects appeal: *Clunet,* 52, and *Inquiry, 1898,* Tome I, 326
220	Letter of Drs. Brunton, Frazer, McHardy: *TIMES,* 10-16-93; *Law Journal* protests arrest: *ibid.,* 3-23-95 5:6
220	"Is this poor man, conscious of his innocence . . .": *Great Britain, Foreign Office,* 20-21, reprint of Lewis and Lewis letter to Home Secretary
221	Activity in Parliament; Griffith-Boscawen questions Asquith: *TIMES,* 5-25-95 10:6
221	Extradition treaty amendment permits hearing outside of Bow Street: *ibid.,* 2-20-96 5:3 and 2-26-96 5:6
221	Bedside hearing for Herz: *ibid.,* 4-28-96 8:3
221	Sir John Bridge sets writ aside, frees Herz: *ibid.,* 5-4-96 3:6 to 4:1
222	Decision "contrary to good will . . .", Herz free " . . . to try his hand again . . ." against France: *Inquiry, 1898,* Tome I, 337-38
222	Arton arrested in London: *TRIB,* 11-18-95 4:4; trial begins in Paris: *TIMES,* 7-8-96 2:4; fined and sentenced: *ibid.,* 7-11-96 2:4; volunteers to face trial for Panama bribes: *ibid.,* 11-9-96 6:1
223	Arton begins to sing: 12-15-96 5:5
223	New trial of Arton and legislators: *ibid.,* 12-20-96 5:6 and following days

223   All freed: *ibid.,* 12-28-97 3:3; courtroom crowd shouts, *"Vive la République": ibid.,* 12-31-97 3:3

223   Footnote, Arton suicide: *TIMES,* 7-18-1905 10:6

223   "It is clear that Arton put . . .": *ibid.*

223-224   Imbert was Herz's principal accuser: *Inquiry, 1898,* Tome I, 298-99; "We have found a note from Baron de Reinach. . .": *ibid.,* Tome III, 38; "It is then that in 1888, I believe. . .": *ibid.,* "one speaks of a secret. . . .": *ibid.,* 44; "That does not concern me . . ."; "There was always that menace": *ibid.,* 39

224   "We have shown the Baron de Reinach despite all . . .": *Inquiry, 1898,* Tome I, 341

225   Herz invites committee to Bournemouth: *ibid.,* 300

225   Plichon statement to *Le Soir: TIMES,* 7-16-97 5:3

225   "The majority of the statements therein are lies": *ibid.,* 7-17-97 9:3

225   Valle sets Bournemouth meeting, Herz asks postponement to permit preparation: *Inquiry, 1898* Tome I, 301-303

225   Herz's postponement request published in London: *TIMES,* 7-20-97 12:5; committee en route when contents are learned: *ibid.,* 7-21-97 5:2

226   Junket aborted "when the twenty-five deputies were about to step aboard . . .": *TRIB,* 8-8-97, part II, 1:1

226   Deputies ridiculed, Herz "man of the day": *ibid.*

226   "His photographs are displayed in the shop windows": *ibid.*

226   "If I'd wanted to make fools of them . . .": *Figaro,* 7-21-97, 1

226   " . . . this band of bird brains . . .": *ibid.,* 2:2

226   "Ever since they almost went to Bournemouth, our investigators . . .": *ibid.,* 7-23-97

227   Herz to Faure: "I claim from the French government . . .": *TIMES,* 7-22-97 7:6

227   Herz retains Lauterbach; asks U.S. intervention, denied: correspondence of Lauterbach, Assistant Secretary of State Alvey Adee, and Dittenhoefer, Gerber & James, Aug. 6 and 12, 1897, *Herz, Documents, State*

227-228   Affidavits of Herz's wife, secretary and nurse: *ibid.*

228   State Department reaffirms refusal to intervene: Hay's communication to Lauterbach, 12-12-99, *Herz, Documents, State*

228   Herz dies, buried at Willesden: *TIMES,* 7-7-98 6:6

228   "Charlatan though he was . . .": *PMG*, 7-6-98 7:2

228   "Dr. Herz's brilliant attainments brought him into contact . . .": *San Francisco Examiner,* 7-7-98 6:4

229   Senator Morgan to call up Nicaragua Canal bill: *San Francisco Bulletin,* 7-7-98, 2

Chapter 12

230   Lemarquis appointed attorney for canal company bondholders: *Inquiry, 1898,* Tome I, 31-32

230   Brunet-Monchicourt receivership: *ICC,* 211-13

231   Guillemain commission's report, Wyse buys new concession: *ibid.,* 57

231   Price of the extensions: *Knox,* 171, 174; Wyse's fee: *ibid.,* 131

231   Gautron succeeds Monchicourt: *Inquiry, 1898*, Tome I, 32

231   "Construction could not be carried on . . .": *ibid.,* Tome III, 51

232   "We decided to levy on the undue profits; *ibid.,* Tome III, 51

232   New Panama Canal Company launched: *ibid.,* Tome I, 33; also *ICC,* 58

232   "I engaged the syndicates in the person . . .": *Inquiry, 1898,* Tome III, 53

232-233 Oberndoerffer, sixty-three others settle: *ibid.,* Tome I, 35; earlier syndicators settle: *ibid.,* 54-55; settlement with three banks: *ibid.,* 34-35; levy on de Lesseps company administrators and heirs; *ibid.,* 35

233   "The best case we had. . . .": *Inquiry, 1898,* Tome III, 56

233   Eiffel and other contractors settle: *ibid.,* Tome I, 34-35, 39-41

233   Couvreux & Hersent settlement: *ibid.,* Tome I, 43-44

233-234 New company's stock issue fails; liquidator picks up the balance: *ibid.,* Tome I, 36

234   New company's organization meeting: *Knox,* 218-25

234   Ownership of Panama Railroad shares its shares in trust: *Inquiry, 1898,* Tome I, 36-37; road's 1893 balance sheet: *Knox,* 258

234   Distribution of new company's earnings: *Inquiry, 1898,* Tome I, 38

23-04 1:1; Day and Russell sign for U.S.: *TIMES,* 5-4-04 5:6; $35,000 fee for Morgan services: Curtis speech to Alabama Bar

253   U.S. delivers biggest Treasury warrant: *NYT,* 5-8-04 4:5

253   Old bondholders get about 10 cents on the dollar, new canal company gets money back plus 3 per cent per annum: Curtis speech to Alabama Bar

253   "Doubtless in Paris, and perhaps to a lesser extent . . .": Theodore Roosevelt in *Outlook,* 10-7-11

253   "We did not buy the corporations . . .": *The Works of Theodore Roosevelt, Presidential Addresses, State Papers and European Addresses,* P.F. Collier & Sons, (1910) 1971 *et seq.*

253   U.S. bought archives but no stockholder data: *U.S. 60th Congress 2nd Session, Document No. 589:* letter prepared by Paul Charlton, law officer, Bureau of Insular Affairs, War Department, 12-9-08

254   Cromwell testimony before Senate Committee on Interoceanic Canals: *U.S. Senate Document No. 401, 59th, 2nd, Vol. II,* testimony of 2-27-06

254   "Why must so many efforts . . ."; "At any rate everything will not be lost . . .": *TIMES,* 11-11-03, quoting *Le Gaulois*

254-255   U.S. takes over: *TRIB,* 5-5-04 3:4

—

Index